Cognitive–Behavioral Therapy for Impulsive Children

THE GUILFORD CLINICAL PSYCHOLOGY AND
PSYCHOTHERAPY SERIES
Michael J. Mahoney, Editor

Cognitive–Behavioral Therapy for Impulsive Children

PHILIP C. KENDALL
LAUREN BRASWELL

THE GUILFORD PRESS
New York   London

© 1985 The Guilford Press

A Division of Guilford Publications, Inc.

200 Park Avenue South, New York, N.Y. 10003

Printed in the United States of America

LIBRARY OF CONGRESS CATALOGING IN PUBLICATION DATA

Kendall, Philip C.
    Cognitive-behavioral therapy for impulsive children.

    (The Guilford clinical psychology and psychotherapy series)
    Bibliography: p.
    Includes indexes.
    1. Behavior therapy.   2. Cognitive therapy.
3. Child psychotherapy.   4. Self-control in children.
I. Braswell, Lauren.   II. Title.   III. Series.
RJ505.B4K45   1985   618.92′89142   84-4572
ISBN 0-89862-008-2

To those researchers, clinicians, and children involved in the past, present, and future training of impulse control in children

and to my son, Mark, and wife, Sue (P. C. K.)

and to my parents, Henry and Rachel Braswell (L. B.)

Preface

Many years of empirical research and clinical application, more than I (P. C. K.) care to remember, have gone into the development of the program that serves as the core of this book. The process started at Virginia Commonwealth University (VCU), specifically at the Virginia Treatment Center for Children (VTCC) of VCU's Medical College of Virginia, where I collaborated with Al Finch, a staff researcher–clinician, and where I began working with impulsive children both clinically and in research. Even today, individual cases at VTCC come to mind as both rich sources of the research hypotheses I have since explored and as important experiences in my clinical training. It was at VTCC and with Al Finch that I conducted and published some of the early and formative studies of the methods described herein.

The University of Minnesota provided an exciting opportunity for the continuation of my research. The structure of the academic environment supported research, and the equally supportive community was receptive to research efforts and outcomes. The multitude of undergraduates who assisted in the series of research studies evaluating the outcome of the cognitive–behavioral program as well as the graduate students who collaborated with me were a source of motivation and stimulation. Lauren Braswell emerged from this group.

Eugene Urbain, Lance Wilcox, Brian Zupan, Wendy Padawer, Jim Braith, Chris Vye, Mike Carey, Linda Bream, Chris Brophy, Jeff Gillman, Debby Huntley, Pam Lumsden, Diane Sandum, and others were valued colleagues and assistants. Our special thanks are due Brian Zupan and Wendy Padawer for their efforts in the preparation of the early drafts of the treatment manual which has until now served to guide the application of the cognitive–behavioral therapy for impulsive children, and Carol Reuter for her special efforts and secretarial assistance in preparing the manuscript on a time-saving word-processing system.

Special acknowledgment is due Independent School District 281 of the suburban Minneapolis community of Robbinsdale, Minnesota. Support from their main office, specifically Phyllis Amacher and Bill Forsberg; each of the principals, Will Zimmerman, Lowell Hammer, and Warren Tabor; and the many teachers who have participated, is most appreciated. Literally, progress would not have been made without their cooperation and genuine efforts. It is to all who have contributed in so many ways that we offer one generic "thank you." This thank you includes, of course, the Center for Advanced Study in the Behavioral Sciences, Stanford, California, where the manuscript of this book was begun. I can think of no greater fantasy than to have researched and written every word within that exceptional environment.

Given the integration of research and practice that has guided the development of this program from the outset, it should come as no surprise that we set forth to write this book for the practitioner who appreciates background research. As decisions were made in the drafting of the proposal, in writing sample chapters, and even in the final editing process, we continued to be guided by our preference to tell the reader the ins and outs of the application of the treatment, but not at the expense of the background literature. Our first two chapters cover the overview and background review that we see as essential to the informed application of the treatment, but the remainder of the book is more focused on "how to." Chapter 3 provides a description of what types of children, with what types of impulsivity problems, are most appropriate for our form of treatment. Methods and ideas for assessing these children are presented in Chapter 4. The actual techniques and procedures that constitute the cognitive–behavioral intervention are discussed in general in Chapter 5, and the explicit and specific guidelines for implementation are available in the Appendix. Factors that may enhance treatment effectiveness and generalization, as well as pitfalls to be avoided in the practice of this intervention, are listed and described in Chapter 6, with the concepts and procedures when working with parents or teachers discussed in Chapter 7. We have intended for this book to provide the information necessary for the implementation of the cognitive–behavioral therapy in as competent and thoughtful manner as possible without more direct training and supervision. The reader can now be the judge of whether or not we have achieved this goal.

Popular lyricists often capture the thoughts and feelings of their age peers, and several have expressed in song both an energizing and thought-provoking spirit. William Joel stands out, to this writer (P. C. K.), as a person who, unbeknownst to him, was a musical source of energy. From the time of an interaction in our midteen years, when Joel's talents were already evident, to the present, when there is no longer any novelty to the identification of his talent, his music has been played over and over.

One more thought before we close the preface—a thought about oversimplifying. Unfortunately, what we are about to describe occurs all too often. It occurs after the completion of a time-consuming dissertation, at the termination of a large-scale government research grant, or after several years of systematic study of an intentionally focused topic. It occurs in certain contexts, such as at a family gathering, in a classroom, or over dinner with friends, to name a few. We are referring to the phenomenon of "summarization." Summarization is the by-product of an overly lengthy, exceedingly detailed description of one's research. Once the description is completed the listener condenses the entire effort into a single, often commonsensical sentence. Nothing can be more disheartening for the weak.

The reader of this volume will, upon completion, and at a point when asked to describe it to another, be tempted to condense the program into a brief scenario. We offer the following: "The program tries to teach impulsive kids to stop and think before they act." We cannot offer a more economical yet accurate summary. However, the pages that follow add substantially to the content.

Philip C. Kendall
Temple University

Lauren Braswell
University of Minnesota Hospitals
and Human Services, Inc.,
of Washington County

Contents

CHAPTER 1

Overview

The judge says to the juvenile who is appearing in court, "How do I know that the next time you walk past a fire alarm at school you won't try to set it off again?" The boy of 12 looks at his feet and then looks up and says, "Well, Sir, next time I get the urge to set one off, I will think of what happened the last time—like having to be here in court—and I will walk on by it." In a separate example, a mother sighs with relief and says, "Son, I'm so glad you came and told me your little brother has been taking your race cars again, instead of just hitting him," and in yet another context a fourth grader thinks to herself, "Wow! I did OK on the social studies test. It did help to read each question real slow and look at all the answers before I marked one."

Impossible to achieve? No. Difficult to achieve? Yes, but these three brief vignettes provide examples of the behavioral goals toward which cognitive–behavioral self-control training is directed. Simply stated, this book is about teaching children to slow down and cognitively examine their behavioral alternatives before acting.

Cognitive–behavioral approaches to the treatment of behavioral, emotional, and academic problems are not restricted to any *one* theoretical tenet or single-minded applied technique. Rather, the emerging cognitive–behavioral procedures are diverse yet interrelated strategies for providing new learning experiences which involve enactive procedures and a cognitive analysis (see Beck, 1970; Goldfried, 1979; Kendall & Hollon, 1979; Kendall & Bemis, 1983; Mahoney & Arnkoff, 1978; Meichenbaum, 1977). The client and therapist work together to think through and behaviorally practice solutions to personal, academic, and interpersonal problems with a consideration of the affect involved.

Although different themes have emerged from the literature on cognitive–behavioral therapy, there appear to be a few principles that serve to guide the cognitive–behavioral therapist, theoretician, and researcher. The following list is adapted from Kendall and Bemis (1983) and Mahoney (1977b), among others.

1

1. Cognitive mediational processes are involved in human learning.

2. Thoughts, feelings, and behaviors are causally interrelated (the program, thus, has a cognitive–affective–behavioral slant).

3. Cognitive activities, such as expectations, self-statements, and attributions, are important in understanding and predicting psychopathology and psychotherapeutic change.

4. Cognitions and behaviors are compatible: (a) Cognitive processes can be interpreted into behavioral paradigms, and (b) cognitive techniques can be combined with behavioral procedures.

5. The task of the cognitive–behavioral therapist is to collaborate with the client to assess distorted or deficient cognitive processes and behaviors and to design new learning experiences to remediate the dysfunctional or deficient cognitions, behaviors, and affective patterns.

More specific definitions of the cognitive–behavioral perspective abound. Unfortunately definitional consensus is more difficult to locate, for definitions appear to vary in the extent to which they emphasize the cognitive versus behavioral aspects of this approach. At one extreme, Ledwidge (1978), in his often criticized review (Meichenbaum, 1979a; Locke, 1979), offered a definition of *cognitive*-behavioral therapy when he suggested that such approaches are "cognitive therapy with a behavioral twist" (p. 354). Ledwidge argued that the primary focus of these approaches is change in patterns of thought, not change in behavior. Hobbs, Moguin, Tyroler, and Lahey (1980) also offered a definition of *cognitive*-behavioral therapy by suggesting that the essential feature of this approach is the teaching of mediation responses that constitute a general strategy for directing or controlling behavior in diverse situations. Urbain and Kendall (1980) proposed that the emphasis on *thinking processes* is the distinguishing feature of cognitive–behavioral approaches with children, but were quick to add that changes in behavior were the desired outcome. Kendall and Hollon (1979) suggested a balanced emphasis in conceiving the cognitive–behavioral approach as "a purposeful attempt to preserve the demonstrated efficiencies of behavior modification within a less doctrinaire context and to incorporate the cognitive activities of the client in the effort to produce therapeutic change" (p. 1).

The cognitive–*behavioral* perspective is presented by Wilson (1978) who, in examining the same techniques considered by Ledwidge (1978), suggested that there is no need for the term "cognitive–behavioral therapy," as these procedures fall within the realm of behavior therapy. Wilson views cognitive–behavioral approaches as mere elaborations of a mediational theme initially introduced in the context of social-learning theory. At the present juncture, the cognitive–behavioral approach does appear to be chiefly distinguished from the behavioral perspective by the emphasis on cognitive activities, such as beliefs, expectancies, self-statements, and problem solving; yet concern with overt behavior, both in treatment and as an indication of outcome (whether manifested in the use of behavioral contingencies or in explicit skills training), differentiates it from cognitive and insight-oriented approaches.

The definitional variations in emphasis on the cognitive versus behavioral aspects of the cognitive–behavioral perspective grew out of two major historical antecedents: (1) the development of behavioristic interest in the phenomenon of self-control, and (2) the emergence of cognitive learning theories of psychotherapy. As noted by Mahoney and Arnkoff (1978), Skinner had written a chapter on self-control in 1953, yet behaviorists displayed very little interest in the topic until the mid-1960s. Stuart (1967), building on the work of Ferster, Nurnberger, and Levitt (1962), employed self-regulatory processes in a weight loss program. Within a few years, Bandura (1969, 1971) and Kanfer (1970) were exploring behavioral self-control in a series of laboratory studies. In the area of interventions with children, the shift from external to self-regulation was explored with a variety of disorders, but most attention focused on self-regulation of disruptive classroom behavior (e.g., Bolstad & Johnson, 1972, Broden, Hall, & Mitts 1971; Drabman, Spitalnik, & O'Leary, 1973; Turkewitz, O'Leary, & Ironsmith, 1975). During this transition period, behaviorists became (pardon the expression) desensitized to concepts that acknowledge the complex interrelationship of the organism and its environment, such as reciprocal determinism (Bandura, 1969). The notion of "coverant control" (Homme, 1965) also became acceptable and enabled behaviorists to study and manipulate long neglected "private events," such as thoughts, feelings, and images. This shift away from strict S-R formulations of human behavior was made explicit in Bandura's (1969) *Principles of Behavior Modification*. In this work, Bandura argued for a cognitive–symbolic mechanism governing the basic processes of behavior change. As Mahoney and Arnkoff (1978) summarized:

Within a very short period of time cognitive terms and themes became a major aspect of behavioral research. Thus earlier conditioning analyses of self-control began to be replaced by more mediational accounts, and behavior therapists began exploring the relevance of social and cognitive psychology for their clinical endeavors. (p. 692)

The second major historical antecedent, the development of cognitive learning models of psychotherapy, occurred largely outside the domain of strict behavioristic psychology. Two examples of these models are Ellis's (1962) rational–emotive therapy and Beck's (1970, 1976) cognitive therapy. According to Ellis, psychological disturbances are largely the result of illogical, irrational thinking. Such disturbances can be ended if the individual learns to increase rational and to decrease irrational thought. This view assumes that thinking and emotion are integrally related and cannot be entirely separated from each other. In a similar vein, Beck's cognitive therapy, as applied to depression, posits that depression is the result of a negative cognitive set that includes negative beliefs about the self, the world, and the future. The maintenance of these beliefs is the result of distortions in information processing, such as arbitrary inferences or overgeneralizations. Cognitive therapy treats these distortions by assisting the client in testing his/her distorted beliefs. The theories of Ellis and Beck and the procedures following from these theories have had a tremendous impact on the field of clinical psychology. Clearly, both views stress the crucial role of the individual's thoughts or beliefs in the determination of behavior and consider change in these thoughts or beliefs as a necessary step in achieving and/or maintaining behavioral change.

While such definitional discussions and historical summaries serve to describe the general characteristics of cognitive–behavioral therapy, a more delineated description is appropriate for work with children. Perhaps the most distinguishing characteristic of cognitive–behavioral approaches *with children* is the therapeutic emphasis on teaching *thinking processes* (Urbain & Kendall, 1980). This emphasis is in contrast to an emphasis on relieving internal conflicts, as in the psychodynamic approach, or to the training of specific behaviors, as in the behavioral approaches. These thinking processes are seen as cognitive–behavioral in that they are the cognitions involved in behavioral adjustment. In stressing the need to modify thinking processes, cognitive–behavioral child therapists teach strategies that are appropriate aids to adjustment across a variety of settings. Specific behaviors are desired end products that are shaped and rewarded throughout treatment, but an essential characteristic of the model is the belief that training at the level of the cognitive processes that mediate competent adjustment across situations will, as an inherent agent of treatment, build in generalizable skills.

In addition to the more delimited description of cognitive-behavioral treatments for children, these procedures also differ somewhat from the cognitive–behavioral strategies used with adult clients. It should be noted at the outset that cognitive–behavioral interventions with children are not merely the downward simplification of the approaches used with adults. Rather, children differ from adults in important ways, and these differences require alteration in the manner with which the therapist treats the client (Kendall, 1981a).

First, the nature of the cognitive problem requiring treatment differs for adults and children. The targets of adult cognitive–behavioral therapies are typically *cognitive errors* (cognitive distortions): irrational beliefs, faulty cognitive processes, inaccurate internal dialogues. The adult's cognitive errors can also be described as illogical interpretations of the environment, exceedingly high standards for personal performance, and inaccurate perceptions of life's routine demands. Thought processes exist and are active, but the outcomes are faulty. In children, the cognitive problems that our treatment is designed for are *cognitive absences* (cognitive deficiencies): The child does not have or does not employ the cognitive skills needed to perform certain desirable actions. In other terms, the child seemingly fails to engage in the information-processing activities of an effective problem solver and fails to initiate the reflective thinking process that can govern behavior. In this instance we are referring to the type of children for whom our cognitive-behavioral treatment is designed: impulsive, non-self-controlled, attention-disordered children. Other types of childhood maladjustment, such as isolation, withdrawal, and depression, may involve cognitive errors.

The distinction between adult cognitive distortions and children's cognitive deficiencies has a direct implication for treatment. Unlike therapy with adult clients, where the therapist has to identify faulty and maladaptive cognitive processes, remove the dysfunctional thinking style, and teach a more adaptive thinking style, the cognitive-behavioral therapist working with impulsive children can proceed more directly to identifying the cognitive absences and teaching the cognitive skills that will help remedy the problem in adjustment.

Child and adult clients also differ in their level of cognitive development. Many of the cognitive strategies that are appropriate with adult clients cannot be fully understood by children and preschoolers. Some adolescents will be cognitively prepared for more adultlike interventions, but the problem is a genuine one for youngsters. For instance, the confrontation of irrational beliefs, as in rational–emotive therapies, would likely be perceived by a child as a scolding. Not only would the reason for this scolding be unclear, but also the intended outcome—philosophical change—would be somewhat foreign.

Another important distinction between working with children and adults, whatever one's therapeutic approach, is that children do not self-refer for their problems in lacking self-control. We have never had a child call for an appointment in order for us to help him/her overcome hyperactivity. Parents and teachers are typically the adults who decide for the child that he/she requires treatment. As a result, the therapist is not seen as a sought-after "helper," as is true for the help-seeking adult client, but rather is seen as another "teacher" who is likely to "tell me what to do." Special attention must be paid to this inequity in order to ensure that the child comes to perceive the therapeutic experience as enjoyable, if not inviting.

Continuing with a focus on children, other streams of influence relevant to the emergence of cognitive–behavioral procedures can be found within the developmental literature. For instance, developmental psychologists have devoted increasing amounts of attention to the study of the development of social cognition (Shantz, 1975), "social cognition" designating the internal events that are believed to mediate actions related to other people and their affairs as the topics for research inquiry. The currently intensifying study of social cognition is in contrast to the concern with physical and logical–mathematical cognitive events that had dominated prior cognitive–developmental research.

Social perspective taking represents an active research domain that is accompanied by general theories to explain the development and functional role of skills in social perspective taking (Piaget, 1926). For example, Piaget (1926) described the young child as egocentric, operating from a personal perspective, and both ignorant of and unconcerned about the perspectives of others. Role-taking (decentering) skills are believed to develop through a maturational process that results from the child's active involvement with the environment, particularly peer social exchanges. Although the unitary nature of the egocentric concept has been questioned (Ford, 1979; Hudson, 1978; Kurdek, 1977; Shantz, 1975), reasonable consensus exists about the stagelike sequence one moves through in the process of acquiring social perspective-taking abilities.

Four basic levels have been described (Selman, 1980; Selman & Byrne, 1974; Shantz, 1975). First, the child lacks social perspective taking and simply does not consider the point of view of the other person. Next, the child can consider another's ideas and realize that these thoughts may be different from his/her own; however, the child has only a rudimentary awareness of other perspectives and has difficulty taking another's role. In the next level the child continues to have difficulty considering different perspectives simultaneously but can sequentially consider his/her own perspective and then consider the perspective of another. In the final level, the child has developed social perspective-taking skills and now has the ability to take both perspectives as well as taking what Selman (1980) calls the "third-person" perspective in social interaction. This involves stepping back from a social interaction and looking at both persons' points of view.

Research with samples of children displaying maladaptive behavior patterns has often revealed perspective-taking deficits (Chandler, 1973; Little, 1979; Urbain & Kendall, 1980), and, of relevance to the concern of this book, some investigators have seized upon the implications for intervention suggested by these theories and the deficits observed in certain children. Perspective-taking intervention programs emerged from developmental psychology but nevertheless have a number of similarities with other cognitive–behavioral treatments, particularly in their emphasis on the generation of alternatives, role-taking practice, and some form of affective education.

As will be discussed in Chapter 2, developmentalists Luria (1961) and Vygotsky (1962) also contributed substantially to the study of children's self-talk and subsequently to the emergence and refinement of self-instructional training procedures. Vygotsky (1962), for example, described a progression from audible talking to "internalized" talking, and finally to silence, where internalization of self-talk is fully accomplished. Vygotsky underscored that the content of the self-talk was important because its primary function was self-guidance.

Luria (1961) took an experimental approach to the descriptive writings of others such as Vygotsky. Luria provided children with verbal self-instructions while they performed laboratory tasks and thereby explored the effects of specific self-talk. Luria identified an important developmental influence: With increasing age, children were able to inhibit behavior not only following adult instructions, but also in response to their own self-directed instructions. Though not the sole influences, developmental topics such as social cognition and self-verbalization contributed to the emergence of the cognitive–behavioral treatment strategies for children.

CHAPTER 2

Background Review

This book really is about how to teach children to "stop and think," and we shall explain just what you can do to get children to slow themselves down and examine behavioral alternatives. However, we feel that it is worthwhile first to review what others have done and what they have reported to be their findings. Accordingly, this chapter presents a review of the research literature with an eye toward the successes and failures of cognitive–behavioral interventions and the possible factors that moderate these differences in outcome.

There have been other reviews published to date (e.g., Abikoff, 1979; Craighead, Craighead, & Meyers, 1978; Hobbs *et al.*, 1980; Kendall, 1981a; Kendall & Finch, 1979b; Pressley, Reynolds, Stark, & Gettinger, 1983; Reynolds & Stark, 1983; Urbain & Kendall, 1980). In addition, there have been special issues of journals devoted to the topic (e.g., *School Psychology Review*, 1982; *Exceptional Education Quarterly*, 1980) and several chapters in which the authors discuss various topics in reference to cognitive–behavioral interventions with children. For instance, Bobbitt and Keating (1983) take a cognitive–developmental perspective, Copeland (1983) examines the theoretical role ascribed to and the methods for the measurement of children's self-verbalizations, and Meichenbaum and Asarnow (1979) bring the issues of metacognitive development to bear on cognitive–behavioral training.

Why, given the existing reviews, do we provide another? First, the field is far from static. New developments in the strategies for intervention, current data on the effectiveness of the procedures, and recent advances in defining and identifying the types of children for whom the types of cognitive–behavioral training are most efficacious are appearing in the literature. Second, there are, perhaps, more profitable ways to look at the existing data. For example, the present review divides the background literature in terms of self-instructional training and problem-solving training. Also, the literature is analyzed in terms of the degree of involvement between the child and the therapist–

experimenter. We also make a distinction between studies that do and do not employ explicit behavioral contingencies as a component of the intervention. In so doing we highlight some of the reasons for the differential outcomes that have appeared in the literature. There is one other reason for our review—to serve the reader. Without a background review of the existing information we would be doing a disservice to the readers of this work. It is rare that we do not learn something new when we examine what others have done before us.

There have been several specific influences on the cognitive-behavioral literature dealing with children. First, self-instructional training came on the scene (Meichenbaum & Goodman, 1971). Accordingly, the factors that led to the self-instructional procedures are important factors in the development of cognitive–behavioral training in general. Second, the focus on problem solving as a form of prevention and treatment made an impressive dent on the field of child clinical psychology. The antecedents of problem solving are therefore also relevant to the development of cognitive–behavioral procedures with children.

At a later point we will be describing the procedures of self-instructional training and problem-solving training but at this time we will provide a brief historical analysis, a review of pertinent literature, and a synthesis of the available data. It is hoped that this material will provide the reader with sufficient background information to gain an understanding of the field at present and to allow for the initiation of research to determine its future.

SELF-INSTRUCTIONAL TRAINING

Compared to other cognitive–behavioral interventions with children, self-instructional procedures have been applied with a broader range of childhood disorders and with samples at various levels of severity within a given class of disorders. As we will discuss later in this chapter, the breadth of the literature allows for some analyses of the influence of subject variables and specific treatment components.

In addition to the historical–theoretical underpinnings of cognitive–behavioral approaches cited in Chapter 1, Meichenbaum (1979b) and Craighead (1982) highlighted areas of theorizing and research that contributed specifically to the development of self-instructional training. We have already mentioned the first and most significant influence that these authors highlighted—the study of the functional relationship between language and behavior that occurred within the field of child development. The most frequently cited examples, as noted briefly in Chapter 1, are the theories of Soviet psychologists Luria (1959, 1961) and Vygotsky (1962). Vygotsky proposed that internalization of verbal commands is the crucial step in a child's establishment of voluntary control over behavior. Luria, Vygotsky's student, elaborated a developmental theory of verbal control that focuses on two interrelated developmental shifts. One shift concerns the origin and nature of the speech that does the controlling. Luria suggested a sequence in which the child's behavior is initially controlled by the verbalizations of others, usually adults (other-external). In the next stage, the child's own overt verbalizations direct his/her behavior (self-external), and finally, by age 5 or 6, the child's behavior is controlled by his/her own covert self-verbalizations (self-internal). The second type of shift or change concerns the type of control provided by these verbalizations. Luria theorized that during the other-external and self-external phases verbal control is primarily impulsive rather than semantic. Impulsive control refers to speech as a physical stimulus that can inhibit or disinhibit responses. As the child develops, the type of control shifts to semantic, with the child learning to respond to speech as a carrier of specific symbolic meaning. As a result of these two shifts, by approximately age 6, the normally developing child acquires self-internal regulating speech and is responsive to the content of verbalizations. Mussen (1963) has also argued for a sequential model of development of verbal control of behavior that is very similar to that of Luria. In addition, other investigators such as Lovaas (1964) and Bem (1967) obtained results supportive of such a developmental progression. This work, along with that of Meacham (1978) and Rondal (1976), does suggest, however, that the age ranges in which the different types of verbal control are demonstrated may vary with the nature of the behavioral task. In a review of theories and studies of private speech, Kohlberg, Yaeger, and Hjentholm (1968) emphasized the importance of private speech in self-initiated regulation and direction of ongoing overt motor behavior. However, this view of the role of private speech is not without its critics. Flavell (1977) objected to interpreting the source of self-control as exclusively verbal, pointing to the importance of nonverbal control via gestures and environmental manipulations. In the applied sector, however, practitioners have typically ignored any shortcomings in the Lurian formulation of verbal self-regulation and have used such formulations as the theoretical bases for self-instructional interventions. A book by Zivin (1979) and a chapter by Copeland (1983) provide reviews of the developmental significance of children's talking to themselves.

The second influence noted by Meichenbaum was research on the child's self-mediated cognitive strategies, such as the work of Mischel and his colleagues on delay of gratification. In a 1974 review, Mischel summarized evidence that self-generated strategies, such as self-instructions and self-praise, helped children reduce frustration during delay of gratification tasks. In this type of research, the "training" in self-instruction is very brief; in fact, it usually involves the experimenter's simply instructing the child to say a particular sentence or think a particular thought. Patterson and Mischel also examined verbal self-control in a series of studies on verbal strategies for resisting distraction (Mischel & Patterson, 1976; Patterson & Mischel, 1976). The findings suggested that preschoolers did not spontaneously produce self-instructions to help them cope with highly distracting stimuli, but when provided with a specific cognitive plan the children were able to work longer in the distracting situation. Very similar research strategies have also been utilized in studies of rule-following behavior (Monohan & O'Leary, 1971; O'Leary, 1968), with results suggesting verbalization of simple self-instructions can reduce rule breaking in children.

While the findings of these two different areas of research are basically complementary, different styles or methods of training in self-instructions have followed from these approaches. In an effort to bring clarity and organization to this growing body of research, studies are grouped for discussion according to the particular type of self-instructional training being implemented. Studies in which training resembles that employed in delay of gratification and resistance to distraction research are termed *noninteractive*, for training involves the experimenter's merely telling the child what to do or say. Studies that reflect more of the influence of Luria's stage theory approach are labeled *interactive*, for training involves more child–experimenter exchange. Within the interactive category, further subgroups can be distinguished. One group refers to self-instructions as self-directed verbal commands. Training in this group of studies is more involved than training provided in the noninteractive studies, but it is still relatively simple and unelaborated. A second subgroup within the interactive class also employs the self-instructional procedures but this training is provided within the context of more operant formulations of self-control. In these studies self-instructions are taught as a skill on par with self-monitoring, self-evaluation, and self-reinforcement. The third and largest group of studies employs a version of training that is designed to more closely imitate the hypothesized processes in Luria's stage theory. This is accomplished by having the trainer first model the desired actions while speaking the self-instructions. The trainer then says the self-instructions with the child as the child carries out the actions. Finally, the child states the self-instructions while accomplishing the task activities. Within each class and subgrouping studies are organized by the disorder or problem of the sample.

Noninteractive Training

As stated earlier, the group of studies described as noninteractive is distinguished from other self-instructional approaches by the simplicity of the training. "Simplicity" is not intended to connote a pejorative stance, but to describe a straightforward type of application. Basically, this training involves the experimenter's or therapist's telling the child exactly what to say and the child merely repeating this statement at the appropriate point. Several studies have employed this procedure in the treatment of children's fears, and two other efforts utilized similar procedures in the treatment of disruptive–aggressive behavior.

FEARS

Kanfer, Karoly, and Newman (1975) compared two types of verbal controlling responses in their research on increasing fearful children's tolerance of the dark. The subjects were selected from among all kindergarten students at a middle-class parochial school. Subject selection was based on the behavioral criterion of inability to tolerate the dark for a brief period; however, subjects who manifested intense emotional reactions were excused from participation because of their high level of discomfort. The 45 selected subjects (30 males, 15 females) were all 5 to 6 years old. Controlling for sex, the children were randomly assigned to one of three conditions. In the *competence* condition, children were instructed to say, "I am a brave boy (girl). I can take care of myself in the dark." Those in the *stimulus* group were asked to say, "The dark is a fun place to be. There are many good things in the dark." The neutral group was asked to repeat, "Mary had a little lamb. Its fleece was white as snow." Each child was then placed in the pretest setting, a dark room with an intercom through which the child could communicate with the experimenter. The length of time the child remained in the room prior to signaling for the experimenter was then measured. This test situation was repeated twice. Next, the child was returned to the same room and given a dial to control the room's illumination. The child was then asked to lower the illumination level as much as he/she could when the experimenter left the room. Two trials in this situation were conducted. On the duration measure, both the competence and stimulus groups showed improvement over the neutral group on the first trial. During the second posttest exposure, all three groups showed increased tolerance, with the competence group showing the greatest increase. On the illumination measure, the competence group tolerated lower levels of illumination than the other two groups on the first trial. On the second trial, the competence and stimulus groups both achieved lower levels than the controls. The authors suggested that the competence statements had the greatest impact because they constituted self-instructions to act like a brave boy or girl and thus are associated with expectations of social and self-approval based on past experience. Subjects were not instructed to rehearse their assigned statements *during* the dark tolerance tests (and monitoring via the intercom system indicated that the children were not overtly verbalizing). The extent of the effects would likely be maximized if the children were reminded, or reminded themselves, to be brave.

Unlike Kanfer *et al.*, Graziano, Mooney, Huber, and Ignasiak (1979) selected severely fearful children as subjects for a multiple-case study of the efficacy of a cognitive change strategy for fear reduction. This sample included seven children (five males, two females) ranging in age from 8.7 to 12.8 years. The parents described their children's problem as highly disruptive nighttime fears of long duration (3 to 6 years). These children had no other major psychological symptoms and all were in age-appropriate grades. The intervention involved five weekly sessions, with the first and last sessions for assessment and the middle three for instruction and discussion. Parents and children were seen separately, but both groups were conducted as classes with an educational focus. The children's meetings were presented as classes on how to learn to be less afraid. Children were instructed in relaxation techniques ("Lie down and relax muscles") and positive imagery ("Choose and imagine a pleasant scene"). They were also asked to say, "I am brave. I can take care of myself when I am in the dark." The children were then told that by practicing these exercises every night they could earn bravery tokens from their parents. They could also earn tokens each morning for having been brave throughout the preceding night. A self-monitoring component was added by giving the children a special book in which to record their earnings. Once a certain total had been achieved, tokens could be cashed in for a hamburger party to celebrate the child's bravery. In the parents' meeting, the children's exercises were explained, and the parents were instructed in the administration of the token system and social reinforcement for correct performance. At posttest the parents' ratings indicated reductions in the number and intensity of fears. All parents also rated the program as being very to extremely helpful. The authors had designated ten consecutive "fearless" nights as the behavioral goal of treatment, and all children reached this goal. The number of weeks required to reach criterion ranged from 3 to 19 with a mean of 8.7. At 1-year follow-up, six of the seven children were completely free of nighttime fears and the seventh was exhibiting a reduced level of fear. This study's combination of cognitive and behavioral components appears extremely effective, but the lack of any type of control group qualifies the conclusions that can be drawn. Finally, given the multicomponent nature of the intervention (relaxation, imagery, self-statements), it is impossible to assess the specific effect, if any, of the self-statements.

Graziano and Mooney (1980) followed the Graziano et al. (1979) multiple-case study with a group comparison study. The subjects were 33 families with severely fearful children between the ages of 6 and 13 years. In all families, "going to bed" was described as a highly emotional and disruptive nightly event. Families were randomly assigned to the experimental or waiting-list control conditions. With one exception, assessment and intervention were virtually identical to that in the Graziano et al. (1979) study. In the current effort, parents were also asked to complete home observation sheets for seven consecutive nights before and after the intervention. At posttest, the experimental group showed significant reductions in fear strength and obtained significantly greater ratings of improvement. The groups did not differ in number of fears. The parental observations indicated that the experimental group displayed significantly less fear behavior at posttreatment. At 2-month follow-up, 14 of the 17 experimental subjects had met the behavioral criterion of ten consecutive fearless nights. By the 1-year follow-up, the figure was 15 of 17 and contact with one of the two noncriterion subjects had been lost. Following treatment of the experimental group, the control group underwent training. Their results were not statistically analyzed, but at 6-month follow-up 11 of the 13 children had achieved the behavioral criterion. These results clearly suggest the effectiveness of the treatment with severely fearful children, but, as stated above, given the numerous elements in this intervention, it is very difficult to discern the actual role of the children's self-verbalizations.

On the whole, these studies provide evidence that cognitive strategies, especially when accompanied by behavioral contingencies, can be effective in the treatment of children's fears. The effects of self-verbalizations alone with severely fearful children are not known.

HYPERACTIVE AND DISRUPTIVE BEHAVIOR

Goodwin and Mahoney (1975) trained hyperactive boys to control their responses to verbal taunts via self-statements. The authors described this intervention as behavioral modeling combined with the modeling of "private responses" consonant with adaptive coping. Three hyperactive boys, aged 6 to 11 years, were asked by the experimenter to play a game in which each one was, in turn, verbally assaulted by the other subjects. Baseline observations indicated that all three had marked difficulty handling this situation. One week after baseline, the subjects viewed a film of a young boy participating in the same verbal taunting game. This model remained calm and appeared to cope with the taunts through a series of self-statements, such as "I'm not going to let them bug me." After this viewing subjects participated in the verbal taunting game again. A few days later, the same film was shown, but at this viewing the therapist pointed out and discussed the thoughts and actions of the model. The boys were then asked to recall as many coping statements as they could, and the taunting game was again conducted. A final game was also conducted 1 week later. Observations of the game situation indicated an improvement continued at the 1-week follow-up session. Observations of disruptive behavior in the classroom also reflected improvement. It is interesting that improvement seemed to occur after the model's self-statements had been emphasized, but it seems equally plausible that the children became habituated to the situation and later sessions simply failed to arouse the anger levels present in the earlier sessions. Also, the absence of any type of control group makes it very difficult to interpret these findings. The modeling component distinguishes this study from the other research discussed in this section; however, the function of self-statements (i.e., to help the child endure a difficult situation) is similar to the use of self-statements in the treatment of nighttime fears.

Palkes, Stewart, and Kahana (1968) examined the impact of self-directed verbal commands on the Porteus Maze (Porteus, 1955) performance of hyperactive boys. Twenty white, middle-class males who were currently under psychiatric care for hyperactivity served as the subjects. Children were reported to be of average intelligence and ranged in age from 8 years 2 months to 9 years 11 months. During the course of the study, medications were discontinued for all children who had been receiving them. Subjects were randomly assigned to either the verbal training or attention control group. Verbal training involved teaching the subjects to use self-directed verbal commands, such as "stop, look, and think" before responding. Visual reminder cards with these commands printed on them were used as aids. The children were trained on materials such as the Matching Familiar Figures Test (MFF; Kagan, 1966) and other cognitive and visual–motor tasks. The control group was exposed to the same materials but received no verbal training. Both groups were seen for two 1-hour sessions on successive days. While the groups did not differ on the Porteus Test Quotient (TQ) and Qualitative (Q) scores at pretreatment, posttreatment assessment indicated that the experimental group obtained a significantly higher mean TQ and a significantly lower Q score than the control group. Thus, the self-directed verbal commands resulted in a more careful and controlled performance on the task.

Palkes, Stewart, and Freedman (1972) attempted to replicate Palkes *et al.* (1968) and examine the importance of the actual vocalization of the verbal commands. The subjects were 30 boys highly similar to those involved in the previous study but the current effort included a larger age range (7 to 13 years). The subjects were randomly assigned to one of three conditions: verbal training, silent reading, or attention control. Verbal training was identical to that conducted in Palkes *et al.* (1968), but the silent reading condition involved using the cue cards as aids but avoiding any verbalization of the commands. Posttreatment assessment indicated that the verbal training group obtained a significantly better Q score on the Porteus, but there were no significant group differences on the TQ. At 2-week follow-up the performance of the verbal training group had deteriorated, resulting in no significant group differences. These results offer slight support for the importance of the vocalization of the self-directed verbal commands; however, the overall "clinical" impact of the intervention is hardly impressive.

Unimpressive results were reported from an effort to use self-directed verbal commands on arithmetic performance and activity level in hyperactive children (Burns, 1972). The 45 elementary-school-aged subjects had been identified by their teachers as hyperactive and were referred for treatment. Subjects were randomly assigned to one of three conditions. In the two verbal training conditions, the children were given either (1) 20 trials or (2) 40 trials using self-directed verbal commands to solve arithmetic problems. These trials were administered in two training sessions that occurred on successive days. The attention control group simply worked on arithmetic problems without any training. Dependent measures included the child's score on the computation and problems sections of a standardized achievement test and the child's motor activity during testing, as rated concurrently by an observer. The posttesting occurred immediately after the second training session. The results indicated no significant effects on the sections of the math achievement test or on motor activity during the testing.

The studies utilizing the noninteractive type of self-instructional training for fear reduction achieved positive treatment outcomes. In contrast, while some of the studies with hyperactive children reported successes, the extent of the change was not impressive. Only one study (Kanfer *et al.*, 1975), however, relied exclusively on self-statements as the mode of intervention. Most employed behavioral procedures, such as modeling and explicit contingencies, in addition to the self-instructional training. Thus, we know little about the effects of noninteractive self-instructional procedures that are not combined with behavioral procedures.

Interactive Training

Cognitive–behavioral training of the interactive type involves more explicit instruction in the use of self-instructions, modeling, and practice. As stated earlier, there are two variants of interactive training. One line of research provides training in self-instructional procedures within the context of a more operant formulation of self-control, with self-instructions being taught along with self-monitoring, self-evaluation, and self-reinforcement, whereas the other line imitates the processes outlined in Luria's stage theory. The second line provides a more elaborated form of training.

OPERANT FORMULATIONS OF SELF-CONTROL

Neilans and Israel (1981) studied the impact of a self-regulation package containing self-monitoring, self-goal-setting, self-evaluation, and self-reinforcement skills. In addition, this package incorporated the use of self-statements. Six residents (two female, four male) of a group home for behavior-problem children, aged 7 to 13, were the subjects. The intervention was conducted for a respectable duration—daily 50-minute sessions, 5 days a week for 3 months. The class time was divided into two 20-minute periods in which the children worked on math and reading, with a 10-minute break separating the periods. Treatment was conducted only during math, and the reading period was used to assess generalization. Dependent measures included paper-and-pencil measures, observations of disruptive and on-task behavior, and assessments of the number of task items completed and percentage correct. When the token economy was in effect, disruptive behavior during the math period decreased to 59% of the baseline level, whereas disruptive behavior in reading showed some increase over baseline levels. During a return to baseline, disruptive behavior increased to 81% of the initial baseline. Self-charting reduced disruptive behavior to 33% of baseline. When the self-statements were introduced in reading, a dramatic drop in disruptive behavior in this period also occurred. Change in on-task behavior mirrored the changes in disruptive behavior, with on-task increasing whenever disruptive behavior decreased.

The Neilans and Israel (1981) study allowed for some interesting comparisons. For example, while the conventional token economy did decrease disruptive behavior and increase on-task behavior, these changes did not maintain after the withdrawal of the system. On the other hand, the self-regulation system produced greater positive changes in behavior and academic performance, and these improvements obtained during the withdrawal of teacher control. As these authors suggested, the very nature of the self-regulation system "programs for maintenance." These results are qualified by the small sample size. The inclusion of an attention control group would have been desirable, but the residential treatment status of these subjects suggests that their behavior difficulties were greater than those of children selected from normal classrooms, so the impact of this intervention is impressive. The effects are, however, due to a combined cognitive–behavioral program so it is not possible to isolate the effects of the self-instructions.

Varni and Henker (1979) examined the effects of the sequential application of self-instructions, self-monitoring, and self-reinforcement procedures on the academic performance and behavior patterns of hyperactive children. The subjects were three 8- to 10-year-old males diagnosed as hyperactive and enrolled in a school for learning-disabled children. The academic performance of the children was assessed using their programmed reading and math texts. A count of the number of items completed and the percent correct was made after each session. Hyperactive behavior was assessed via behavioral observations in the training room and in the classroom. Both gross motor behavior and off-task responses were recorded. In addition, a "hyperactivity index" for each child was calculated on the basis of the average number of target behaviors occurring per interval of observation. The three children experienced 10 to 19 baseline sessions (35 minutes) in the training room and 21 to 30 sessions in the classroom. During the baseline sessions, the child was presented with academic materials and given the choice of whether or not to work on these materials. Following baseline, each child was exposed to a one-session "instructional control probe" to assess the impact of the experimenter's simply requesting the child to work on the academic materials. Following this session, each subject was given three sessions of self-instructional training using materials such as the MFF, Porteus Mazes, and the programmed reading text. The impact of this training was then assessed in posttraining sessions. Next, self-monitoring was introduced. In this phase, the child was provided a wrist counter and a clock and was instructed in how to use the counter to keep track of points earned by number of minutes worked. At the end of the last self-monitoring session, the therapist explained the rate of exchange of points for prizes. In subsequent sessions, the child continued to self-monitor but was also responsible for self-reinforcement. The entire self-regulation package was applied first with reading and then with math. The authors report that self-instructional training had no significant impact on the children's academic or behavioral performance. The introduction of self-monitoring yielded minor, but consistent positive effects, and self-reinforcement resulted in increased academic performance and decreased hyperactive responding. Thus, the major effects appeared to be specific to self-reinforcement.

A number of factors could explain the absence of effects following self-instructional training. First, self-instructional training as applied in other studies typically includes a self-reinforcement component as a part of training, rather than separate as in this instance. Also, the detailed description of the self-instructional training provided in this study suggests that the training was conducted in a somewhat non-interactive or rigid manner. The authors did require a criterion level of performance in terms of correct problem solutions, but there was no attempt to directly assess the child's knowledge of the self-instructions. Nevertheless, this study offers some interesting information about the relative effectiveness of the various self-regulation components, and requires that attention be given to self-reinforcement.

A training program that emphasized both self-instructional procedures and other self-management strategies was evaluated by Cameron and Robinson (1980). The subjects were four 7- to 8-year-old children selected by their teachers as demonstrating academic and behavior problems. Using a multiple-baseline, across-individuals design, the authors assessed on-task behavior during math class, math performance in terms of percent accurate, and self-correction rate in reading. Each child received 12 individual 30-minute sessions over 3 weeks. Self-instructional training procedures were applied to math problems and additional training was provided in self-monitoring and self-reinforcement for correct performance. The training resulted in significant increases in on-task behavior for two of the three children, and all three showed gains in math accuracy. Training did seem to generalize to reading, but the authors cautioned that factors such as the nature of the reading program and simple maturation might also explain the improved reading. These findings provide support for self-instructional plus other self-regulation skills as a method of improving on-task behavior and academic performance in specific subject areas, but the absence of a control group does make it difficult to successfully rule out other reasons for the improvements.

ELABORATED SELF-INSTRUCTIONAL TRAINING

The second line of research or interactive self-instructional training considers self-instructions as cognitive schemata that are capable of guiding, directing, and coordinating other aspects of self-regulatory behavior. Research with this conceptualization of self-instructions provides the most elaborate versions of training. The majority of the studies reviewed in this section employed self-instructional training in which the child is taught a series of self-statements to aid in task performance, with the therapist serving as a model for thinking through problems.

The prototype for these studies was conducted by Meichenbaum and Goodman (1971) and elaborated by Kendall and Finch (1979b). As described by Meichenbaum (1975, 1977), in the first stage of training the therapist or tutor models the behaviors associated with successful task performance while talking to himself/herself out loud. These verbalizations of self-instructions relate to the specifics of the task and include statements of problem definition (i.e., clarifying and understanding the exact requirements of the task at hand), problem approach (planning a general strategy for solving the problem), focusing attention, selecting an answer, and self-reinforcing for correct performance or using a coping statement for incorrect performance. After observing the therapist perform several items, children then perform the task while talking to themselves out loud. Usually at this point the therapist assists the child in remembering to employ the modeled sequence of self-verbalizations. The therapist and child typically alternate performing task items, and as they proceed through the task, the therapist gradually fades these verbalizations to a whisper and encourages the child to do the same. Eventually, the therapist and child self-instruct covertly, using the internalized statements to control and direct task performance. Thus, self-instructional procedures include training in the use of task-directing verbalizations, self-reinforcing statements, and modeling of task-appropriate behavior. The effectiveness of this approach has been evaluated with cognitively impulsive children, as well as with aggressive, hyperactive, non-self-controlled, and behavior-problem children.

Some self-instructional intervention studies have identified their samples solely on the basis of cognitive impulsivity as defined as task performance on a measure such as the MFF. This measure is a match-to-sample task in which the child's latency to first response and number of incorrect responses are recorded. Typically a child is judged impulsive if his/her latency is below and reponse errors above the respective medians of a same-aged sample. The MFF is also frequently used as an outcome measure, and some evidence for a relationship between cognitive and behavioral impulsivity does exist (see review by Messer, 1976; Egeland, Bielke, & Kendall, 1980); however, there is controversy over the construct validity of this measure (Bentler & McClain, 1976; Block, Block, & Harrington, 1974; Kagan & Messer, 1975; Messer, 1976). Given this controversy, studies using only the MFF or similar measures of cognitive impulsivity for case identification will be discussed separately from investigations using more "clinical" criteria such as parent or teacher referral.

Test-Selected Subjects. Meichenbaum and Goodman's prototype self-instructional training (1971, Study II) used MFF-selected kindergarten and first grade subjects in an examination of the efficacy of the cognitive self-instructional training relative to a modeling-only and control group. The self-instructional training condition employed the procedures just described; the modeling condition was identical to the self-instructional condition except for the absence of any verbal self-instructions. Relative to the control group, both treatment groups demonstrated significant increases in response latency following four 30-minute training sessions, but only the self-instructional group obtained a decrease in errors. This finding suggests that self-instructions do have an impact beyond that obtained by simply modeling successful task behavior. Abikoff (1979) has suggested that the results of this study are qualified by the high degree of overlap between the test, the MFF, and the picture-matching materials used in training. This critique does have relevance for evaluating the overall level of improved performance, but the overlap between training and test materials does not necessarily qualify the contrast between the self-instructional and modeling conditions.

Although Cullinan, Epstein, and Silver (1977) also compared the impact of modeling and modeling-plus-self-verbalization on MFF performance, their results, as we will see in a moment, may require cautious consideration. From a population of learning-disabled children, 33 impulsive males (aged 9 to 12) were selected on the basis of their MFF scores. Subjects were then randomly assigned to the modeling, modeling-plus-self-verbalization, or control conditions. In both the modeling conditions, subjects observed a video tape of a boy solving MFF problems reflectively. In this tape, the model overtly verbalized self-instructions to delay selecting an answer until he/she had carefully checked each possibility. Subjects in the modeling-plus-self-verbalization condition not only watched the video tape but were also required to repeat the model's reflective self-instructions as soon as they were spoken. The control group observed a video tape of MFF items but no model was shown. Immediately after exposure to the video tapes, all subjects were readministered the MFF and a follow-up administration occurred 3 weeks later. At immediate posttest, both modeling conditions performed significantly better than the control group in terms of MFF errors, with no significant group differences observed for MFF latencies. At follow-up, there were no significant group differences on either errors or latency. While these results are not encouraging and suggest at best the equivalence of self-instructions and modeling procedures, the study is different from other self-instructional interventions in several important respects. First, the models were video-taped rather than live. The absence of a one-to-one learning relationship may have been crucial. Second, the subjects were never required to use the self-instructions while actually solving problems. Also, even in a field where brief treatments are the norm, this intervention was unusually short-lived. Thus, the absence of interactive features seems to be related to less impressive results.

Data presented by Bender (1976) included a contrast of tutor-verbalized versus self-verbalized strategies and this comparison lends support to the need for interactive training with participatory subjects. Controlling for sex, Bender randomly assigned 70 impulsive first graders to verbal self-instructional strategy training, tutor-verbalized strategy training, verbal self-instruction without explicit strategy training, attentional–materials control, and in-class control conditions. While all the outcomes were not consistent, the results of the immediate posttests indicated self-verbalization was more effective than tutor verbalization in terms both of decreasing MFF errors and of increasing response time. A comparison of the strategy versus nonstrategy self-verbalization conditions revealed that strategy training was more effective in increasing response time. These results tentatively suggest that self-verbalization of explicit strategies may be the most effective of these methods in modifying cognitive impulsivity in first graders.

Kendall and Finch (1978) compared self-instructional procedures combined with a response-cost contingency with an attention control. Twenty impulsive emotionally disturbed children (16 males, 4 females) served as subjects. The treatment group received six 20-minute sessions of self-instructional training accompanied by a response-cost procedure contingent upon errors. The control group was exposed to the same materials, psychoeducational tasks, for six sessions and given non-contingent rewards. The treatment group demonstrated increased MFF latencies and decreased MFF errors at posttest and 3-month follow-up. No group differences were observed on two self-report measures of impulsivity. The treated children were rated by teachers blind to conditions as significantly less impulsive at follow-up on the Impulsive Classroom Behavior Scale (ICBS; Weinreich, 1975), suggesting the treatment had generalized to classroom behavior. It was later recognized, however (Abikoff & Ramsey, 1979; Kendall & Finch, 1979c), that the treatment and control groups differed significantly on this measure prior to treatment. While the intervention was successful in improving task performance, the psychoeducational focus of the training materials and, perhaps, the limited amount of instruction were, in retrospect, less than maximal. The pretreatment group differences detracts from conclusions regarding the generalization of treatment effects.

In a series of studies conducted by Meyers, Cohen, Schlesser, and colleagues, children identified as cognitively impulsive and stratified according to Piagetian stage of cognitive development (preoperational vs. concrete operations) have been studied to determine how best to enhance generalization of treatment effects. In a recent study (Cohen, Meyers, Schlesser, & Rodick, 1982) the cognitive level of the children was found to interact with different types of training. Importantly, some interesting findings emerged regarding generalization: Only the concrete operational children who received a "directed discovery" type of training demonstrated significant generalization of this training to other cognitive tasks. Children in the directed discovery training were led by their therapist to "discover" the self-instructional statements that would guide problem solving. A series of prepared questions were employed to facilitate each child's discovery. An apparent conclusion, and one that is consistent with our review of the literature, is that an active involved training, with cognitively prepared children, is most likely to produce generalization.

A few studies have begun to examine the relative contributions of certain features of the self-instructional training approach. The effects of self-reinforcing self-statements and of explicit response-cost contingencies have been investigated. Other similar comparisons have also appeared, but keep in mind that we are here only reviewing those studies where the sample was cognitively impulsive based on their performance of the MFF.

Speculating on the special role of the self-reinforcement component in self-instructional procedures, Nelson and Birkimer (1978) compared the effects of self-instructions alone with self-instructions plus self-reinforcement. Forty-eight black, cognitively impulsive second and third graders were randomly assigned to one of four conditions: (1) self-instructional training; (2) self-instructional training with self-reinforcement; (3) attentional control; and (4) assessment control. At posttest assessment, only the self-instructional training with self-reinforcement resulted in significant improvement on the MFF, with change occurring in both the response latency and the number of errors. Apparently, the self-reinforcement component adds meaningfully to the training procedures.

A different match-to-sample task, the Kansas Reflection–Impulsivity Scale for Preschoolers (KRISP; Wright, 1973) was used to select 32 impulsive 4- and 5-year-olds out of a population of low-income preschoolers. Arnold and Forehand (1978) then compared the effectiveness of cognitive self-control training and response-cost procedures by randomly assigning subjects to conditions (cognitive training, response-cost, cognitive training and response-cost, or placebo control). The response-cost procedures, for some reason, were executed only during the post- and follow-up assessment. Training involved four 20- to 30-minute sessions conducted over a 2-week period. Dependent measures included the KRISP and a group-administered classroom matching test. On the KRISP, all groups, including the placebo control, showed improvement with repeated administration. On the classroom test, however, only the two cognitive training groups showed significant improvement. These results suggest that cognitive training can improve the impulsive response style of preschool children in the immediate training situation and in the classroom, whereas response-cost enhances task performance only in the immediate situation.

On the whole, interventions with test-selected samples of cognitively impulsive children tend to be briefer and more circumscribed than interventions with subjects selected for their social problem behavior, as will be seen when the latter studies are considered. Research with cognitively impulsive children, however, has provided some information about the relative effectiveness of various treatment components, and has been fairly consistent when examined in the following light—interventions where the procedures are interactive and involving for the child and/or where behavioral contingencies are systematically applied produce more gains than when these conditions are absent. The studies reviewed thus far are limited by the manner of selecting subjects and by the lack of extensive assessment of generalization. Nevertheless, the hints that emerge here are worth pursuing further as we examine studies with behavior-problem children.

Clinical Samples. In addition to the studies of procedures to help cognitively impulsive children, a large and ever growing number of studies have utilized variations of self-instructional training with children who have difficulty controlling their social behavior. These children have been described with various labels including impulsive, hyperactive, non-self-controlled, or behavior problem. Generally, children such as these are selected for participation in research on the basis of social, rather than test performance, criteria. Undoubtedly, some important differences exist among the various subject samples considered in this section; however, the focus on behavior as the selection criterion makes it reasonable to group these studies together.

As previously stated, Meichenbaum and Goodman's (1971) research was one of the earlier studies in this area—a study that stimulated many later investigations. In Study I, the subjects were second grade children who were teacher-identified as hyperactive or lacking in self-control and randomly assigned to cognitive training, attention control, or assessment control conditions. Subjects in the experimental and attention control groups received four 30-minute training sessions with both groups using the same training tasks but only the experimental group being taught self-instructions. Two types of dependent measures were employed. Task performance measures included the Porteus Maze Test, the MFF, and the Picture Arrangement (PA), Block Design (BD), and Coding subtests of the Wechsler Intelligence Scale for Children (WISC; Wechsler, 1949). Measures of classroom behavior included behavioral observations and a teacher questionnaire designed to assess the child's level of self-control. Posttesting indicated the self-instructional group improved significantly more than the two control groups on MFF latency and WISC PA and Coding subtests. Both the self-instructional and attention control groups made significantly fewer qualitative errors on the Porteus than did the assessment control group. The pattern of relatively positive results was basically maintained at 4-week follow up. However, the classroom measures revealed no significant group differences for the behavioral observations or teacher ratings of classroom behavior. Self-instructions seemed to improve task performance on certain tests, but, perhaps because of the limited number of sessions or the nature of the training materials, generalization to classroom behavior did not occur.

Numerous case studies and group treatment studies have followed and many have sought to develop improved methods for attaining this elusive generalization. As we review several of these studies we will keep an eye on features of the study and features of the method of providing the intervention to determine what might be important prescriptive characteristics to enhance generalization in future applications.

Bornstein and Quevillon (1976) employed self-instructional training with three hyperactive preschool children enrolled in a Head Start program. This intervention also included self-reinforcement paired with external reinforcement (candy) that was faded over the course of the training. The treatment emphasized teaching the children to complete tasks assigned by the teacher. The intervention involved only one 2-hour session, and training materials focused on sensorimotor skills such as drawing figures, block design tasks, and conceptual grouping problems. Behavioral observations indicated a dramatic increase in on-task behavior in the classroom, and this improvement was maintained at 5-month follow-up. The impact of these findings is qualified by the lack of a control group.

Friedling and O'Leary (1979) attempted to replicate the findings of Bornstein and Quevillon (1976) with nonmedicated second and third grade hyperactive children (seven male, one female). Children were assigned to either self-instructional training or attention control conditions. The intervention was applied in two "doses." Initially, one 90-minute session of self-instructional training was conducted, as was done in Bornstein and Quevillon. The children's behavior was then observed for 10 days. Observers recorded on-task behavior, academic behavior (percent accurate, quantity completed, percent skipped), and teacher attention. Next, self-instructional training was repeated in two

40-minute sessions on consecutive days, and observations were repeated for another 10-day period. Unlike Bornstein and Quevillon, no change in on-task behavior was obtained. The general lack of impact of the training provides little support for the self-instructional intervention; however, several differences between this study, the Bornstein and Quevillon effort, and the other case studies noted earlier are worth considering. From the authors' description of their training procedures, it seems possible that Friedling and O'Leary administered the self-instructional training in a very rote, structured, and noninteractive manner, thus allowing little opportunity for tailoring the instructions and statements to the level of the child. If we assume that this potential shortcoming does not explain the results, then we must look elsewhere. One apparent possibility concerns the lack of behavioral contingencies. Bornstein and Quevillon (1976) used a behavioral contingency with the self-instructional training, as did Kendall and colleagues, so that the different results obtained by Friedling and O'Leary might be caused by their omission of the behavioral contingency component of the training.

A case reported by Kendall and Finch (1976) combined self-instructional training with a response-cost contingency and, via a multiple-baseline design, demonstrated that the changes in rates of switching behavior were associated with the implementation of the cognitive–behavioral training. Generalization probes, as well as a serendipitous report from the school teacher, provided some data on the generalization of the effects of the training program.

In another case report, Kendall and Urbain (1981) employed the combined cognitive–behavioral training procedures (self-instructions and response-cost contingencies) but added a more direct focus on problem-solving and perspective-taking training. The client was a 7-year-old hyperactive girl. The training in this case was more extensive than that typically reported in the literature. Initial training lasted 3 months (weekly meetings) with therapeutic contact continuing for 1 year. Self-evaluation and role plays in which the child taught the therapist how to use the self-talk were also part of the intervention package. Desired gains were evident in a reduction of disruptive behaviors and, to a lesser extent, in the ratings of home and school behavior. Although this single-subject design did not permit clear-cut conclusions, the data suggest that the inclusion of the response-cost component of the training was an important factor in the achievement of behavioral control.

Thus far, small-n or single-case studies of a reasonable degree of experimental rigor have been reviewed. The effects of well-elaborated, interactive self-instructional training have also been examined in group treatment studies. As was the case with the research just reviewed, these group outcome studies have typically been concerned with identifying factors associated with treatment generalization as well as with the production of treatment effects.

The contribution of different types of self-instructional training to the attainment of generalized change was examined in a study by Kendall and Wilcox (1980). The study compared self-instructional training that focuses on the specific training task (concrete labeling) with training that was relevant to the task but was also general and could thus be applied to other situations (conceptual labeling). The 33 8- to 12-year-old subjects were referred for treatment by their teachers owing to a problematic lack of self-control (using the Self-Control Rating Scale—SCRS; Kendall & Wilcox, 1979; see also Figure 4-1 in Chapter 4) that interfered with both academic performance and classroom deportment. Using a randomized block procedure, with teacher-blind SCRS ratings as the blocking factor, the subjects were assigned to one of the two treatment conditions or an attention control group. All subjects were seen for six 40-minute sessions, but only the two treatment groups received self-instructional training with modeling and a response-cost contingency. The training materials for sessions 1 through 4 were psychoeducational tasks, and in sessions 5 and 6 training focused on interpersonal play situations that required cooperation. At posttest and 1-month follow-up, teachers' blind ratings of self-control and hyperactivity evidenced significant change due to treatment, with the treatment effects stronger for the conceptual labeling group. Thus, generalization of treatment effects to the classroom was found. A self-report measure of impulsivity showed no change, and all three groups improved on the MFF and Porteus Mazes. In addition, Kendall and Wilcox provided data on the self-control ratings of nonreferred children to give some guidelines or norms for assessing treatment impact (see also Kendall & Norton-Ford, 1982b, for more detailed discussion of the methods of normative comparisons). At posttreatment and follow-up, the conceptual treatment group fell within one standard deviation of the mean for the nonreferred children (see also Thackwray, Meyers, Schlesser, & Cohen, in press).

At 1-year follow-up (Kendall, 1981b), numerous improvements were found for subjects in all treatment groups—perhaps due to increased age. Teacher ratings showed differences favoring the conceptually trained children, but with a small number of children available, the differences did not reach statistical significance. However, it was found that conceptually trained children showed significantly better recall of the material they had learned than either the concrete or the control group. Conceptually trained children were rated by their new classroom teachers as not sufficiently lacking in self-control to warrant referral. Although the documentation of long-term effects was not compelling, there was a suggestive pattern of relationships between the age of the subject and long-term maintenance of gains.

In a study of the relative effectiveness of individual and group application of the cognitive–behavioral intervention procedures, Kendall and Zupan (1981) employed twice as many treatment sessions (12) as had Kendall and Wilcox (1980). Would the provision of the treatment in settings similar to the settings in which generalization is desired (i.e., groups of children) enhance the attainment of generalized behavior change? After all, in the small-group setting, the children see others learning similar skills and are exposed to multiple peer models. In contrast, the individual attention and the additional time allowed for rehearsal provided in a one-to-one therapy might more effectively facilitate desirable behavior change.

In order to compare individual versus group application of the cognitive–behavioral procedures, 30 teacher-referred, non-self-controlled classroom problem children from grades 3 to 5 were assigned according to a randomized block procedure to either the individual treatment condition, the group treatment condition, or a nonspecified group treatment (control) condition. All children received twelve 45- to 55-minute sessions, averaging twice a week for 6 weeks. Except for the instructions relating to the cognitive–behavioral self-control training proper, children in all three conditions were given similar tasks, task instructions, and performance feedback. However, only the children in either the individual or group self-control conditions received training in the cognitive–behavioral strategies.

Multiple-method assessments were used to evaluate the treatment procedures, including measures of children's task performance and cognitive skills and two teacher ratings (teachers blind to treatment conditions) of classroom behavior. In addition to children's perform-ance (latencies and errors) on the MFF, two tasks for assessing cognitive interpersonal skills were utilized: the Means–Ends Problem Solving (MEPS) task (Shure & Spivack, 1972) and Chandler's (1973) bystander cartoons (measure of social perspective taking). Teachers who were blind to subjects' conditions completed the SCRS and Conners hyper-activity index. Each of these assessment measures was administered pretreatment, posttreatment, and at 2-month follow-up. The Peabody

Picture Vocabulary Test (PPVT; Dunn, 1965) was administered pre-treatment to acquire a general index of each child's intellectual abilities.

The most striking gains were seen in pretreatment to posttreatment changes on the teachers' blind ratings (i.e., SCRS and hyperactivity). Analysis of the teachers' blind ratings of self-control indicated that the children in the group and individual treatment conditions demonstrated significant improvements that were significantly superior to the changes in the nonspecific treatment condition. These findings provide evidence of the generalized effects of the treatment to classroom behavior. The changes in teachers' ratings of hyperactivity parallel somewhat the self-control ratings; however, the changes were significant for all three treatment conditions. Analysis of maintenance effects indicated that both self-control and hyperactivity ratings showed significant improvements, but that the improvement at follow-up was independent of the child's treatment condition.

Improvements that were independent of the child's treatment condition were seen in performance on the MFF. However, while changes in MFF latency scores were not maintained at follow-up, improvements in MFF scores were. That is, when MFF latencies and errors are considered together, the results indicated that children were performing in a somewhat fast and accurate manner, a style that is more desirable than either the fast inaccurate (impulsive) or slow accurate (reflective) styles. Changes in perspective taking at follow-up were positive. Both individual and group treatments produced lasting improvements; the nonspecific control condition did not. Changes in MEPS test performance were in the opposite direction from what would be expected. This trend was likely the result of the use of the same test material for repeated administration and the tendency of the children to tell shorter stories on each administration. Shorter stories resulted in lower MEPS scores.

It should be noted, however, that the significant improvements across the assessment periods for children in all three groups were not surprising. The nonspecific (group treatment) control condition was included to control for the effects of group participation; it was intended as an attention–placebo condition in a group context. Because of the problems that arose in the control group of non-self-controlled children, therapists eventually employed reprimands, forceful comments, and other group control techniques to maintain order. As a result of these procedures and the children's response to the training materials, some gains were expected.

In terms of normative comparisons using the teachers' blind-ratings data, the mean SCRS scores of the cognitive–behavioral treatment conditions at posttreatment were within one standard deviation of the normative mean. Similarly, the hyperactivity ratings for the cognitive–behavioral treatment conditions were brought within the normative range. These normative comparisons suggest that the children receiving the cognitive–behavioral treatment (individually or in groups) evidence improvements that brought them (at posttreatment) within a normal range of self-control and hyperactivity. These improvements, resulting from lengthier treatments, were greater than those reported in Kendall and Wilcox (1980).

At 1-year follow-up (Kendall, 1982b), improvements were found for subjects across treatment conditions. Only the children receiving group treatment were not significantly different from nonproblem children on ratings of self-control; only the children receiving individual treatment were not significantly different from nonproblem children on hyperactivity ratings. Structured interviews indicated that individually treated children showed significantly better recall of the ideas they had learned, and produced significantly more illustrations of use of the ideas than children in either the group treatment or the nonspecific treatment conditions. Apparently, there is evidence for generalization to the classroom (as evident in the teachers' ratings) but an absence of compelling evidence for long-term maintenance.

Drummond (1974, cited in Meichenbaum, 1976a) employed training materials with a more social or interpersonal focus and compared the efficacy of self-instructional training with discussion and assessment control groups in the reduction of disruptive classroom behavior among 30 third and fourth grade classroom problem children. Self-instructional training focused on developing self-talk that could be used in classroom problem situations, such as talking out, leaving the desk, hitting other children. In the discussion control the subjects talked about general issues such as school problems and getting along with other children. Both treatments were administered in two groups of five, and each group met twice a week for 3 weeks. At posttreatment and 12-week follow-up, the self-instructional groups showed significant improvement on teachers' blind ratings of classroom behavior. Both the self-instructional and discussion groups showed improvement in behavioral observations of actual classroom behavior. Finer comparisons between the behavior of the two groups were not possible since the behaviors actually taught in the self-instructional group were not included in the observational coding system (Urbain & Kendall, 1980). No group differences were found on the MFF or a self-esteem inventory. The comparability of the treatment and discussion control groups on the behavior ratings is puzzling in light of the differential teacher ratings. This pattern of results appears relatively consistent with the treatment's focus on changing problem behaviors rather than improving cognitive task performance, and points to the relevance of interpersonal training tasks.

Moore and Cole (1978) conducted self-instructional training with 8- to 12-year-old children in residential treatment. Training consisted of six 30-minute sessions that focused exclusively on the use of self-instructions with cognitive and visual–motor tasks such as mazes, dot connection, and hidden-figures problems. Posttreatment assessment indicated that the self-instructional group was significantly improved relative to attention and assessment controls on MFF latency, the Children's Embedded Figures Test (CEFT; Witkin, Oltman, Raskin, & Karp, 1971), and the WISC PA and Coding subtests. There was no reported change in classroom behavior as measured by the Conners Teacher Rating Scale (Conners, 1969). No follow-up was conducted. Again it appears that the exclusively cognitive nature of the training materials did not encourage generalization of effects to classroom behavior.

In a comprehensive effort, Douglas, Parry, Marton, and Garson (1976) employed self-instructional procedures with hyperactive boys. To be included in the study, both the child's parents and teacher had to agree that the child demonstrated symptoms of hyperactivity, such as attentional problems, excessive motor activity level, and impulsivity. In addition the child had to be rated above the cutoff score on the Conners Parent and Teacher Rating Scales for Hyperactivity and demonstrate a mean latency of less than 10 seconds on the MFF. All subjects were from upper-lower-class or middle-class homes, and no child with an IQ below 80 was included. Subjects ranged in age from 6 years 1 month to 10 years 11 months. The experimental group included 18 subjects, and the control group contained 11, with groups not differing on age, IQ, and Conners score. Training involved two 1-hour sessions per week for 12 weeks. Self-instructional procedures were applied to a broad range of training materials, including the child's actual homework and interpersonal problem situations. In addition, a minimum of 12 consultation sessions with each child's parents and six sessions with classroom teachers were held. These sessions explained the training to parents and teachers and provided instructions in the implementation of self-instructional procedures at home and at school. On occasion, parents or teachers observed and participated in the child's training session.

Treatment impact was assessed via an extensive test battery, including the MFF, Porteus Mazes, Story Completion Test (Parry, 1973),

Bender Visual–Motor Gestalt Test (Bender, 1938), Memory tests from the Detroit Tests of Learning Aptitude (Baker & Leland, 1967), Durrell Analysis of Reading Difficulty (Durrell, 1955), the Wide Range Achievement Test (Jastak, Bijou, & Jastak, 1965), and the parent and teacher versions of the Conners. At posttest the treatment group showed significant improvement over its pretreatment performance on nine of ten task performance measures, whereas the control group showed significant improvement on only one measure. The treatment group did not show improvement on either the parent or teacher behavior ratings. At 3-month follow-up, the treatment group maintained its improved level on eight of ten measures, and the control group maintained its one improved score. As the authors point out, improvements were observed in the treatment group on measures that were not the specific focus of training, such as the reading and Story Completion Tests. The failure to obtain change on the Conners indicates a lack of generalization of treatment effects to the home or school setting. These data are particularly worrisome in light of the involvement of teachers and parents and the use of training material focusing on social–interpersonal problems. On the other hand, there was no explicit program of behavioral contingencies to accompany the training of self-instructional procedures. The Douglas *et al.* (1976) investigation can be credited for careful subject selection and thorough assessment of treatment effects. The lack of impact on home or school behavior is disappointing, but the results do support the efficacy of self-instructional training for producing lasting improvement in performance on certain cognitive and visual–motor tests.

As noted above, another feature of several of the self-instructional studies that may be potentially beneficial in terms of generalization concerns the concurrent application of some form of behavioral contingencies. Several studies, such as those reported by Kendall and colleagues, have used a response-cost contingency along with social praise. Others have used variations of reward contingencies. It is worth noting in advance that authors reporting studies without systematic behavioral procedures often mention this in the discussion as a suggestion for inclusion in future research.

Considering the hypothesized importance of behavioral contingencies, Kendall and Braswell (1982b) compared the efficacy of an intervention involving self-instructional training with response-cost contingencies, role plays, and modeling with an intervention utilizing only the behavioral techniques. Twenty-seven non-self-controlled problem children (8 to 12 years old) were randomly assigned to the cognitive–behavioral treatment, the behavioral-only treatment, or the attention control group. All children received 12 sessions of individual therapist contact focusing on psychoeducational, play, and interpersonal tasks and situations. The children receiving the cognitive–behavioral intervention improved teacher's blind ratings of self-control, and both the cognitive–behavioral and behavioral treatments improved teachers' blind ratings of hyperactivity. Parent ratings did not show that treatment produced behavioral improvement in the home setting. Several performance measures (cognitive style, academic achievement) showed improvements for the cognitive–behavioral and behavioral conditions whereas only the cognitive–behavioral treatment improved children's self-reported self-concept. Naturalistic observations in the classroom showed significant variability, but off-task verbal and off-task physical behaviors showed some decrease in frequency as a result of both of the treatments. Some of these improvements were maintained at 10-week follow-up for the cognitive–behavioral condition; however, 1-year follow-up data did not show significant differences across conditions. These results argue for the effectiveness of the combined cognitive and behavioral components of the intervention.

At this juncture, it would be reasonable to draw a tentative conclusion that the available studies document the success of cognitive–behavioral procedures. It would also be reasonable to suggest that there is some consistency across types of studies: Treatment gains are greatest when cognitive training is combined with behavioral contingencies and when the cognitive training is conducted as an interactive process between the therapist and child. We are comfortable with these conclusions, but we recognize that there are other studies with conclusions that further restrict the supporting evidence and with generally less favorable outcomes. These studies, nevertheless, offer interesting suggestions for pinpointing those clients most responsive to the intervention and identifying potential areas in need of improvement within the training format.

In a study of the role of expectations and the differential effectiveness of external versus internal monitoring, Bugental, Whalen, and Henker (1977) provided treatment for 36 7- to 12-year-old hyperactive and impulsive boys, half of whom were receiving methylphenidate. Treatment was conducted twice a week for 8 weeks, with the experimenter–tutors utilizing either self-instructional training or contingent social reinforcement. Both interventions were aimed at increasing the child's attention and correct performance on academic tasks. The results indicated that children whose attributional styles were congruent with their treatment (high personal control/self-control training or high external control/social contingency management) achieved better Porteus scores than those in noncongruent combinations. Also, self-instructional training was more effective with nonmedicated children, whereas external control was superior with the medicated subjects. As Bugental *et al.* (1977) stated, "Change strategies (behavioral management, educational programs, psychotherapy, medical intervention) have implicit attributional textures which interact with the attributional network of the individual to influence treatment impact" (p. 881). Thus children who were already somewhat internal in their attributional styles responded more positively to an internally oriented intervention whereas an externally managed intervention proved to be most effective with children manifesting external attributional styles. Unfortunately, neither intervention produced changes on a teacher rating scale. Bugental, Collins, Collins, and Chaney (1978) carried out a 6-month follow-up with these children. Subjects receiving self-instructional training had increased their perceptions of personal control; however, according to teacher ratings, the social contingency group had changed in the direction of reduced hyperactivity. All subjects improved on the Porteus. The authors suggested that the ideal intervention might be some combination of self-control procedures and social contingencies.

Self-instructional procedures have also been applied with children identified as a result of their aggressive behavior. Camp and her colleagues (Camp, Blom, Hebert, & van Doorninck, 1977) developed the "Think Aloud" program in an effort to teach verbal mediation skills to aggressive second grade boys. Camp (1977) found that this group of subjects possessed some skills in verbal mediation but that they failed to use these skills in problematic situations. Accordingly, the treatment involved 30 half-hour sessions that focused on self-instructional training with impersonal tasks and interpersonal problem situations. In addition, training in problem-solving skills was also provided. Twelve treated subjects were compared with ten who were untreated, and, as another control, Camp *et al.* (1977) also evaluated 12 "normal" boys selected from the same age group and geographical area. The dependent measures included teacher ratings of aggression and achievement; tests of intellectual ability, achievement, auditory perception, and interpersonal problem solving; and ratings of private speech during testing. At posttest, the treated group showed a significant increase in the teacher ratings of prosocial behavior relative to the control group but no decrease in aggressive behavior. Unfortunately the teachers were aware of which boys were receiving treatment, so they were not blind

raters. The treated subjects showed an increase in the number of solutions provided on the measure of interpersonal problem solving, but
these solutions were not of improved quality and frequently included
aggressive responses. On the more cognitive measures the treated subjects showed an increase in the number of solutions provided on the
measure of interpersonal problem solving, but these solutions were not
of improved quality and frequently included aggressive responses. On
the more cognitive measures the treated subjects showed a general
pattern of improvement relative to the aggressive control group. Thus,
while the treatment program appeared to have some impact on the
children's cognitive functioning, the behavioral effects were much less
clear.

Coats (1979) applied self-instructional procedures to the reduction
of impulsive and disruptive classroom behavior in 16 third grade boys
who were referred for aggressive behavior based on teacher ratings of
impulsive–aggressive behavior and poor self-control *and* behavioral
observations. Subjects in the treatment and attention control groups
were equated on the frequency of aggressive and motor behavior, as
indicated in the pretreatment observations. The children in both groups
were seen for eight 30-minute sessions over a 2-week period. Training
materials began with simple sensorimotor tasks, such as maze drawing,
and gradually expanded to include reasoning tasks and interpersonal
problem-solving situation. The attention control group engaged in the
same activities without self-instructional training. The classroom
behavior of the subjects was assessed via behavioral observations in the
classroom, teacher ratings of classroom behavior, and behavioral observation of performance in a staged interpersonal conflict situation.
The results indicated no group differences on behavioral observations
in the classroom or on teacher ratings. In the staged situation, the
treatment subjects demonstrated an increased frequency of appropriate
waiting behavior and a decreased frequency of verbal aggression, but
there were no differences in requests, negotiations, or physical aggression. Unfortunately, the subjects were not pretested in the staged problem situation, so these results are difficult to interpret in terms of the
effects of intervention. Considering all three measures, there is little
support for the efficacy of the training in reducing impulsive–aggressive
behavior, despite the inclusion of interpersonal problem situations in
the training.

In a study conducted by Urbain and Kendall (1981), group training procedures were employed and social perspective-taking and inter-

personal problem-solving training approaches were compared. Similar to the study by Coats (1979), the target children were aggressive. Both of the training procedures included behavioral contingencies within the group treatment and an emphasis on modeling, role playing, and self-instruction. A third treatment condition employed only the behavioral contingencies in groups without cognitive training. The behavioral contingencies in all three groups included the possibility of both earning reward chips for appropriate participation and losing chips for inappropriate behavior.

The target subjects were second and third grade impulsive–aggressive children selected according to teacher ratings of aggressive behavior. There were 44 target children and an additional 18 non-problem children—included as peer models of adaptive social behavior—assigned to the training conditions. Treatments were provided for twelve 45- to 50-minute sessions over a 6-week period to groups of three to six impulsive–aggressive subjects and two peer models. Children's performance on Chandler's bystander cartoons and the MEPS were recorded at pretreatment, posttreatment, and 2-month follow-up. Teachers, blind to specific children's assignment to conditions, rated each subject on the Checklist of Socially Impulsive–Aggressive Behaviors (CSIAB) developed for the study.

Within the interpersonal problem-solving training groups, children were exposed to structured lessons and activities designed to teach the following components of problem solving: (1) initial inhibition of impulsive responding—"stop and think"; (2) evaluating consequences —"think ahead"; (3) problem identification—ways to recognize problems were discussed and children shared problems within the group; (4) generating alternative—"brainstorm"; and (5) making a plan. Within the social perspective-taking training groups children were again exposed to structured lessons and activities, in these cases designed to teach the hypothesized components of social perspective taking: (1) awareness of feelings—a "feelings dictionary" of words; (2) social–causal reasoning—using role plays and pictures of inter-personal situations, children discussed the reasons and motives for different types of feelings; and (3) awareness of others (role switching). Different points of view and the fact that people are different were emphasized, and discussion centered on "fairness" and "putting yourself in other guy's shoes." The reward and response-cost contingencies (token program) used in the cognitive training groups were used alone in the behavioral contingencies groups. Children engaged in structured activities and group leaders provided solutions to interpersonal conflicts, but there was a minimal amount of discussion of the alternatives, consequences, or feelings involved.

Analyses of the effects of treatment did not provide evidence for the superiority of either interpersonal problem solving, social perspective taking, or behavioral contingency procedures alone. All three training groups led equally to improved performance on the social–cognitive tasks, but none led to significant behavioral change on teachers' ratings of impulsive–aggressive behavior. Improvements on the social–cognitive tasks were significantly correlated with behavioral improvements.

The absence of change in the classroom—the lack of treatment generalization—appears to be a common finding in research in which the target children are identified as aggressive even when the treatment package includes behavioral contingencies. Such results are less encouraging than the work with non-self-controlled children. Although the exact features that distinguish aggressive children from children who manifest their lack of self-control in other ways are as yet unknown to us, aggression does appear more resistant to treatment. Indeed, much lengthier or qualitatively different treatments may be necessary with truly aggressive youngsters.

Outcome Inconsistency and Moderator Variables

Our journey through the literature involving self-instructional training has taken several paths. We have examined noninteractive and interactive forms of intervention and have found a relatively diverse pattern of outcome results. We have sought a few central themes to guide future work and we have identified the apparent benefits of including interactive efforts and a behavioral contingency program and the differential effectiveness of the procedures with different problem behaviors (e.g., cognitive impulsivity, behavioral impulsivity, hyperactivity, and aggression). Beyond these comments, are there other factors that might help us understand treatment outcome? Are there any factors that might be moderating treatment effects? In light of available data, an exploration of both subject and training variables appears feasible and potentially fruitful.

SUBJECT VARIABLES

Several authors have called attention to the need for examining individual differences in the broad field of self-management with children (Karoly, 1977) and the specific area of self-instructional training (Kendall, 1977, 1982a; Kendall & Finch, 1979b). The most comprehensive review of subject variables in relation to self-instructional training was compiled by Copeland (1981, 1982; Copeland & Hammel, 1981). In her review, Copeland examined not only the self-instructional literature but also the research on other self-control interventions, delay of gratification studies, and resistance to temptation investigations. Some of Copeland's conclusions regarding selected major subject variables, as well as conclusions of our own, are presented below.

Age. As the reader may have noted, self-instructional training has been most frequently employed with elementary school children, although there are examples of training with preschoolers (e.g., Bornstein & Quevillon, 1976) and adolescents (e.g., Williams & Akamatsu, 1978). Copeland concluded that a broad age range of children do appear to benefit from self-instructional training, but also specified that younger children may require more structured and specific training than would be appropriate for older children. In a 1979 review, Pressley also discussed the need for more concrete training with younger children. In support of this view, Bender (1976) found explicit strategy training more effective than a more general type of training with a sample of impulsive first graders, whereas Kendall and Wilcox (1980) found conceptual training more effective than concrete training with an older group of children (non-self-controlled 8- to 12-year-olds).

Sex. Unfortunately, this section is all too brief. In an amazingly high percentage of studies no analyses of possible sex differences are reported. In one treatment study where sex effects were examined (Genshaft & Hirt, 1979), no sex differences were noted. The study of sex differences is somewhat hampered by the highly significant difference in the number of boys versus girls who are identified as in need of such interventions (see Chapter 3 for prevalence estimates).

Race and Socioeconomic Status. As Copeland has indicated, given the confounding of race and socioeconomic status (SES) (and frequently geographic residence) in our culture, it is not always possible to consider these factors separately. The majority of self-instructional training studies do not report the racial or SES makeup of their samples. Two studies on resistance to rule breaking provide potentially relevant information. Monohan and O'Leary (1971) found that self-instructional training was effective in preventing rule breaking among rural Midwestern white children; however, in a second experiment such training was unsuccessful with urban, Northern black children. The role of SES in cognitive–behavioral training was addressed by Braswell, Kendall, and Urbain (1982b). The subjects of this study were homogeneous with respect to race (white), despite SES variation. Examining the results of three outcome studies involving 58 treated children, significant SES differences in some of the pre- and posttreatment measures were found. Despite these differences in level of performance, there were no differences in the improvement and generalization rates of high- versus low-SES subjects, indicating that low SES did not interfere with or hinder treatment. Genshaft and Hirt (1979) examined the effects of race of subject and race of therapist with SES held constant (all subjects were low SES). Both black and white children trained by white tutors improved on one task performance measure, but only children trained by same-race models improved their scores on the other task performance measure. These findings tentatively suggest that race of subject (and therapist) may be an important mediating variable; however, it seems only logical that the effect of race on treatment outcome would depend on what particular type of outcome that is being measured. For example, one might hypothesize that subject–tutor racial similarity would affect improvement on self-esteem and self-concept measures more than it would influence change on measures of academic achievement or other cognitive task performance measures.

Cognitive Level. Kendall (1977) has emphasized the importance of considering the cognitive capacity of the child when designing a self-instructional training program. This is not to say that such training would not be reasonable and effective with retarded or learning-disabled children, for there are examples of its effectiveness with such populations (e.g., Guralnick, 1976; Wagner, 1975). Cognitive capacity may operate much like the age factor, with lower-IQ children requiring more task-specific and concrete training, and brighter children responding best to more abstract training. Research by Cohen et al. (1982) found that cognitive level, as assessed from a Piagetian stage perspective, interacts with type of training in predicting outcome, thus underscoring the role of level of cognitive development. Based on anecdotal accounts from our own work, trainers working with borderline retarded children found it effective to increase the amount of tutor modeling in each session and to apply the self-instructional steps to sports or games that the subjects already knew how to play. With these alterations of the program, the less intellectually developed children mastered the self-instructional approach to problems by the sixth or seventh session, though the average-range children typically master the steps by the second or third session. It thus seems extremely important for the tutor to work at the child's pace, not the experimenter's, if the ultimate goal is the child's mastery of the material. As obvious as this point may sound, the format utilized in some self-instructional intervention programs appears, unfortunately, to allow little opportunity for attention to the individual learning rate or style of the child.

Attributional Style. Kopel and Arkowitz (1975) noted that a child's feeling of personal control over his/her life might influence his/her responsiveness to any type of self-control intervention. This possibility was examined with respect to self-instructional training by Bugental *et al.* (1977). As previously described, attributional and medication status were found to interact with treatment approach (self-instructions vs. social reinforcement) on a task performance measure of impulsivity at posttest but not at 6-month follow-up. In addition, self-instructional training produced more durable increases in perceived control than the social reinforcement condition, but the latter condition produced longer-lasting improvement in teacher ratings of hyperactivity (Bugental *et al.*, 1978). The finding that those high in personal control improved more with self-instructional training is consistent with the work of Schallow (1975) who found that undergraduates high in internal orientation, as measured by Rotter's Locus of Control Scale (Rotter, 1966), were more successful in self-modification of a number of behaviors. Braswell, Kendall, and Koehler (1982a) reported that children who tended to attribute positive behavior change to *effort* also tended to obtain positive change on the teacher's ratings of classroom behavior. Correspondingly, attributing positive behavior change to *luck* was negatively associated with change on teacher ratings.

Child Involvement. We have discussed the importance of implementing self-instructional training in an interactive format, but what about the child's level of interaction or involvement? Braswell, Kendall, Braith, Carey, and Vye (1984b) addressed this issue in a study in which the therapist's and child's verbal behaviors were rated during self-instructional training sessions. Those children who offered the most suggestions regarding what should happen during the training sessions and who might therefore be perceived as the most actively involved tended to display the greatest improvement on the teacher ratings of their classroom behavior. Child involvement was the best prediction of treatment gains from among the rated verbal behaviors.

TREATMENT VARIABLES

The training programs that we have described include several distinguishable treatment components that could independently account for treatment effects. In addition to these specific components, treatments also vary in other factors that could influence the efficacy of the intervention.

Modeling. Cole and Kazdin (1980) speculated that the modeling component alone could account for treatment effects, as modeling is often considered an intervention in its own right (e.g., Rosenthal & Bandura, 1978). In recognition of this possibility, we recall the study by Meichenbaum and Goodman (1971, Study II) in which the authors compared self-instructional training and modeling alone. Both interventions produced increased MFF latencies, but only the self-instructional training decreased MFF errors. Finch, Wilkinson, Nelson, and Montgomery (1975b) obtained a very similar pattern of results. Cullinan *et al.* (1977) found no differences between a modeling and self-instructional intervention, but the version of self-instructional training applied in this study was somewhat atypical; in fact, it was little more than modeling itself. To some extent, many of the studies utilizing attention–materials control groups may be controlling for the modeling of successful task performance and therefore imparting a "treatment." Modeling in such conditions may be particularly influential in the relatively longer interventions. Such an explanation would account for the improved task performance in the attention control groups as reported by Kendall and Zupan (1981) following a 12-session intervention. Thus, recognizing the impact of modeling is very important, even if it does not account for all the effects of the cognitive–behavioral training.

Self-Reinforcement. The typical self-instructional intervention incorporates a self-reinforcement component. However, one investigation has specifically contrasted the effects of self-instructional training with and without self-reinforcement (Nelson & Birkimer, 1978) and reported that self-instructions with self-reinforcement produced improvement on the MFF, whereas self-instructions alone did not. The general findings of the more operant self-regulation studies discussed previously also suggest that self-instructions are most effective in achieving behavior change when the treatment package includes a self-reinforcement component. These interventions, however, also included self-monitoring and self-evaluation activities, so the specific effects of self-instructions versus self-reinforcement remain unclear. One might conceptualize the self-reinforcement component as providing a specific goal toward which the child can direct his/her behavior. When self-instructions are taught as a means of achieving this goal, they may be more effective than if presented in a more ambiguous or "goal-less" framework in which the advantage of using the self-instructions is not obvious to the child.

Verbalization of Self-Instructions. At least two studies have examined the importance of having the child actually verbalize the self-instructions. Palkes *et al.* (1972) found that the verbalizing group obtained significantly better IQ scores on the Porteus Maze than a silent reading group. Bender (1976) found self-verbalization more effective than tutor verbalization in improving performance on MFF-type tests given immediately after each session, but no effects were obtained on a final posttest administration of the MFF. Thus, both studies suggest that self-verbalization is an important factor, but given the generally weak overall effects obtained in both studies, this conclusion must be guarded.

Type of Self-Instructions. Studies of the effectiveness of different types of self-instructions suggest that the specificity–generality of the self-instructions interacts with the age of the subject. Bender (1976) found that explicit rather than general strategies were more successful with impulsive first graders, while Kendall and Wilcox (1980) found conceptual rather than concrete self-instructions most effective with 8- to 12-year-olds. When we consider data presented by Schlesser, Meyers, and Cohen (1981) an important finding emerges. Schlesser *et al.* provided a replication of some of the findings reported in Kendall and Wilcox (1980). Schlesser *et al.* found that a general self-instructional approach was superior to an approach providing specific self-instructions. Accordingly, unless the children are very young, conceptual (general) self-instructions represent a procedural improvement within the self-instructional paradigm that merits further research attention and clinical application.

Individual versus Group Interventions. Studies conducting both individual and group training in self-instructional procedures have achieved some positive results, but only the Kendall and Zupan (1981) study specifically contrasted these two modes of training. Although the results indicated that relatively comparable change was achieved by both individual and group training, the "group" condition may not have maximized its potential. That is, children in the group training "took turns" as opposed to engaging each other in the use of stop-and-think self-talk. Procedures described in Chapter 7 provide more group opportunities for practice and learning of the cognitive skills.

PROBLEM-SOLVING APPROACHES

A second major class of interventions within the cognitive–behavioral realm emphasizes a problem-solving approach to social and interpersonal difficulties. As the reader will have recognized by this point, self-instructional training has a problem-solving focus, but there are other problem-solving interventions that do not emphasize self-instructions but which constitute cognitive–behavioral interventions. This portion of the present review will examine the outcomes of problem-solving training—looking first at training children individually and second at training them within the family.

Jahoda (1953, 1958) is frequently cited as one of the first to suggest that the ability to solve real-life interpersonal problems is one criterion of mental health. The 1970s witnessed a series of attempts to formulate problem solving as a set of skills relevant for clinical endeavors. Interpreting problem solving within a behavioral framework, D'Zurilla and Goldfried (1971) defined it as "a *behavioral process . . . which* (a) *makes available a variety of potentially effective response alternatives for dealing with the problematic situation and* (b) *increases the probability of selecting the most effective response from among these various alternatives*" (p. 108; italics in original). D'Zurilla and Goldfried went on to outline five stages of problem solving, including general orientation, problem definition and formulation, generation of alternatives, decision making, and verification. Mahoney (1977) described a seven-step problem-solving sequence. The stages he elaborated include specification of problem, collection of information, identification of causes, examination of options, narrowing of options and experimentation, comparison of data, and extension, revision, or replacement of the solution. Spivack, Shure, Platt, and their associates at Hahnemann Community Mental Health Center (Shure & Spivack, 1978; Spivack, Platt, & Shure, 1976; Spivack & Shure, 1974) have theorized that effective interpersonal cognitive problem solving requires the subskills of sensitivity to human problems, the ability to generate alternative solutions, the conceptualization of the appropriate means to achieve a given solution, and a sensitivity to consequences and cause–effect relationships in human behavior. These three systems evidence a high degree of similarity and, perhaps, reflect the beginnings of a consensus on the nature of interpersonal problem solving.

The Hahnemann research group has studied the nature of the relationship between these skills and overt social adjustment. Positive relationships between these Interpersonal Cognitive Problem-Solving (ICPS) skills and adjustment have been demonstrated in 4- and 5-year-olds (Shure & Spivack, 1970; Shure, Spivack, & Jaeger, 1971; Spivack & Shure, 1974), 10-year-olds (Larcen, Spivack, & Shure, 1972), adolescents (Platt, Spivack, Altman, Altman, & Peizer, 1974; Spivack & Levine, 1963), and adults (Platt & Spivack, 1972a, 1972b, 1973). It should be noted, however, that negligible relationships with adjustment were reported from a study of 6- to 11-year-old children from a normal school and with IQ controlled (Kendall & Fischler, 1984). In the Kendall and Fischler (1984) study ICPS skills were scored quantitatively, as suggested by Spivack and Shure (1973). Significant relationships between problem solving and adjustment were found, however, when the skills were scored according to variations in the *quality* of the children's solutions (Fischler & Kendall, 1984). In relating their positive findings to the development of a training program, Spivack and Shure (1974) state their hypothesis as "one should be able to enhance the personal adjustment of young children if one can enhance their ability to see a human problem, their appreciation of different ways of handling it, and their sensitivity to the potential consequences of what they do" (p. 21).

Several studies have examined the impact of social problem-solving training with a focus on prevention. Recently, for example, Weissberg, Gesten, Rapkin, Cowen, Davids, de Apodaca, and McKim (1981) examined the effects of intensive social problem-solving training with suburban and inner-city third graders. The intervention was found to be effective with the suburban but not the urban children. The interested reader can examine the impact of such preventive programs with "normal" children in a number of other investigations (Allen, Chinsky, Larcen, Lochman, & Selinger, 1976; Feldhusen & Houtz, 1975; McClure, Chinsky, & Larcen, 1978; Stone, Hinds, & Schmidt, 1975).

Nonfamilial Problem-Solving Interventions

The vast majority of the research in this area has been conducted since 1970; however, one investigator anticipated the interest in this topic by almost 30 years. Chittenden (1942) designed a training program to help children learn to analyze social situations objectively and select their responses on the bases of this careful analysis. Chittenden believed such training would decrease a child's attempts at domination of social activities and increase cooperative assertiveness. Using a special behavioral situation, Chittenden tested 71 3- to 6-year-olds and selected every child who was in the upper fifth of the sample in dominative initiations or responses and in the lower fifth in cooperative initiations or responses. Children were then matched on age and classroom teacher and assigned to the experimental or control group. Those in the experimental group attended individual sessions in which doll play was used to act out social problem situations. These sessions had three specific aims: (1) to teach the child to discriminate between situations in which satisfactory agreements had been reached and those involving no such agreement; (2) to teach the child ways to working out disagreements in play situations, such as taking turns, common use, or cooperative use; and (3) to make the child aware of successful ways of approaching another child in such play situations. The children were seen daily for approximately 15 minutes over 11 days. The control children were also periodically removed from the classroom to keep the teachers blind to condition assignments. At posttest, the trained children demonstrated significantly less dominant behavior than at pretest. There was also significantly more cooperative behavior in trained subjects at posttest. At 1-month follow-up, however, only the change in dominance persisted. Unfortunately, data on the control group were not presented for comparison with the experimental group. This intervention represents an interesting cross between traditional play therapy techniques and problem-solving training. Despite its early appearance, it incorporates several methodological features, such as age-matched groups, attention controls, and follow-up testing, which, unfortunately, are not always present in more recent studies. The method of subject selection, however, makes it unclear how impaired these children actually were and how many of them were in need of treatment.

In an effort to apply their theoretical formulations, Spivack and Shure (1974) developed a training program to be used by preschool teachers for instructing children in ICPS skills. The program included dialogues, games, and activities for the teacher to use with the children in a series of 46 daily lessons, each lesson lasting approximately 20 minutes. The early sessions focused on developing what Spivack and Shure believe to be prerequisites for problem-solving skills, such as the ability to identify and discriminate emotions. Later sessions teach alternative, consequential, and means–ends thinking as applied to interpersonal problem situations. This intervention was implemented with 113 preschool children who had been teacher-classified as impulsive, inhibited, or adjusted. At posttreatment these children were compared with no-treatment controls. The experimental subjects demonstrated significant improvement in generation of alternative solutions and consequential thinking. Improvement on the teacher ratings of behavior was also noted, but the teachers were not blind to the treatment status of the children. Certain subgroups within the treated sample demonstrated improvement on particular measures. For example, the children rated as inhibited improved on behavioral ratings of concern for others, and females improved in ratings of popularity with peers. At 1-year follow-up, teachers who were not informed of the children's treatment status also rated the trained subjects as better adjusted than the controls. These results are extremely interesting, but the absence of an attention control group, particularly given the lengthy nature of treatment, makes it difficult to rule out alternative explanations of change. Other comments on the Spivack and Shure research program will be presented subsequently.

Pitkanen (1974) tested the effectiveness of a form of problem-solving training as a means of helping aggressive children recognize behavioral alternatives. Twenty-four aggressive boys (mean age of 8.4 years) were the subjects, and 12 extraverted, well-controlled boys were selected as a criterion group. The 24 subjects were assigned to experimental and control groups, with the experimental group receiving eight training sessions over a 4-week period. Training included three phases: (1) recognition of the factors causing a situation, generation of alternative actions, and examination of the consequences of these actions; (2) discussions of pictorial presentations of conflict situations; and (3) role play of conflict situations using the discussed problem-solving strategies. The impact of the intervention was assessed via behavioral observations of the subjects performing a series of tasks in a group context. Both aggressive and constructive behaviors were rated. At posttest the experimental group demonstrated a significant reduction in aggression relative to the control group, although the rate of aggression in the experimental group still exceeded that of the criterion group. Significant increases in the use of strategies in the experimental group were also noted. The use of special behavioral situations as a dependent measure is an interesting assessment method; however, in this study the same situations were not used at both pre- and posttesting, so the actual effects of the intervention are more difficult to interpret.

The use of problem-solving training with severely hyperactive boys was examined by Kirmil-Gray, Duckham-Shoor, and Thoresen (1980). Eight hyperactive boys, aged 7 to 10 years, currently on stimulant medication, were selected to participate in this intervention. Subject selection included screening interviews with parents, teachers, and physicians, as well as double-blind placebo trials to ensure that medication was effective in controlling the behavior of these children. The intervention had two components: problem-solving training for the children, and behavior management training for the parents. The problem-solving training involved 48 sessions designed to teach social problem solving as well as motor inhibition, attending behavior, and self-direction skills. Each 45-minute session included explanation, modeling, role playing, and game playing. During training a reinforcement system was operational in order to reward the child for appropriate behavior and use of new skills. The parent training in behavior management involved eight 2- to 3-hour sessions in which parents received instruction in implementing behavioral techniques with their children. The children's teachers were also provided consultation on the behavioral management of hyperactive children. Four subjects received both the problem-solving and parent training interventions, two received only parent training, and the remaining two were assessment controls. An individualized medication reduction schedule was developed for each of the six treatment subjects, with the goal for all being complete medication withdrawal by the end of training. All subjects were observed over an 18-week period, including 3 to 4 weeks of baseline, 12 weeks of treatment, and 2 weeks of follow-up. Both disruptive behavior and social interactions were observed. Teachers and parents also completed daily reports on the child's behavior. In addition, these children were assessed with a number of task performance measures of intelligence, school achievement, impulsivity, and self-esteem. Measures of each child's interactions with the teacher and classmates were also obtained.

The basic findings from these multiple outcome measures indicated that acceptable behavior was maintained with the complete withdrawal or significant reduction of medications in all six treated subjects; however, there was no indication that the problem-solving training with the children added to the effects of the behavior management classes for parents. There were no noteworthy pre–post differences on the academic measures or the measures of social interaction. On the whole, the authors noted that the children tended to respond in a highly individualized manner. For example, those subjects for whom behavioral management was most effective in controlling behavior at school were not necessarily those who demonstrated the greatest behavior change at home. Given the length of the problem-solving intervention and the use of behavioral techniques to reward demonstration of new problem-solving skills, it is particularly puzzling that no effects of the intervention were obtained. The small number of children involved certainly qualify the strength of the findings, but the failure of the intervention to produce effects on any of the multiple outcome measures is striking.

The turtle technique (Robin & Schneider, 1974; Robin, Schneider, & Dolnick, 1976; Schneider & Robin, 1976) is another type of problem-solving approach developed to help emotionally disturbed children inhibit aggressive or impulsive responding in social situations and generate alternative responses. This training is presented in four phases. First the children are taught the "turtle response" of pulling in one's limbs and lowering the head to withdraw from a provoking situation. Next, the children are instructed in relaxation skills they can utilize while "doing the turtle." This program was designed to require 15 minutes of instruction per day for 3 weeks. At the end of the 3-week period, sessions can be reduced to twice a week and then gradually faded. Robin and Schneider (1974) evaluated this procedure by teaching the turtle technique to 15 emotionally disturbed children in three special-education classrooms. Behavioral observations in two of the classrooms indicated significant reductions in aggressive behavior, with aggressive incidents reduced 46% to 54% from baseline levels. The technique was introduced later in the third classroom, and the authors stated that apparently it was too late in the semester to provide meaningful results. These findings are encouraging, but given the absence of controls and the strong possibility that the observers were not blind to the treatment status of each child (for "doing the turtle" is a very noticeable activity), this report provides little more than anecdotal support for the effectiveness of the technique.

Robin *et al.* (1976) also evaluated this procedure with 11 children from two primary level classrooms for emotionally disturbed children. These subjects were selected on the basis of teacher reports of aggressive behavior. The training was introduced to the two classrooms in a multiple-baseline design. Classroom A experienced 2 weeks of baseline and 8 weeks of treatment; classroom B underwent 7 weeks of baseline and 3 weeks of treatment. The chief dependent measure was the observation of aggressive behavior. With the implementation of treatment, classroom A showed a 41% decrement in aggressive behavior, and classroom B obtained a 45% decrement. All target children decreased their aggressive behavior, with rates of decrease ranging from 34% to 70%. These results are certainly consistent with those obtained by Robin and Schneider (1974). The multiple-baseline design of this study adds support to the contention that it was the training that reduced aggressive behavior, yet the addition of some type of attention control group would have strengthened the study. Again, it seems unlikely that the observers were truly blind to the identities of the target children. Neither of these two studies included follow-up assessments. Finally, it is impossible to discern the actual effect of the problem-solving component of training, especially since the dependent measure concerned rate of aggressive behavior and change in this rate could easily be explained by use of the turtle response alone to simply inhibit such behaviors.

A small number of investigators have employed problem-solving techniques with children and adolescents in institutional settings. Russell and Thoresen (1976) described a program for teaching problem-solving skills and used this program with 8- to 12-year-old children in a behaviorally oriented residential treatment setting. Residents of this setting are typically neglected, acting-out children. This training uses a workbook format to teach problem-solving components such as identifying the problem, generating choices, collecting information, recognizing personal values, selecting the best choice, and then reviewing the decision at a later time. The workbook is organized into six sections, each section requiring about 30 to 45 minutes to complete. The success of the intervention has been evaluated in terms of the child's knowledge of the workbook content and the child's ability to generate choices and examine the consequences of each choice in a simulated problem situation. By the authors' own admission, no controlled comparisons have been conducted, but anecdotal evidence suggests that children using the workbook have made significant improvements in the number of alternatives generated and the valuation of consequences. Additional research on this technique is clearly needed, but the combination of problem-solving training in the context of an ongoing behavioral program would appear to be a potentially powerful intervention.

Giebink, Stover, and Fahl (1968) attempted to increase the number of alternative responses that emotionally disturbed children could generate in response to a potentially frustrating situation. Four of the six subjects (boys aged 10 to 12) were diagnosed neurotic, and the other two were diagnosed schizophrenic. Problem-solving training involved meeting four times to play a board game that fostered generation of alternative responses to provoking situations. The problem situations used in training were randomly selected from a group of eight frustrating situations that occurred regularly in the residential setting. Four other situations were not used as training examples but were used to assess treatment generalization. The subjects were also assessed via a "frustration questionnaire" consisting of 14 problematic situations. Following treatment the authors reported an increase in the number of acceptable alternatives provided on the "frustration questionnaire." Slight behavioral improvement in the experimental situations was also noted, but there was no generalization of effects to the nontrained situations. The absence of any type of control group limits the conclusions that can be drawn from these findings. Given the severe impairment of this sample, as suggested by their presence in residential treatment and their diagnoses (at least in the case of the two schizophrenic children), it seems improbable that any four-session intervention, problem-solving or otherwise, would produce behaviorally significant effects.

Sarason (1968) and Sarason and Ganzer (1973) conducted problem-solving training with institutionalized delinquents. In his pilot work, Sarason (1968) found that a program emphasizing a problem-solving approach to problematic situations via modeling and role playing was effective in producing improved staff ratings of behavior. Sarason and Ganzer (1973) examined the effectiveness of this same program in a more extensive investigation. The subjects were 192 male first offenders ranging in age from 15 to 18 years. Subjects were matched for age, IQ, diagnostic classification, and severity of delinquent behavior, and were then randomly assigned to one of two treatments or a no-treatment control condition. The modeling condition, as the authors labeled it, emphasized a practical approach to social problems. The subjects met in groups of four, with two models or tutors per group. The models demonstrated positive and negative approaches to certain problem situations and then the subjects would role-play the same situations. These role plays were taped and played back for discussion. The discussion treatment condition covered the same content as the modeling group but no role play was involved. Both treatment groups met for 16 1-hour sessions over 5 weeks, and within each treatment, half the groups received audio-taped and half video-taped feedback of their group behavior. The results indicated that significantly more subjects in the audio-taped modeling group received favorable case dispositions than all other groups. Those in either the audio- or video-taped modeling groups were significantly more likely to evaluate their insitutional experience as positive. Also, modeling subjects were more likely to recall the content and goals of treatment compared to the discussion group (79% vs. 38%) when asked 18 months following treatment. In terms of recidivism, significantly more recidivists were in the control group than were present in either treatment group.

In addition to treatment results, this study yielded some interesting subject-by-treatment interactions. The test anxiety of all subjects had been assessed, and it was hypothesized that high-test-anxious subjects would be upset by televised feedback of their role-playing performance. In support of this hypothesis, only one of 15 high-test-anxious subjects in the televised modeling group received positive behavior ratings, whereas 14 of the 19 high-test-anxious subjects in the nontelevised modeling group received positive ratings. The authors also noted that subjects who improved in the modeling condition tended to be diagnosed neurotic or passive–dependent personality, whereas those improving in the discussion group condition tended to have the diagnosis of passive–aggressive or sociopathic personality. These results indicate that subject participation in the modeling or discussion groups produced more positive concurrent and long-term effects than did the institutional program alone. In addition, the results suggest that the two treatments had different impacts on subgroups within the sample.

Sarason and Sarason (1981) examined how effective a cognitive–behavioral problem-solving intervention could be in teaching more adaptive problem approaches to high school students at high risk for dropout and delinquency. The intervention was presented as a special unit within a regularly required course and involved 13 class sessions, with the first and last sessions devoted primarily to assessment. The training procedure involved the modeling of both the overt behaviors and the cognitive antecedents of adaptive problem solving in both social and cognitive problem situations. These modeled behaviors were then rehearsed. In one condition subjects viewed live models; in the other treatment condition subjects observed video-tape models. A control group received no problem-solving training. At posttest, the treated subjects were able to generate more adaptive alternatives for approaching problematic situations and were able to make more effective self-presentations in a job interview situation than the controls. In addition, at 1-year follow-up the treated students tended to have fewer absences, less tardiness, and fewer referrals for misbehavior. These results are of special interest for they suggest that the intervention was effective at the level of the subjects' cognitive processes and at the level of specific behaviors in real-life problem situations.

Family Interventions

Because interpersonal problem solving is often called for within the family context, many practitioners and researchers have examined the impact of training the target child *and* his/her parents in problem-solving skills. For example, following a successful pilot study, Shure and Spivack (1978) examined the effectiveness of having mothers train their preschool children in the use of ICPS skills. Forty mother–child pairs were selected on the basis of the child's demonstrating overly impulsive or overly inhibited behavior in the preschool setting and being low on measures of the ICPS skills. Mother–child pairs were then matched on the mother's pretest scores, the child's school adjustment, the child's ICPS test scores, and the child's sex and age. Half of the mothers were trained in workshops like those used to train the teachers in Spivack and Shure (1974). Each mother administered the program games and dialogues at home with her child for 20 minutes a day over a 3-month period.

The results are reported in terms of child, mother, and mother–child outcomes. On the ICPS tests, the experimental children improved significantly more than the controls in their ability to generate alternative solutions and demonstrate consequential thinking. There were no significant changes in sensitivity to the existence of an interpersonal problem, and the authors suggest that this skill could be too developmentally advanced for the average preschool child. Also, the trained children did not differ from the control children at posttest on measures of impersonal thinking skills, indicating that treatment effects were specific to interpersonal thinking skills. At pretest, 17 of the 20 experimental children were rated as not adjusted by their teachers, but at posttest only five were still so rated. In contrast, 16 of 20 controls were rated as not adjusted at pretest, and posttest ratings indicated 11 of the 20 remained not adjusted. There were no sex differences in improvement on these children whose school behavior improved with the five who did not show such improvement in terms of their ICPS test scores. The improved group did demonstrate significantly greater change in the ICPS skills than the nonimproved group.

Interview data from the mothers suggested the trained mothers changed their problem-solving style in dealing with their children as a result of exposure to the program. The mothers also demonstrated significantly improved means–ends thinking at posttreatment. In term of mother–child outcomes, the children's significantly improved alternative thinking abilities were correlated with both the mothers' improved child-rearing style and increased means–ends thinking scores. The mothers' means–ends thinking scores were also related to the children's improvement in consequential thinking. The research of Spivack, Shure, and their colleagues demonstrates many laudable features, such as regular analyses for possible sex differences, explicit examination of the link between changes in ICPS skills and change in behavior, and a generally programmatic approach to their topic of study. Unfortunately, their failure to utilize attention controls makes it more difficult to rule out competing explanations, such as the possible effects of a consistent increase in maternal attention and mother–child interaction, whatever the nature of this interaction. Also, while the authors provide beautifully detailed descriptions of the intervention, evaluation procedures are rather loosely described, making accurate replication quite difficult.

Blechman and colleagues (Blechman, Olson, Schornagel, Halsdorf, & Turner, 1976b; Blechman, Olson, & Hellman, 1976a) examined the impact of a procedure called the Family Contract Game. This technique uses a board-game format to develop problem-solving and contingency contracting skills in families. Component problem-solving skills, such as identifying problems in behavioral terms, gathering relevant information, generating behavioral alternatives, choosing a specific alternative, and evaluating the outcome of the selected alternative, are taught within the game context. Blechman et al. (1976b) utilized this procedure with a 56-year-old mother and her 14-year-old son who were experiencing considerable conflict. The pair were seen for two baseline sessions during which two 5-minute unstructured problem discussions were video-taped. The pair were then seen for seven weekly 40-minute sessions in which the Family Contract Game was played. Following this intervention phase, unstructured problems discussions were again recorded in two posttreatment assessment sessions. The authors reported that the improved interaction patterns resulting from the game generalized to the posttreatment sessions. In addition, the child showed a substantial reduction of fears and anxiety on the Fear Survey Schedule (Scherer & Nakamura, 1968) and moved from the severely pathological to the normal range on the Devereux Adolescent Behavior Rating Scale (Spivack, Haimes, & Spotts, 1967). The mother's and son's self-reports also indicated satisfaction. These findings are certainly encouraging, but the case study nature of the report limits the generalizability of the findings.

Blechman et al. (1976a) implemented the Family Contract Game with six mother–child dyads. The children (four boys and two girls) ranged in age from 8 to 15 years. The mothers were all employed single parents, ranging in age from 33 to 56 years. These dyads were selected for treatment as a result of parent–child conflict over rules, schoolwork, personal hygiene, and sibling relations. As in Blechman et al. (1976b), unstructured videotaped problem discussions were used as pre–post measures. The intervention was conducted for five 40-minute sessions. As in the case study, the use of the game procedure resulted in a significant increase in on-task behavior and decreased off-task behavior during problem discussion. This change was apparent in the first intervention session and remained fairly constant throughout treatment. Unlike the Blechman *et al.* (1976b) study, these changes did not persist in the posttreatment problem discussions. Decreasing the number of intervention sessions might be responsible for this failure of generalization. It's also plausible that, given the diverse ages of both children and mothers, the game would need to be modified slightly for use with each particular dyad in order for generalization to occur. These authors should be credited for the extent to which they described their sample of mothers, as well as children, for demographic data on parents are frequently not provided in such studies.

Robin, Kent, O'Leary, Foster, and Prinz (1977) also examined problem-solving training with parent–child dyads. Twelve mother–daughter and twelve mother–son dyads were selected according to the child's age (11 to 14), reports of excessive parent–child conflict, absence of psychiatric history, and the willingness of both parent and adolescent to attend sessions together. These pairs were then randomly assigned to treatment or waiting-list control groups, with groups matched for socioeconomic status and severity of communication deficits as rated by the parent. The treatment was designed to incorporate the problem-solving model of D'Zurilla and Goldfried (1971) with the communication models of G. W. Piaget (1972) and Gordon (1970). The training emphasized "(1) mutual resolution of disagreements, (2) equalization of decision-making power, and (3) systematic instruction in 'independence-seeking' and 'independence-granting' skills" (Robin *et al.*, 1977, p. 640). Training included five 1-hour sessions and involved activities such as modeling guided practice, role playing, and social reinforcement of correct problem-solving performance. Pre- and posttreatment assessment included audio-taped discussions of a hypothetical and a real conflict and checklists of home problem-solving and communication skills that were completed by both parents and adolescents. The intervention produced highly significant increases in the use of problem-solving behaviors in the audio-taped discussions of both real and hypothetical conflicts, whereas the control group families showed no positive change or worsened slightly. Specific items on the checklists showed some improvement, but overall the ratings failed to indicate improvement in home problem-solving and communication behaviors. Thus, this intervention appears capable of altering behavior but these altered patterns didn't generalize to "real-world" settings.

Foster (1979) studied the impact of procedures specifically designed to enhance generalization of these communication and problem-solving skills. Foster's subjects were 28 families complaining of excessive arguing. In this study both one- and two-parent families were included and the children ranged in age from 10 to 14 years. Families were matched according to pretreatment measures of severity and were randomly assigned to one of two treatment groups or a waiting-list control condition. The treatment groups both utilized the procedures described in Robin *et al.* (1977); however, one group also experienced procedures believed to enhance generalization, such as homework assignments and weekly discussions of various factors influencing the use of communication and problem-solving skills at home. Training for both groups included seven 1-hour sessions. Dependent measures included audiotaped discussions of real conflict situations, self-reports of recent conflict behavior, global ratings of satisfaction with the relationship, and self-report ratings of family-specific goals, communication targets, and conflict situations addressed within the treatment sessions. At posttest, the audio-taped discussions indicated a decrease in negative communication in the generalization group, whereas the other treatment and the control group worsened slightly. The problem-solving behaviors coded on these tapes showed no change for any group. The global improvement ratings and the self-report ratings of goals, communication targets, and conflict situations showed significantly greater improvement in both treatment groups than in the control group. Also, both groups reported use of the skills at home. At 6- to 8-week follow-up, both treatment groups appeared to maintain their treatment gains with the regular treatment group continuing to improve on some of the measures from post to follow-up whereas the generalization group worsened slightly on the same measures. These results are somewhat encouraging with respect to the intervention, but the generalization issue remains puzzling. The increased number of sessions for both groups, relative to the Robin *et al.* (1977) intervention, might have influenced these results, and the use of family-specific measures of change may have resulted in greater sensitivity to treatment effects, but the reason for the nongeneralization group's continued improvement is still unclear.

Several problem-solving interventions have also been attempted in families with a delinquent child. Kifer, Lewis, Green, and Phillips (1974) sought to determine if negotiation skills could be taught to mother–child dyads simultaneously. Their subjects were two mother–daughter and one mother–son pairs in which the children had all had at least one contact with juvenile court. Pre- and posttreatment each pair was observed in the home discussing conflict situations. Also, discussions of simulated conflict situations were recorded prior to and following each session. In both samples of discussions, observers recorded negotiation behaviors (complete communication, identification

of issues, suggestion of options) and agreements (compliant vs. nego-
tiated). A multiple-baseline, across-pairs design was used to evaluate
the influence of training on the occurrence of negotiation behaviors
and agreements. Training followed a model that focused on generating
different responses to a given situation, examining the consequences of
each response, selecting the desired consequence, and then practicing
the chosen response–consequence sequence. Training with each pair
continued until the stopping criterion was reached. This criterion was
two consecutive presession simulated discussions in which all three
negotiation behaviors were used between the two pair members. Subjects required from four to six sessions to reach criterion. All three pairs
substantially increased their use of negotiation behaviors over baseline
levels but only one pair reached this level of performance prior to being
informed of the nature of the termination criterion. In the home
observations of real conflict discussions, all pairs showed significant
posttreatment increases in negotiation skills and agreements. This
study's use of a termination criterion is an interesting technique, but
the failure of two pairs to reach this criterion before being informed of
its existence suggests that a motivation to end treatment, as well as
improved negotiation skills, may have been responsible for the change.
The results also indicated, however, that the negotiation behaviors
generalized to home discussions without any explicit generalization
training, although the presence of an observer may well have served as
a discriminative stimulus for the display of such behavior. The small
sample size and the absence of a control group once again lessen the
strength of any conclusions that can be drawn regarding the effectiveness of this intervention.

Alexander, Parsons, and colleagues (Alexander & Parsons, 1973;
Parsons & Alexander, 1973; Klein, Alexander, & Parsons, 1977) worked
with delinquent adolescents in a program referred to as a short-term
behavioral intervention that focused attention on contingency contracting. In addition, this intervention stressed the modification of
family communication patterns with respect to clarity, precision, and
clarification, and emphasized the generation of alternative solutions to
family conflicts. Alexander and Parsons (1973) conducted their research
with the 86 families of 38 male and 48 female delinquents. The children
ranged from 13 to 16 years of age and had been arrested or detained for
offenses such as running away; shoplifting; habitual truancy; posses-
sion of alcohol, soft drugs, or tobacco; or being declared ungovernable.
Thus the treatment sample was diverse in sex, age, and nature of
offense. Forty-six families were assigned to the short-term behavioral
intervention, 19 participated in a client-centered program, 11 were

assigned to a psychodynamically oriented program, and ten served as no-treatment controls. Treatment effects were assessed via coded video tapes of family interactions and in terms of the recidivism rates of the delinquents. As predicted by the authors, families receiving the short-term behavioral intervention demonstrated significantly more equality of interaction, less silence (more activity), and more interruptions in the video-taped interactions. Recidivism rates were examined during a 6- to 18-month follow-up period. The short-term behavioral, client-centered, psychodynamic, and no-treatment groups obtained recidivism rates of 26%, 47%, 73%, and 50%, respectively. Thus, the short-term behavioral group demonstrated a significantly lower recidivism rate. Given the long interval during which these recidivism statistics were gathered (12 months), it is hoped the groups were equivalent on the mean length of time to follow-up contact; otherwise these reported recidivism rates could be biased. To study the relationship between the family interaction variables and recidivism, all cases were divided into recidivism and nonrecidivism groups, regardless of condition. It was observed that the nonrecidivism group obtained significantly better interaction scores.

Parsons and Alexander (1973) compared the short-term behavioral intervention with a control group using a sample similar to that of Alexander and Parsons (1973). Again, the treatment resulted in significantly improved family interaction. Using an interesting follow-up procedure, Klein *et al.* (1977) searched for indications of sibling court contact in the 86 families participating in the Alexander and Parsons (1973) intervention. Juvenile court records were examined at a 30- to 42-month interval following the completion of the intervention. The rates of sibling court involvement for the short-term behavioral, client-centered, psychodynamic, and no-treatment groups were 20%, 59%, 63%, and 40%, respectively. These data suggest the positive impact of the short-term behavioral intervention on the family system. Given the long follow-up interval, these data are subject to the same potential for bias noted in regard to the Alexander and Parsons (1973) recidivism rates.

Outcome Inconsistency and Moderator Variables

Given the smaller number of studies in this area, relative to the self-instructional training literature, the available data on variables that mediate outcome are necessarily more limited. In addition, some of these interventions were conducted with very small samples. The current summary considers only the studies just reviewed, but the literature on problem-solving training with "normal" children is another source of data. The interested reader is referred to the research with non-problem samples that was cited previously in this section (see also D'Zurilla & Nezu, 1982; Fischler, 1984).

SUBJECT VARIABLES

As was the case with self-instructional training, subject characteristics constitute a meaningful class of potential moderator variables.

Age. Problem-solving interventions have been conducted with a wide age range of children and adolescents. If one groups these studies into four age categories (preschool children, elementary school children, preteens and early adolescents, and adolescents), there appear to be studies obtaining positive and not-so-positive results in each age category. Developmental features seem to have been ignored, as no study has directly addressed the issue of age effects on treatment outcome (see also Kendall, 1984). Spivack, Shure, and colleagues have suggested that the various components of problem-solving may vary in their significance for social adjustment depending on the age or development level of the child; however, while some differences in component skills over the years have been found, the data are far from clear-cut (Kendall & Fischler, 1984). A recognition of the child's developmental level would be particularly important if a given intervention requires certain prerequisite skills. Spivack and colleagues, in their work with preschoolers, assume that such skills must be trained prior to the formal intervention, but other investigators working with older samples typically assume the existence of skills such as affective identification and differentiation.

Nature of Disorder. An interesting relationship occurs between age and nature of disorder. Within each age category, children were selected as requiring treatment for demonstrating their developmental level's version of acting-out behavior or conflict with authority. Preschoolers and elementary school children were treated for overly aggressive and impulsive behavior, as typically judged by their classroom teacher. Preteens and early adolescents were selected for intervention on the basis of parent–child conflict, and the adolescent samples were receiving treatment by virtue of being delinquent. Interestingly, even when the subjects were diagnosed as neurotic or schizophrenic, as in Giebink *et al.* (1968), training was forced on the inhibition of aggressive responses to frustrating situations. The only exception to this pattern was Spivack and Shure's surprising inclusion of overly inhibited children in the treatment sample. While a number of more behavioral social-skills training programs have been implemented with the inhibited or socially isolated child (see Combs & Slaby, 1977), problem-solving approaches have generally not been applied with this group.

The problem-solving literature did yield a few specific treatment by disorder interactions. For example, Spivack and Shure (1974) found that overly inhibited children tended to improve on ratings of concern for others following interpersonal problem-solving training, while the impulsive and adjusted children did not improve on this measure. Sarason and Ganzer (1973) found that their modeling intervention (that emphasized role playing) tended to produce improvement in delinquents diagnosed as neurotic or passive–dependent personality disorder, and that the discussion treatment group resulted in improvement in those diagnosed as sociopathic or passive–aggressive personality disorder.

Sex. Few of the problem-solving interventions considered the possible influence of the child's gender on treatment outcome. In fact, only Spivack and associates regularly analyzed for sex differences. The only notable difference these investigators obtained was a tendency for female preschoolers to improve on ratings of popularity with peers while males did not. The importance of gender differences deserves closer scrutiny from future researchers.

Race and Socioeconomic Status. This review included reports of treatment success with racially and economically diverse samples, although no intervention actually included upper-SES subjects. The impact of these variables on outcome, however, is not clearly understood. For example, Spivack and Shure's investigations all involve predominantly black, inner-city samples of preschool children and positive results are typically reported, but Weissberg *et al.* (1981) reported improvement in suburban but not inner-city third grade children following a training program highly similar to the Spivack and Shure intervention. Again, the issue of higher-order interactions appears relevant, with race and SES influences possibly related to factors such as age of subject, as well as features of the intervention.

Intelligence. While studies typically describe their samples as being of average intelligence, few other data on the intellectual level of the child are presented. Perhaps in the effort to distinguish interpersonal cognitive problem solving from impersonal problem solving, investigators have tended to forsake assessment of the child's intellectual level. Whether or not the two domains are independent, however, the child's intellectual level, like his/her age level, is bound to affect his or her ability to comprehend the training—whatever the focus of the training.

TREATMENT VARIABLES

As was the case with subject variables, the relatively small number of studies limits the number and strength of conclusions that can be drawn regarding various treatment components. In addition, the problem-solving approach has not been subject to the kinds of "dismantling" studies found in the self-instructional training literature. The following discussion represents a brief attempt at "comparative dismantling."

Training Skills. The most common focus of problem-solving training was teaching children to generate behavioral alternatives to problem situations. Several interventions (Giebink *et al.*, 1968; Sarason & Sarason, 1981; Spivack & Shure, 1974; Shure & Spivack, 1978) explicitly assessed this skill at pre- and posttreatment, and all three studies reported increased generation of alternatives following treatment. Spivack and Shure took the next step of ascertaining whether or not the *individual* children improving in generation of alternatives were also demonstrating behavioral improvements. These authors found that children improving in generation of alternatives were also more likely to be rated as behaviorally adjusted following treatment.

The interventions conducted with parent–child pairs tended to emphasize communication and negotiation skills in addition to problem-solving techniques. Alexander and Parsons (1973) conducted an analysis similar to that of Spivack and Shure by assessing whether those parent–child dyads who demonstrated improved communication skills were actually the families with lower recidivism rates. Their findings did indicate a significant relationship between better skills and lower rates of recidivism. On the other hand, Foster (1979) found that one of her treatment groups displayed slightly worse communication skills at posttest, yet this group showed the most long-lasting improvement on self-report measures of the mainly specific goals, communication targets, and conflict situations. Thus, in some cases, the role of the skills emphasized in training remains unclear.

Role Play. Most of the interventions in this section included role play of problem situations or simulated problem discussions. As noted above, Sarason and Ganzer's (1973) was the only study to examine the effects of the role play variable specifically. The results of this study indicated that subjects in the role-playing condition were more likely to evaluate their institutional experience as positive and recall the content and goals of treatment when asked 18 months later. The role-play group was, however, comparable to the other treatment group in rates of recidivism.

Game Format. Several investigators provided problem-solving training in a game format (Blechman *et al.*, 1976a, 1976b; Giebink *et al.*, 1968). Interestingly, only in the Blechman *et al.* (1976b) case study were there any significant indications of generalization of problem-solving skills to nontraining settings. These findings suggest that a brief, game-format intervention alone may not build in the components necessary for generalization of treatment effects, and that the game-format intervention should be coupled with other strategies. Indeed, a game format might enhance the involvement of the child in the treatment, a factor that Braswell *et al.* (1984b) found related to degree of improvement.

Therapist or Tutor. Typically special experimental personnel provide the problem-solving training. Robin and Schneider (1974), however, used the classroom teacher to successfully train emotionally disturbed children in the use of the "turtle technique." The efforts of Spivack and Shure also suggest that both teachers and mothers can be successfully trained to impart interpersonal cognitive problem-solving skills. The use of parents as trainers for their own children is an interesting approach worthy of further research. At present, results are not tied to the type of trainer.

Use of Explicit Behavioral Contingencies. The use of explicit behavior contingencies is not as common in the problem-solving training literature as it is in the self-instructional training research, but a few examples do exist. Kirmil-Gray, Duckham-Shoor, and Thoresen (1980) incorporated rewards for the use of problem-solving skills, yet their results indicated that problem-solving training added nothing to the effects achieved via parental use of behavioral management techniques. Robin *et al.* (1976) trained their subjects to provide each other with peer reinforcement for the appropriate use of the turtle technique. This intervention did obtain positive effects. However, in the absence of any follow-up data it is impossible to know if the peer reinforcement actually helped maintain the desired response. To the extent that such contingencies did help maintain appropriate problem-solving behavior, they would constitute useful additions to a training program. The research is incomplete, but it is our opinion that behavioral contingencies are a valuable facet of any program designed to teach interpersonal problem-solving skills.

CONCLUSIONS

What do we know as a result of these studies of self-instructional and problem-solving interventions? First, it appears that several of these treatments have affected both the cognitive and behavioral activities of their subjects. These findings are exciting and encouraging for they offer data indicating that some of the treatments are quite effective. The evidence for continued enthusiasm aside, many important questions remain. For example, few studies have ascertained whether or not the subjects showing the most change on the cognitive skills or tasks were also showing the most behavioral change. Clarification of this link in the treatment requires further study.

Given that all children do not respond the same way to cognitive-behavioral training, what subject factors affect outcome? The subject's age and cognitive level continually appear in discussions of moderator variables and there are already data to suggest that these factors contribute to the extent to which the cognitive training is best presented in a concrete or conceptual manner. Younger and/or cognitively less mature children appear to benefit from a more concrete approach whereas older and/or cognitively sophisticated children appear to profit from a conceptual approach. The child's sex does not appear to affect outcome and although the effects of the variables of race and socio-economics are not fully understood, it appears that children from diverse racial and economic backgrounds are capable of deriving some benefit from these cognitive–behavioral interventions.

In terms of the nature of the child's problem, it seems that as the child's level of aggression increases so does the difficulty of achieving a positive outcome. Future studies might examine how the outcome could be improved for more aggressive youngsters. For example, one might calibrate the emphasis on "behavioral" aspects of the treatment with the child's level of aggression, providing the most aggressive children with a "behavioral–cognitive" treatment while those with less aggressive behavior would receive cognitive–behavioral training. A second slant on the problem would focus on the role of emotions in treatment outcome. For instance, variations in degree of affective education provided to the children or in the extent of anger-arousing role plays might influence the final gains. Clearly, more effort needs to be assigned to the analysis of affect in the treatment of the more aggressive youngster.

Just as one recognizes that all children do not respond uniformly, so too we must acknowledge that treatments, even when described as similar in written format, are often provided in ways that result in slight to major variations. What, then, are the treatment factors that affect outcome? Modeling appears to be a very important component, as does the opportunity for the child to self-reinforce for correct performance. Both self-instructional and problem-solving studies that include role playing also seem to obtain more positive results. The use of a gamelike format may foster initial interest, but if the intervention is very brief and never progresses beyond the game, there may be little generalization. At the present time we lack information about what type (or types) might be more effective, but there is much reason to hold that the trainer should include a performance base and behavioral contingencies since these factors seem to enhance treatment effectiveness.

Our conclusions are tentative. Nevertheless, they do provide helpful guideposts for the further application and evaluation of cognitive–behavioral training programs with children. We hope too that our review guides the reader's formulation of further hypotheses regarding the interplay of cognitive and behavioral training and the influences of affect and subject and treatment variables.

CHAPTER 3

Nature of the Deficit: The Target Sample for the Treatment

Treatments are optimal to the degree that they are directed toward and focus on the nature of the deficit troubling the target child. What do we mean by this statement? We intend to urge that treatments not be prescribed according to the therapists' theoretical allegiances or professional affiliations, but, rather, that the deficit shown by the child and, more specifically, the exact features associated with the deficit, should determine the type of treatment that is provided. No one intervention strategy can be optimal for the various types of childhood disorders. As we will describe in this chapter, there are features of the non-self-controlled, impulsive child that make him/her a prime candidate for the cognitive–behavioral treatment we are presenting.

The cognitive–behavioral procedures detailed in this book were developed for use with children manifesting deficits in self-control. Children falling into this group are often described as impulsive, attention-disordered, overactive, disobedient to adult authorities, externalizing or undercontrolled (Achenbach, 1966; Achenbach & Edelbrock, 1978), and/or aggressive toward others. They may carry psychiatric diagnoses of attention deficit disorder with or without hyperactivity or conduct disorder, and learning problems are often present.

Describing the target group is not a difficult task, but certain complexities are present. For instance, while the intervention described herein has its main historical antecedents within behavioral attempts to enhance self-management of discrete behaviors, the recipients of the intervention have frequently been described in terms of the traditional psychiatric labels or labels more associated with trait or temperament theories (Buss & Plomin, 1975; Chess, Thomas, & Birch, 1968) than

with behavioral formulations. In our description of the target population and the nature of its deficits, we are comfortable with a blending of
perspectives; but our comfort rests on certain assumptions that we shall
share. We recognize that certain patterns of behavior that may be
reflective of problems in self-management (e.g., blurting out in class,
inability to sit still, difficulties in effective attention deployment) could
also be viewed as symptoms of some psychiatric syndromes. We acknowledge that some diagnostic labels are accompanied by assumptions
regarding etiology and prognosis that are abhorrent to many behaviorists. Current thought regarding the diagnoses of attention deficit disorder and conduct disorder, however, suggests that these syndromes
may be the final common manifestation of a wide range of etiological
agents. Thus, using a diagnostic label does not imply acceptance of a
specific theory of causation. On the other hand, we also agree with
Karoly's statement that "prior to systematic assessments, there is no
reason for interpreting certain clinical disorders (such as hyperactivity,
antisocial or criminal behavior, depression, or academic failure) as
being self-management disorders by definition" (1981, pp. 92–93). Using
one of Karoly's examples, a child's antisocial behavior, such as vandal-
ism, may not be the result of an inability to manage or control his/her
behavior but rather the result of a decision to imitate a peer model, even
while cognizant of the potential long-term consequences. Thus, we
shall employ behavioral descriptions while also using more general
labels as we attempt to describe our target population. Our description
of non-self-controlled, externalizing children will include prevalence,
behavioral pattern or symptomatology, cognitive deficits, course of
disorder, and the role of family variables.

PREVALENCE

Difficulties in self-management appear to be extremely common in
both clinic and nonclinic child samples. Conners (1980) estimates that
60% to 70% of the clients at child guidance clinics are referred by parents
or teachers because the child's externalizing behavior has made him/her
a management problem. Based on teacher ratings of nonclinic samples
of school-aged children, Werry and Quay (1971) report that 30% of
males and 13% of females were described as overactive, 46% of males and
22% of females were rated as disruptive, 43% of males and 25% of females
were said to have short attention spans, and 26% of males and 11% of
females were rated as disobedient and difficult to discipline.

In a series of treatment outcome studies, Kendall and his colleagues asked second through sixth grade teachers to refer those children displaying a problematic lack of self-control that interfered with their social and/or academic functioning in the classroom. This selection criterion typically yielded a referral rate of three children per 30-student classroom, or 10% of a sample of unselected school children.

In terms of the traditional diagnostic categories of hyperactivity and conduct disorder, prevalence estimates vary from 1% to 15% of school-aged children (Schrag & Divoky, 1975), with most of the figures falling into the 5% to 12% range.

Examination of prevalence rates across studies indicates these rates are strongly influenced by the type and number of raters. Using the Conners Teacher Rating Scale, Trites (1979) had classroom teachers rate over 14,000 children between the ages of 4 and 12 years. Using the standard 1.5 cutoff, 14.3% of the children were rated hyperactive. A 3:1 male:female ratio was observed in this sample. Interestingly, Trites found a high degree of stability of prevalence ratings for both sexes across all included ages. Other investigators using teacher ratings have also produced estimates in the 10% to 20% range (Huessy, 1967, 1974). The scoring of the hyperactivity factor has been varied. However, scoring the four frequency categories as 0, 1, 2, and 3 for ten items, and dividing the total by ten yields a score which, if over 1.5, has been said to indicate hyperactivity.

The prevalence rates observed in studies where the raters are trained mental health professionals or where multiple raters are employed tend to be lower than those produced in studies using teachers as raters. For example, Nichols (1976, cited in Rapoport, Quinn, Burg, & Bartley, 1979) reported a rate of 6%, whereas Lambert, Sandoval, and Sassone (1977) identified only 1.9% of their sample as hyperactive. Rutter, Cox, Tupling, Berger, and Yule (1975) observed a rate of conduct disorder of only 4% among 10- and 11-year-old children on the Isle of Wight, although a rate of 8% was obtained in a sample of children from an inner London borough. Thus, it appears that the prevalence rates for the syndromes of hyperactivity and conduct disorder are both approximately 1% to 4% for school-aged children; however, problematic behaviors, in the absence of the full syndrome, are much more common.

As will be discussed more fully in the next section of this chapter, the most current diagnostic formulations (DSM-III) refer to hyperactivity as part of Attention Deficit Disorder (ADD), with the primary difficulty being viewed as one of attention instead of overactivity. ADD is believed to occur both with and without hyperactivity, and the prevalence rate of ADD *without* hyperactivity is uncertain. The results of research by Kendall and Brophy (1981) suggest that one of the standard measures of hyperactivity, the Conners Teacher Rating Scale, assesses only the motor behavior or activity level component of the disorder. Prevalence studies based on this measure, therefore, yield little or no information regarding the rate of ADD that occurs without hyperactivity.

BEHAVIORAL PATTERN

A blend of the behavioral and traditional psychopathology perspectives is particularly valuable in considering the behavior patterns and symptoms of the target population. Adopting a behavioral self-control view, it is helpful to think of children displaying a problematic lack of self-control in terms of Kanfer's two-stage model. In this model, Kanfer (1977) distinguishes between decisional self-control, which involves the decision to select the self-controlling response from among alternatives, and protracted self-control, which involves the specific behaviors necessary to actually accomplish the relevant behavior changes, such as self-monitoring, self-evaluation, and self-reinforcement. Some children with difficulties managing their behavior may lack both decisional self-control and protracted self-control, while others may lack only protracted self-control. Children of the former type would not make an initial decision favoring a self-controlling response, and even if they did they couldn't carry it out. Children of the latter type could verbalize a desire to control their own behavior ("OK, Mom, I won't hit baby brother anymore"), but they don't have the component skills necessary to accomplish this goal. In fact, not only do they lack the appropriate behaviors but they also have what Meichenbaum (1976b) has described as an "automatized" chain of events that leads to maladaptive responding. Borrowing from Kopp's (1982) discussion of self-regulation, this maladaptive responding might include difficulty in complying with a request, initiating or ceasing activities according to situational demands, modulating the intensity, duration, and frequency of verbal and motoric acts in educational as well as social settings, postponing action toward a desired object or goal, and generating socially appropriate behavior in the absence of external monitors.

From a more symptom-oriented perspective, this target population is frequently described in terms of the symptom pattern known as hyperactivity. There is some general agreement that overactivity, difficulties with attention deployment, impulsivity, and excitability are the most frequently noted symptoms of this disorder (Cantwell, 1977; Routh, 1980; Stewart, Pitts, Craig, & Dieruf, 1966; Werry, 1968). It should also be acknowledged, however, that the clinical picture of children labeled hyperactive "varies from the little boy who is silly, immature and not performing academically up to expected standards to the markedly active, aggressive, and anti-social child who is unable to be managed in a regular classroom setting" (Cantwell, 1977, p. 525). We have had clinical experiences in which the level of aggression displayed by the client far outweighed any attentional difficulties, yet hyperactivity was the "diagnosis." At a later point in this section we shall discuss efforts that have been made to determine the association between the construct of hyperactivity and the concept of aggression. Now, however, we shall focus on the increased emphasis on attentional difficulties rather than overactivity as the primary problem or deficit with children who have been labeled hyperactive in the past.

In recent years, a growing body of research and clinical observations has suggested that hyperactive behavior is one potential result of an attentional deficit. Diagnostic standards have changed to reflect this shift in emphasis, so that according to DSM-III children previously diagnosed as hyperactive are now labeled as having ADD with hyperactivity.[1] This deficit in attention is manifested as distractibility, inability to listen, difficulty concentrating and completing projects, and difficulty sticking with play activities. These problems are more likely to be displayed in situations that require greater self-application, such as the classroom. They may not be observed when the child is in a novel or one-to-one work situation. As indicated previously, many children with such problems are also overly active, but some are not. The child with ADD *without* hyperactivity does not have unusual difficulty remaining still, but he/she is likely to have trouble completing assignments and organizing or planning activities.

While many investigators agree that a deficit in attention deployment is the primary problem, there is not unanimity of thought regarding how to describe the exact nature of this problem. Some authors

1. While "Attention Deficit Disorder with Hyperactivity" is the correct diagnostic term, it is unclear whether or not the children labeled hyperactive or hyperkinetic in previous research would necessarily fit the diagnostic criteria of ADD with hyperactivity. Therefore, in the interest of being precise we shall continue to use the term "hyperactivity" and the label "hyperactives" when making reference to research conducted prior to the establishment of ADD with hyperactivity as a diagnostic entity.

label it distractibility, as indicated by greater reactions to external events, difficulty persevering with schoolwork, and frequent daydreaming (Cantwell, 1977; Routh, 1980). In a related vein, these children have been described as "stimulus-driven" (Goldstein & Sheerer, 1941) or as having forced responsiveness to stimuli (Cruikshank, 1966/1977). As will be discussed in the section on cognitive deficits, however, other investigators, such as Douglas and Peters (1979), question the data supporting the hypothesis that hyperactives are stimulus-driven or more distractible than their normal peers. Douglas and Peters contend that the available data are more consistent with the notion that hyperactives have an unusual need for stimulation and show a tendency to have their attention so "captured" by the more obvious aspects of a task or situation that they fail to attend to the more subtle aspects.

While attentional difficulties appear to be primary, the hyperactive behavior that some children manifest is clearly the most obvious symptom. This overactivity is typically manifested by intense and undirected energy, fidgetiness, inability to sit still, and, in some cases, a reduced need for sleep (Cantwell, 1977). In the classroom this overactivity often takes the form of running, jumping, and remaining out of seat without permission. In an observation of 26 hyperactive preschool children and 26 controls, Schleifer, Weiss, Cohen, Elman, Cvejic, and Kruger (1975) rated behavior that occurred during periods of free play and structured play. No differences were observed between the hyperactives and controls in the free-play situation, but in the structured-play situation hyperactives exhibited significantly higher rates of "up" and "away" behaviors. Weiss (1975) also has difficulty distinguishing hyperactives from normals in a free-play situation. Jacob, O'Leary, and Rosenblad (1978) observed hyperactives and normals in both open and traditional classrooms. The hyperactive children displayed the same activity levels in both settings, but normals were less active in the more structured, traditional settings. In light of these findings it seems the overactivity of these children becomes problematic because of their inability to modulate or manage their activity level in accordance with the demands of their environment rather than simply because of the absolute amount of activity they display.

Our target group is also notable for its impulsivity, which is conceptualized as an inability to think before acting. Impulsivity may be displayed via a wide range of behaviors, including impulsive responding on psychoeducational tasks, verbal blurting out and interrupting, and physically irritating others. It is also manifested as a tendency to shift excessively from one activity to another and an inability to await one's turn in a group or game situation. In some situations impulsiveness may be tantamount to recklessness. Cognitive impulsivity is further discussed in a later section.

Our target children also demonstrate excitability. They appear to have low frustration tolerance which results in temper tantrums and fits over unimportant matters and a tendency to become "revved up" or overexcited, particularly in the presence of large groups of other children (Cantwell, 1977).

In addition to these four major symptom areas (attention problems, overactivity, impulsivity, and excitability), investigators studying the nature of hyperactivity or attention deficit disorder have increasingly recognized the socially inappropriate nature of the child's behavior and the deficits in self-control implied by such behavior (Barkley, 1982; Routh, 1980). In addition, other factors that frequently accompany the four major symptoms include poor school achievement and specific learning disabilities. Mendelson, Johnson, and Stewart (1971) found that 58% of the hyperactive children in their sample had failed one or more grades in school by the time they reached adolescence. Poor school performance has been observed by many other investigators (Hechtman, Weiss, Finkelstein, Werner, & Benn, 1976; Minde, Lewin, Weiss, Lavigueur, Douglas, & Sykes, 1971; Weiss, Minde, Werry, Douglas, & Nemeth, 1971), and it is particularly surprising when a large number of these children obtain relatively high scores on individually administered IQ tests.

Physical and verbal aggression have also been observed more frequently in children exhibiting the four symptoms previously discussed than in controls (Abikoff, Gittelman-Klein, & Klein, 1977). Clearly, however, not all children who display attentional difficulties, overactivity, impulsivity, and excitability are also aggressive, and many of those who do commit aggressive acts do not display these other symptoms. Some hyperactivity researchers have attempted to explicitly determine the characteristics of hyperactivity that are essentially independent of aggression (e.g., Milich, Loney, & Landau, 1982; O'Leary & Steen, 1982; Prinz, Connor, & Wilson, 1981; Roberts, Milich, Loney, & Caputo, 1981). While the results remain somewhat equivocal (see Lahey, Green, & Forehand, 1980), the weight of the evidence from these studies suggests that while features of hyperactivity and aggression are quite similar, these two dimensions of behavior are not redundant.

As an example of such research, Milich et al. (1982) examined observational data gathered in a playroom situation. Ninety boys referred to an outpatient psychiatry service served as subjects. By DSM-III diagnoses, 22 were ADD, 22 conduct disorder, eight received both of these diagnoses, and 38 were assigned other diagnoses. The 90 boys participated in two 15-minute playroom observation periods: a free-play situation and a restricted academic situation. The playroom floor was marked into grids and several behaviors were coded (e.g., grid crossing, out of seat, fidgeting, attention shifts). Chart ratings similar to those employed in Loney, Langhorne, and Paternite (1978) were examined (e.g., frequency and severity of attention problems, impulsivity, aggressive interpersonal), and mother and teacher ratings were gathered. Factor analysis yielded three factors: hyperactivity, anxiety-depression, and aggression. Regarding demographic data, SES was related to the aggression factor but not the hyperactivity factor. The hyperactivity factor helped account for variations in mothers' and teachers' ratings of hyperactivity and inattention, but did not add to the prediction of conduct problems. Similarly, the hyperactivity factor added to the prediction of the observation data, beyond the common variance with the aggression factor. Thus, while aggression is often observed in children who also manifest hyperactivity and related attentional difficulties, these symptom groups do not always coexist in the same child.

Several authors have pointed out the importance of recognizing developmental shifts in symptomatology (Cantwell, 1977; Denhoff, 1973; Ross & Ross, 1976; Wender, 1971). The mothers of children who were later diagnosed as hyperactive often report that these children were particularly demanding and irritable infants (Ross & Ross, 1976). These babies tended to be irregular in their physiological functioning as demonstrated by sleeping and eating disturbances, colic, and frequent crying. Ross and Ross (1976) have reported that using Sanders's (1962) five levels of adaptation, hyperactive children and their mothers appear more vulnerable to difficulties in establishing regular patterns. It should be noted, however, that these disturbances are not characteristic of hyperactive, acting-out children alone (Thomas, Chess, & Birch, 1968).

During the preschool years the symptoms of overactivity, attentional difficulties, and low frustration tolerance may appear. In addition, these children may continue to exhibit irregularity of mood and physiological functioning. These children may also seem to have no sense of danger and to be unaffected by disciplinary efforts that are successful with other children (Cantwell, 1977). As mentioned previously, Schleifer and his colleagues (1971) did observe differences of certain off-task behaviors in preschool children in structured but not free-play situations. Again, it must be cautioned that single symptoms such as overactivity are relatively common at this age. Weiss (1971) has concluded that preschool hyperactives are a heterogeneous group and that it might be reasonable to expect that a certain percentage of these children will "outgrow" their problems, but that another subgroup will develop ADD with hyperactivity in their elementary school years.

During these early school years, the behaviors noted previously persist and may become much more noticeable. Given the demands of the classroom environment, children who had not previously exhibited problems of attention or activity level may begin to have such difficulties at school. As mentioned earlier, many of these children develop academic problems. These academic and behavioral difficulties may feed into the development of both poor self-concept and poor peer relations.

Ross and Ross (1976) have suggested that adolescence may represent an even more difficult time for the child than the primary school years, for even though actual activity level may decrease, the attentional, educational, and social difficulties persist and antisocial behavior may appear. In a follow-up study of 64 hyperactive children, Weiss *et al.* (1971) reported that by early adolescence 80% of these children had repeated a grade, many still demonstrated behavior problems, and as a group these children were more likely to display signs of psychopathology than were the controls.

COGNITIVE DEFICITS

Many investigators have written about the cognitive or mediational deficits that are believed to be responsible for the actual deficit in attention that results with observed impulsive or hyperactive behavior. The current authors have been influenced by the research and theorizing of Douglas and her colleagues (Douglas, 1972, 1974, 1976; Douglas & Peters, 1979). Douglas and Peters (1979) hold that the behavioral and cognitive difficulties of these children can be traced to defective functioning in the "three mechanisms that govern (a) sustained attention and effort, (b) inhibitory control, and (c) the modulation of arousal levels to meet task or situational demands" (p. 67). Douglas holds that there are no data that speak to the question of which of the three hypothesized areas of defective functioning is more basic.

Douglas and Peters (1979) question the notion that children observed to be hyperactive are more vulnerable to distractions or more likely to process and remember irrelevant information than are normal controls. They do, however, believe there is support in the observation that hyperactives display a tendency to have their attention so "captured" by the more obvious aspects of a problem or situation that they fail to consider more subtle, but potentially relevant, features. To cite an example from the domain of interpersonal cognitive problem solving, Parry (1973) observed hyperactives on a story completion task. These children displayed an inability to cope with frustrating situations, for they tended to focus (or have their attention "captured") almost entirely on the frustrating event and failed to consider the motives of others. As an aside, hyperactives also tended to choose story endings that allowed the frustrated child to act aggressively.

Douglas and Peters (1979) also have stated that they do not think there is evidence to support the view that hyperactive children are actually "stimulus-driven," as suggested by Goldstein and Sheerer (1941), or that these children display "forced responsiveness to stimuli" (Cruikshank, 1966/1977). Douglas and Peters contend that the data are more consistent with the hypothesis that these children have an unusual need for stimulation and, as a result of this need, they display a tendency to seek heightened levels of stimulation.

Ultimately, Douglas and Peters (1979) feel that the nature of the deficits described earlier involves "an inability to sustain attention and to inhibit impulsive responding on tasks or in social situations that require focused, reflective, organized, and self-directed effort" (p. 173). In summarizing previous research tasks, Douglas (1980) observed that hyperactives do no worse than normals on paired association tasks involving pairs that are meaningfully associated, or, in other words, pairs that provided a "built-in" strategy for remembering. On the other hand, the performance of hyperactives is notably worse when the pairs involve arbitrary associates that require the subject to generate his/her own strategy for remembering. In a review of studies examining the task strategies of impulsive and reflective children, Cameron (1977) reports that the majority of the studies found impulsives less likely to display focusing strategies. In his own research, Cameron found impulsives more likely to approach the task in a disorganized manner and make guesses or attend too narrowly to a particular stimulus dimension, rather than systematically utilizing strategies that would rule out competing alternatives. Interestingly, Cameron also observed that even when impulsives were able to verbalize more effective task approaches, they seemed to have difficulty maintaining attention to their own task rule and would make choices inconsistent with their verbalized strategy. Tant (1978) compared the performance of matched groups of hyperactive, reading-disabled, and normal controls on matrix solution tasks. The hyperactive children were distinguishable from both the other groups, for they appeared to conduct less thorough perceptual analyses of the arrays and displayed a lack of information about what constituted "efficient" questioning. These findings are particularly interesting since the three groups were matched for verbal IQ and an effort was made to help all subjects remain highly motivated.

These findings dovetail nicely with current theorizing about metacognitive development. Brown (1975) and, much earlier, Vygotsky (1962) distinguished between knowledge that is acqired in a non-self-conscious, relatively automatic way and knowledge that must be consciously, deliberately sought. This difference may be of relevance for understanding the cognitive strengths and weaknesses of non-self-controlled, hyperactive children. For instance, Brown (1975) has suggested that successful performance, at least in most Western cultures, demands the application of deliberate, systematic learning strategies, particularly given the fact that most exercises within formal education are likely to appear contrived and serve no obvious purpose from the child's perspective—leaving little chance of spontaneous learning. The hyperactive or impulsive child's reported difficulty with this very type of task is highly consistent with the finding that the majority of these children experience academic difficulties throughout their school careers (Hoy, Weiss, Minde, & Cohen, 1978; Mendelson *et al.*, 1971, Minde *et al.*, 1971; Weiss *et al.*, 1971). As noted earlier, however, hyperactive children can obtain relatively high scores on IQ tests. Several explanations for this discrepancy have been advanced. In a summary of the relevant research, Douglas (1980) concluded that hyperactives do not demonstrate impaired performance on tasks in which the examiner assumes responsibility for eliciting the child's attention or on tasks in which the relevant stimuli are presented until the child has attended to them. In addition, hyperactives appear to have less difficulty on search tasks in which the items are presented one at a time and which require the child to detect only one missing feature. Interestingly, administration of the major individual IQ tests, such as the WISC-R and Stanford–Binet, is consistent with the features outlined by Douglas, and, in fact, both measures include subtests in which items are administered one at a time and have only one missing element. In addition, Torgesen (1977) has noted that a number of items appearing on standard IQ tests, especially those appearing on tests for younger age levels, require information that can be acquired unintentionally or without use of a specific strategy. Douglas goes on to note that if Torgeson's contentions are correct, one would expect to see progressive decrements in the IQ scores of hyperactives since higher test levels demand the actual use of systematic strategies or tap knowledge that can only be acquired through the use of such strategies. Data presented by Loney (1974) supported this hypothesis, for hyperactives and controls obtained similar IQ scores in second grade but significantly different scores in sixth grade. The findings of other investigators are also consistent with this review (Prinz & Loney, 1974; Wikler, Dixon, & Parker, 1970).

The issue of cognitive or mediational deficits also emerges in the consideration of children with externalizing disorders other than hyperactivity. Camp's (1977) research with young aggressive boys has led her to hypothesize that an ineffective linguistic control system may be the basis for the difficulties this population has in inhibiting inappropriate responses on both impersonal and interpersonal tasks. She has suggested that aggressive behavior might follow from an inconsistent or weak response to covert commands and/or as unusually high threshold for initiating self-regulatory statements. Moreover, aggressive children show errors and deficits in social cognition, in particular misperceptions of intention, as suggested by the work of Dodge and colleagues (Dodge & Frame, 1982; Dodge, Murphy, & Buchsbaum, 1984).

This hypothesized difficulty with generation and utilization of task strategies and the activation of self-regulating speech coincides with the problem-solving orientation emphasized by cognitive–behavioral procedures. Indeed, the cognitive training focuses directly on the cognitive deficits of the target sample. Slight variations in the target group require some adjustments in the training, but the central theme remains focused on training to remove deficits in cognitive control.

PROGNOSIS

In terms of prognosis, it was once held that these problems with attention, overactivity, impulsivity, and excitability remitted at puberty (Bakwin & Bakwin, 1966; Bradley, 1957; Laufer & Denhoff, 1957). Subsequent research suggests that while overactivity does generally decrease between the ages of 12 and 16, many of the associated problems persist.

Weiss *et al.* (1971) followed up 64 children who had been diagnosed as hyperactive 4 to 6 years previously. All children had originally been treated with chlorpromazine, thioridazine, dextroamphetamine, methylphenidate, or some combination of these drugs, and 10% of the families had received intensive psychotherapy; however, only five children were still on medication at the point of follow-up. As previously suggested, these authors found that overactivity had diminished with increasing age, but difficulties with attention and concentration *did persist*. Of ancillary interest, chronic and severe underachievement in school, poor self-image, and emotional immaturity were common, and antisocial behavior was present in a substantial subgroup.

Mendelson *et al.* (1971) studied 82 hyperactive children at 2 to 5 years following the initial clinic contact. As with Weiss *et al.* (1971), a large number of these children had received stimulant medication at some point during the follow-up interval. Despite these treatment effects, the majority of these children were still described as more active, impulsive, and defiant than their peers, and they were more likely to have failed one or more grades in school. Similar results were obtained by Minde, Weiss, and Mendelson (1972).

In a more long-term follow-up, Huessy, Metoyer, and Townsend (1974) traced 75 children who had been diagnosed hyperactive 8 to 10 years previously. Of this group, 18 had been institutionalized in mental health or correctional facilities. Only 24 were categorized as having satisfactory academic levels, and only 37 were observed to have satisfactory family relations.

Hechtman *et al.* (1976) conducted a 10-year follow-up of the children observed by Weiss *et al.* (1971). Their results were consistent with those reported by Huessy *et al.* (1974) in that the hyperactives were distinguishable from normal controls in terms of school performance, with the hyperactives reporting fewer years of education, lower academic standing, and more failed grades. These findings strongly suggest that these individuals did not "outgrow" their cognitive deficits. Hechtman *et al.* (1976) did not, however, find the groups to differ significantly in terms of antisocial behavior, drug use or abuse, or incidence of psychosis.

In a follow-up study focused specifically on cognitive style, Hopkins, Perlman, Hechtman, and Weiss (1979) compared 17- to 24-year-old subjects who had been diagnosed hyperactive at least 10 years previously with controls on the cognitive-style dimensions of reflectivity–impulsivity, field independence–dependence, and constricted versus flexible control. Differences persisted on all three dimensions, with the "hyperactive" adults scoring less accurately (though not more quickly) on the reflectivity–impulsivity measure, more field-dependent, and more constricted than the controls.

On the whole, these studies indicate the persistence of difficulties into adolescence and, in some cases, adulthood, even when some form of treatment was attempted. On a cautionary note, some of the studies reported above did not include control groups and none of the studies included a "longitudinal" control group that was assessed when the hyperactive children were initially seen and at each subsequent evaluation. Even in the studies including control groups, few of them employed blind raters or testers. In other words, the experimental personnel were aware of which subjects had been originally diagnosed as hyperactive. While these methodological limitations are serious, the consistency of some of the reported findings, such as chronic academic underachievement, is impressive and certainly argues against minimizing the long-term implications of the cognitive deficits associated with hyperactivity.

ROLE OF THE FAMILY

Each child's family plays a complex and multifaceted role in the etiology, symptom expression, and/or prognosis of the child's non-self-controlled behavior. From a developmental perspective, Kopp (1982) has noted that even though parental or caregiver factors probably do not play a direct causal role in the emergence of self-regulation, these factors may play an important facilitative role. That is, there is nothing that parents do or fail to do that is directly responsible for their child's displaying developmentally appropriate self-regulation, but their actions may reinforce or enhance the natural unfolding of these skills. For example, Lytton (1976) reported that parents' use of language and general approach to caregiving related to their 2-year-old's compliance skills, and the work of Golden, Montane, and Bridger (1977) suggested that parental expectations and use of verbal techniques were influential factors in determining the child's ability to delay his/her behavior in a laboratory task. Kopp (1982) also noted that stressful family events may be associated with changes in demonstrated level of control. Using divorce as an example, Hetherington, Cox, and Cox (1977, cited in Kopp, 1982) found that when newly divorced mothers lowered their demands for child independence and provided less communication and reasoning, child control was impaired. This suggests that family stress is sometimes translated into parental behaviors that have the ultimate effect of reducing the child's demonstrated level of self-control. These findings are interesting in that they identify a possible pathway or mediating link between family stress and child misbehavior.

The families of children with externalizing disorders have frequently been observed to have unusually high rates of a variety of stress-producing factors. Disrupted marriages and interpersonal conflict have been reported to occur at higher than average frequencies among the parents of delinquents or children with conduct disorders (Glueck & Glueck, 1950; Johnson & Lobitz, 1974; McCord, McCord, & Gudeman, 1960; Nye, 1958; Rutter, 1974). The rate of psychiatric illness among the parents of hyperactive children, particularly paternal alcoholism, paternal sociopathy, and maternal hysteria, has been reported as at least twice that observed among the parents of controls (Cantwell, 1972; Morrison & Stewart, 1971). Brandon (1971) compared overactive, timid, and normal controls on a number of home environment variables and found that, compared to the other two groups, the overactive children came from more problematic home situations as indicated by poor parent–child relationships, broken or never established homes, maternal psychiatric disorder, and paternal noninvolvement.

In a more fine-grained analysis, Paternite, Loney, and Langhorne (1976) examined the relationship between parenting variables, SES, and both primary and secondary symptoms associated with hyperactivity. Inattention, fidgetiness, hyperactivity, judgment deficits, negative affect, and incoordination were considered primary symptoms; aggressive interpersonal behavior, control deficits, and self-esteem deficits were labeled secondary symptoms. While boys from low-SES families demonstrated higher rates of secondary symptoms, the parenting variables were found to be even stronger predictors of these symptoms. Thus, the parent's caregiving style was more strongly associated with the presence of aggression, impaired self-control, and low self-esteem than was the family's SES. Interestingly, neither parenting variables nor SES was consistently associated with the presence of primary symptoms, suggesting that family variables are implicated in the expression of some, but not all, of the class of externalizing behaviors.

Family factors have also been associated with response to treatment and general prognosis. Several investigators have reported a positive relationship between quality of parental management and favorable short-term response to stimulant treatment for hyperactivity (Conrad & Insel, 1967; Loney, Comly, & Simon, 1975). With respect to more long-term outcomes; it has frequently been observed that family disturbance and parental abnormalities were associated with more antisocial child outcomes (Mendelson et al., 1971; Minde et al., 1971, 1972; Weiss et al., 1971).

Of course, while parental factors may affect the expression of certain behaviors by the child, there is clearly a reciprocal relationship between the actions of virtually all parents and children. As Barkley (1981) states, "Parent and child behaviors can be viewed as a reciprocal feedback system where the behavior of each serves as both controlling stimuli and consequating events for the behavior of the other" (p. 143). In other words, parents may appear to be poor child managers when they must attempt to control exceptional children. It is not difficult to imagine how the overactive, impulsive behavior of the hyperactive child or the aggression of the conduct-disordered child could quickly elicit very negative responses from the parent. Behavioral observations by various investigators have confirmed the presence of an unusually high rate of coercive interactions within the families of conduct-disordered children (Delfini, Bernal, & Rosen, 1976; Forehand, King, Peed, & Yoder, 1975; Lobitz & Johnson, 1975; Patterson, 1976). As originally described by Patterson (1976), these interactions involve the child engaging in excessive rates of aversive behaviors followed by parental retaliation with responses that are aversive to the child and are intended to halt the child's behavior. Patterson maintains that whether or not the child does halt depends on who escalates their aversive behavior more quickly—the parent or the child. If the parent responds quickly with very negative behavior, perhaps some type of harsh discipline, the child may actually halt. If the child's efforts at resisting compliance (yelling, whining, having tantrums) escalate more quickly than the parent's behavior, the parent may give up his/her attempt to make the child comply. This parental acquiescence then has the effect of reinforcing the child's resistance and increases the probability that the child will demonstrate resistance behavior in the future.

Barkley (1981) has speculated that similar types of coercive interaction patterns are observable in the families of hyperactive children. According to his own experience, he says that the mothers of hyperactive children seem most likely to respond to such spirals of aversive parent–child interactions by giving up their attempts to control the child. The parents may even complete the disputed behavioral goal themselves (e.g., cleaning up the child's room or clearing the table), which further reinforces the child's noncompliance. In addition, the mothers of hyperactive children report withdrawing from interactions with their child in an effort to avoid future confrontations. If the child is, on some rare occasion, playing quietly and appropriately, parents report that they do not wish to interrupt this good behavior and may use this time to take care of other household duties. While this parental reaction is quite understandable, it also perpetuates a cycle of behavior in which the child must act out in order to gain the parents' attention.

Lest we end this section on too dismal a note, there is some evidence to suggest that negative parent–child interaction patterns can be interrupted. For example, Cunningham and Barkley (1978) reported that when hyperactive children increased their levels of compliance, following the onset of treatment with psychostimulant medication, their mothers responded by becoming less commanding and more rewarding of appropriate behavior.

SUMMARY

This chapter has provided a brief overview of the target population for which the intervention described in this book is best suited. In summary, it appears that the prevalence rates of hyperactivity and conduct disorder are both approximately 1% to 4% of the population of elementary school children; however, a higher percentage of children display a problematic lack of self-control without displaying all the symptoms of either disorder. The cardinal symptoms of this target group include attentional difficulties, overactivity, impulsivity, and excitability. Aggressive behavior and poor school achievement may also be present. Current research suggests that the cognitive deficits of these children are most observable in situations or on tasks that require focused, reflective, self-directed effort. Follow-up studies suggest that there are significant long-term difficulties associated with this set of childhood problems, including continued cognitive impulsivity, poor self-esteem, academic underachievement, and, in some cases, antisocial behavior. The expression of symptoms such as aggression and poor self-esteem may also be related to factors within the child's family. Parents and their children may become "locked" into cycles of behavior that perpetuate the child's difficulties.

As the reader may have noted, the shift in focus from overactivity to attentional difficulties which has occurred within current diagnostic standards and the increasing number of studies on the nature of the cognitive deficits in these children are highly consistent with the focus of our intervention. The cognitive–behavioral approach we shall detail represents a shift away from an exclusively behavioral perspective to one that emphasizes the importance of the child's processes of attention deployment and strategies for the solution of social–cognitive problems.

CHAPTER 4

Assessment Issues and Procedures

Proper intervention is dependent upon careful assessment, and the goal of this chapter is to present an overview of information on a wide range of assessment methods that are consistent with and contribute to cognitive–behavioral approaches. While clinical settings vary in the breadth and depth of their standard intake evaluations, we encourage the use of several different forms of assessment with virtually every case. Children who are homogeneous in terms of a lack of self-control will nevertheless vary in level of self-esteem, intellectual ability, and many, many other features. A child who is impulsive but has high self-esteem and good peer relations is different from one who is equally impulsive, but has low self-esteem and poor peer relations. An impulsive child with documented neurological impairments will require very different treatment from an impulsive child who has no neurological signs but has parents who have never been able to set firm and consistent limits. Even if the therapist deemed it appropriate to use the cognitive–behavioral program with most of his/her cases, the varying symptom pictures and histories would demand that the sensitive clinician make some subtle (and probably some not so subtle) variations in the treatment plan for each individual child.

To aid the clinician in formulating individualized treatment plans, we present information on interview, rating scale, task performance, self-report, behavioral, and sociometric assessment tools. In addition, we briefly discuss naturally occurring archival data that can be useful in developing and evaluating cognitive–behavioral interventions.

INTERVIEW ASSESSMENT

The most widely used form of clinical assessment, the intake interview often uncovers pertinent information for any type of intervention. We assume that the clinician already possesses well-developed interview skills, so this section will simply include some of our thoughts on what information is particularly important and useful to gather if one anticipates implementing some type of cognitive–behavioral intervention with the child and/or family.

Parent Interviewing

The parent will, in most cases, be the prime source of information regarding the child's problem behaviors. As in any behavioral interview, it is important to help the parent translate terms such as "hyper," "out of control," or "bad" into some specific behavioral correlates. For example, "hyper" might be translated to "he can't sit still at the dinner table" or "he blurts out comments all the time." "Bad" might be more accurately described as hitting, and more specifically as "she hits her little brother." In traditional behavioral terminology, the antecedents and consequences of these behaviors need to be clarified. Obtaining a history of the current problem is also important, and, if the problems are long-standing, the clinician will want to learn why the family is seeking help at *this* particular time (e.g., pressures from the school, marked increases in the child's concern about his/her behavior, additional personal stresses affecting the parents).

Beyond the discussion of the current problem, we stress the importance of obtaining a developmental history from the parent(s). This information can be crucial in formulating an appropriately comprehensive treatment plan. As part of this developmental history, the mother could be asked about the course of her pregnancy and the birth history of this child, as well as the child's early medical history. The clinician will want to be particularly attentive to factors that suggest possible neurological impairment. The presence of neurologically based problems does *not* contraindicate cognitive–behavioral training, for the child might be in dire need of exactly this type of intervention. Such conditions may, however, require concurrent medical management in order for the child to derive maximal benefit from therapy.

Asking about the child's achievement of early developmental milestones and general temperament as an infant and toddler can yield important information regarding the child's vulnerabilities in certain areas (speech, fine and gross motor coordination, etc.) as well as rich data about the quality of parent–child relationship. Learning that the parent does not remember when the child spoke his/her first words or cannot recall when toilet training was accomplished would cause the clinician to generate very different hypotheses about the parent–child relationship from those that would be produced by learning that both parents recall each phase of the child's development in detail. Have the parents and child been engaged in power struggles ever since the child could walk? Was the family able to successfully negotiate early separations? Whether or not one values attachment theory, obtaining some sense of how the parent coped with the major events of early childhood can be quite useful, for as Karoly (1981) stated, "The fact remains that adults are frequently the 'creators' of children's self-management dilemmas by virtue of their establishing the task demands and by withdrawing (to varying degrees) their explicit guidance" (p. 105). Discussion of the child's developmental history can provide a convenient framework for discerning how this particular parent tended to establish task demands ("All children should be completely toilet-trained by 18 months" vs. "I figure he'll learn when he's ready") and remove explicit guidance ("My 5-year-old loves to play in the park down the street" vs. "We never let him go into the front yard unless we are with him").

Finally, the parent interview is crucial for learning what other stresses the family is coping with at this time. Is there chronic marital discord which fosters inconsistent parenting? Are there special financial or professional pressures on the parents? Is there a seriously ill family member? Learning of these potential stresses, or the lack thereof, may help the clinician ascertain to what extent the parents are emotionally available to the child or are themselves in need of services.

Child Interviewing

Typically a child is brought to see a clinician because some adult (parent, teacher, probation officer, etc.) has deemed the child to be in need of treatment. As we have noted, a child has never called up and said, "Dr. Kendall (or Dr. Braswell), I'm hyperactive. Can you help me?" In spite of this adult-oriented state of affairs (or perhaps because of it), interviewing the child can be quite informative. Regardless of whose report is more "truthful," it is interesting to know if the child admits to any difficulties or if he or she sees the problems as they are viewed by parents and/or teachers. Hearing the child's view of the situation will help the clinician begin to discern whether the current difficulties reflect a skills deficit (the child doesn't know *how* to think through a problem or perform the necessary behavior), a mismatch of expectancies (the child can think through the problem and perform the behavior but doesn't recognize what is expected in the problem situation), and/or a motivational issue (the child can think through the problem, perform the behavior, and know what is expected, but there is no reward for doing so or no consequence for failing to do so).

Karoly (1981) suggests that the clinician elicit the child's clarification of an episode of misbehavior by assuming a puzzled or bemused manner and relating some vague details of the event. Typically the child will help fill in the factual details of the setting and the reactions of others, even when he/she is unwilling to describe his/her own role. Even the sharing of small bits of information such as this may tell the clinician about the child's attitude toward the misbehavior (e.g., defiance vs. guilt). Particularly resistant and psychologically unsophisticated children can sometimes be lured into sharing their view of the situation if the clinician recounts a very exaggerated version of the alleged incident: "What's all this about you not doing any homework for a month?" Or, "Did you really beat up your teacher?" "Beat up my teacher, no, I just bop my brother on the head all the time." This technique can backfire, however, and is only recommended for use with some children.

At a more general level, the clinician can assess the child's problem awareness and other existing problem-solving abilities through the use of fictitious stories (Karoly, 1981; Meichenbaum, 1976b, 1977). This method involves presenting the client with a brief story about a child of the same sex who is involved in a problem situation like that of the referred child. With younger children, it may be more comfortable for them to "play out" the story using puppets or dolls. The client can be urged to describe how the story character is feeling and what he/she is thinking in that situation. As recommended by Meichenbaum (1976b, 1977), these narratives can be tape-recorded in order to preserve the sequence of the child's thoughts as well as the content. Strict behaviorists may be appalled that we would recommend the use of (should we say it?) projective measures, but examining the content of the child's thought, particularly in regard to specific situations, is well within the domain of the cognitive–behaviorist.

Shure and Spivack (1978) have described a process of eliciting the child's thoughts about a particular situation or problem, which they refer to as "dialoguing." Shure and Spivack maintain that via the use of stylistic factors such as a matter-of-fact tone and nonaccusatory questioning the clinician will be able to carefully guide or direct the child to assess the quality of his/her current methods of problem resolution. As Karoly (1981) points out, this type of procedure blurs the distinction between assessment and intervention; however, dialoguing appears to be a potentially productive mode of interacting with the child in the interview setting.

BEHAVIOR RATING SCALES

Behavior rating scales provide a global view of the child's behavior as perceived by significant others in the child's environment, usually parents or teachers. Several features of ratings make them particularly valuable to both clinicians and researchers. Rating scales can typically be completed with very little instruction from the mental health professional. They can be completed quickly, and their subsequent scoring and interpretation are rarely time-consuming. These forms also have the advantage of yielding quantitative data (Atkeson & Forehand, 1981; Haynes, 1978). Finally, they do require the rater, whether parent or teacher, to think about the child's behavior in specific terms. As a result of reading the specific items on the rating scale, the rater may become aware of other problem behaviors that were not included in the initial discussion of the presenting problem (Ciminero & Drabman, 1977). Reading a list of specific problem behaviors may also cause the rater to reconceptualize the child's problematic actions. For example, we have asked teachers to identify impulsive, non-self-controlled children in their classroom by completing a rating scale (Self-Control Rating Scale—SCRS; Kendall & Wilcox, 1979). One teacher shared that as he began reading the scale items and thinking about a particular child whom he had initially planned to refer, he recognized that, while this child did have difficulties, he really wasn't very impulsive. Being forced to complete a rating scale, raters give more detailed consideration to the child's behavior than they would otherwise.

A number of scales are available for use with children presenting the types of disorders we are discussing. The current review is meant to be illustrative rather than exhaustive. Readers should note the variations in format and focus (general screening measure vs. measures of specific factors) among these scales and select those most appropriate for their own client population. In addition to the more standardized rating scales, an example of a more unstructured referral form is also presented.

Child Behavior Checklist

The Child Behavior Checklist (CBCL; Achenbach, 1978; Achenbach & Edelbrock, 1978) was designed to assess 4- to 16-year-old children's behavioral and emotional problems and their adaptive competencies. The parent typically completes the scale by indicating which of 118 symptoms or behaviors are descriptive of his/her child now or within the last year. The parent responds to each item using a 3-point scale, with 0 indicating that the item is never true or never occurs, 1 indicating that the item is somewhat or sometimes true of the child, and 2 indicating that the item is very true or frequently occurs. In addition, the parent completes three social competency scales that indicate the child's level of involvement and quality of participation in school, social relations, and nonacademic activities. Each child's scores are then plotted in relation to sex- and age-appropriate (4–5, 6–11, and 12–16 years) norms. The specific number of subscales produced depends on the age and sex of the child. Factors or subscales that are common to both sexes in age ranges of 6–11 and 12–16 include somatic complaints, withdrawal, hyperactive, aggressive, and delinquent. These authors have also developed a version to be completed by the classroom teacher. While the sensitivity of the CBCL to treatment effects is not yet known, it is a sound method of descriptive classification. The CBCL's concern with areas of strength or competency as well as deviant behavior may provide a more well-rounded picture of the child, as perceived by his/her parents. Knowing about specific strengths could be particularly valuable in treatment planning. For example, if the therapist knows a child excels in a certain subject or recreational activity, he/she can incorporate examples or problems based on the child's area of strength while attempting to introduce a new concept, thus increasing the probability that the child will understand the concept and will remain interested in the therapist's discussion.

Walker Problem Behavior Identification Checklist

The Walker Problem Behavior Identification Checklist (WPBIC) is a 50-item scale that was originally developed to be completed by the teacher and to assess classroom behaviors that interfere with successful academic performance (Walker, 1970), but it has also been utilized with parents as raters (Christophersen, Barnard, Ford, & Wolf, 1976). This scale presents a two-choice response format that requires the rater to indicate whether a given behavior has been observed or not within the last 2 months. The problem behavior descriptions are basically straightforward and require the rater to make few inferences. Factor analysis of the WPBIC has yielded five factors: acting out, withdrawal, distractibility, disturbed peer relations, and immaturity (Walker, cited in Spivack & Swift, 1973). In computing a child's score, the items are weighted and transformed to standard scores, with a mean of 50 and a standard deviation of 10. Potential disturbance is indicated by a score of 60 or more. The scoring process yields separate totals for each factor, and sex- but not age-related norms for each factor are also provided.

The two-choice response format of this scale may restrict its sensitivity for measuring behavior change (Kendall, Pellegrini, & Urbain, 1981a), but there is some evidence suggesting the measure can reflect treatment-produced changes whether it is completed by the teacher (Johnson, Bolstad, & Lobitz, 1976) or the parent (Christophersen et al., 1976). The WPBIC may be useful as an initial screening device that is easily understood by both teachers and parents. In addition, as noted by Atkeson and Forehand (1981), this scale's inclusion of a disturbed peer relations factor, separate from the acting-out and distractibility factors, can provide the clinician useful information. For example, considering the current target population of externalizing children it would be helpful to know that a child referred for hyperactivity is viewed as distractible by his/her teacher, but that this same rater perceives the child as having few problems in peer relations.

Conners Teacher and Parent Questionnaires

The teacher and parent rating scales developed by Conners (1969, 1970, 1973) are perhaps the most frequently used scales in hyperactivity research. The parent scale includes 93 items. When factor-analyzed by Goyette, Conners, and Ulrich (1978), the scale yielded the factor grouping of attentional–learning problems, psychosomatic problems, impulsive–hyperactive behavior, aggressive conduct problems, and anxious–fearful behavior. Scores on the individual factors can be compared with norms. According to Goyette et al. (1978), individual factor scores do appear to be related to the sex and age of the child. These scores are also influenced by which parent completed the rating, for mothers have been found to report more deviant behavior than fathers.

The teacher questionnaire contains 39 items, but in many hyperactivity studies only the ten items of the hyperactivity factor are used. This short form contains items such as "restless or overactive," "disturbs other children," and "fails to finish things he starts—short attention span." Each item is rated on a 0 to 3 scale and a mean rating is then computed. The standard cutoff for labeling a child hyperactive is an average score of 1.5.

Both Conners scales are often used as criteria for subject selection in studies involving hyperactive children. While the standardized cutoff point is useful for research purposes, this method of identifying hyperactive children does tend to yield much higher prevalence rates than other means of subject selection (see Prevalence section of Chapter 3). In addition, this scale typically does not yield information that is particularly helpful in treatment planning, with the exception that hyperactive children who also score highly on the anxiety factor may be less responsive to stimulant drug treatment (Barkley, 1977, 1981; Fish, 1971). Also, the frequently used short-form covers a very circumscribed range of behaviors and, therefore, is not useful for selecting deficits or identifying treatment-produced changes in other areas of functioning.

Self-Control Rating Scale

The SCRS (Kendall & Wilcox, 1979) was specifically developed to assess self-control in elementary school children as rated by their classroom teacher and/or parents (as in Kendall & Braswell, 1982b) (see Figure 4-1). The scale is based on a cognitive–behavioral conceptualization of self-control, wherein self-controlled children are said to possess the cognitive skills necessary to generate and evaluate alternatives *and* the behavioral skills needed to inhibit unwanted behavior and engage in desired action. Of the 33 items, ten are descriptive of self-control (e.g., "Can the child deliberately calm down when he/she is excited or all wound up?"), 13 are indicative of impulsivity (e.g., "Does the child have to have everything right away?"), and the remaining ten present both possibilities (e.g., "In answering questions, does the child give one thoughtful answer, or blurt out several answers all at once?"). Each of the items is rated on a 7-point scale, and all items are summed to yield a total score. The higher the score the greater the child's lack of self-control. The mean of the SCRS often approximates 100.

When first working on the creation, revision, and selection of final items for the SCRS we sought to include those features of behavior that have been identified in the literature as associated with a lack of

FIGURE 4-1. Self-Control Rating Scale. © 1979, Philip C. Kendall, PhD.

Name of Child _____ Grade _____
Rater _____
Please rate this child according to the descriptions below by circling the appropriate number. The underlined 4 in the center of each row represents where the average child would fall on this item. Please do not hesitate to use the entire range of possible ratings.

1. When the child promises to do something, can you count on him/her to do it?

   1 2 3 4 5 6 7
   always   never

2. Does the child butt into games or activities even when he/she hasn't been invited?

   1 2 3 4 5 6 7
   never   often

3. Can the child deliberately calm down when he/she is excited or all wound up?

   1 2 3 4 5 6 7
   yes   no

4. Is the quality of the child's work all about the same or does it vary a lot?

   1 2 3 4 5 6 7
   same   varies

5. Does the child work for long-range goals?

   1 2 3 4 5 6 7
   yes   no

6. When the child asks a question, does he/she wait for an answer, or jump to something else (e.g., a new question) before waiting for an answer?

   1 2 3 4 5 6 7
   waits   jumps

7. Does the child interrupt inappropriately in conversations with peers, or wait his/her turn to speak?

   1 2 3 4 5 6   7
   waits   interrupts

8. Does the child stick to what he/she is doing until he/she is finished with it?

   1 2 3 4 5 6 7
   yes   no

9. Does the child follow the instructions of responsible adults?

   1 2 3 4 5 6 7
   always   never

10. Does the child have to have everything right away?

   1 2 3 4 5 6 7
   no   yes

11. When the child has to wait in line, does he/she do so patiently?

   1 2 3 4 5 6 7
   yes   no

12. Does the child sit still?

   1 2 3 4 5 6 7
   yes   no

13. Can the child follow suggestions of others in group projects, or does he/she insist on imposing his/her own ideas?

   1 2 3 4 5 6 7
   able   imposes
   to follow

14. Does the child have to be reminded several times to do something before he/she does it?

   1 2 3 4 5 6 7
   never   always

FIGURE 4-1. (*Continued*)

15. When reprimanded, does the child answer back inappropriately?

1 2 3 <u>4</u> 5 6 7
never   always

16. Is the child accident-prone?

1 2 3 <u>4</u> 5 6 7
no   yes

17. Does the child neglect or forget regular chores or tasks?

1 2 3 <u>4</u> 5 6 7
never   always

18. Are there days when the child seems incapable of settling down to work?

1 2 3 <u>4</u> 5 6 7
never   often

19. Would the child more likely grab a smaller toy today or wait for a larger toy tomorrow, if given the choice?

1 2 3 <u>4</u> 5 6 7
wait   grab

20. Does the child grab for the belongings of others?

1 2 3 <u>4</u> 5 6 7
never   often

21. Does the child bother others when they're trying to do things?

1 2 3 <u>4</u> 5 6 7
no   yes

22. Does the child break basic rules?

1 2 3 <u>4</u> 5 6 7
never   always

23. Does the child watch where he/she is going?

1 2 3 <u>4</u> 5 6 7
always   never

24. In answering questions, does the child give one thoughtful answer, or blurt out several answers all at once?

1 2 3 <u>4</u> 5 6 7
one   several
answer

25. Is the child easily distracted from his/her work or chores?

1 2 3 <u>4</u> 5 6 7
no   yes

26. Would you describe this child more as careful or careless?

1 2 3 <u>4</u> 5 6 7
careful   careless

27. Does the child play well with peers (follow rules, wait turn, cooperate)?

1 2 3 <u>4</u> 5 6 7
yes   no

28. Does the child jump or switch from activity to activity rather than sticking to one thing at a time?

1 2 3 <u>4</u> 5 6 7
sticks   switches
to one

29. If a task is at first too difficult for the child, will he/she get frustrated and quit, or first seek help with the problem?

1 2 3 <u>4</u> 5 6 7
seek   quit
help

30. Does the child disrupt games?

1 2 3 <u>4</u> 5 6 7
never   often

(*Continued*)

FIGURE 4-1. (Continued)

31. Does the child think before he/she acts?	1 2 3 <u>4</u> 5 6 7 always never
32. If the child paid more attention to his/her work, do you think he/she would do much better than at present?	1 2 3 <u>4</u> 5 6 7 no yes
33. Does the child do too many things at once, or does he/she concentrate on one thing at a time?	1 2 3 <u>4</u> 5 6 7 one too thing many

self-controlled (impulsive) behavior. For instance, data suggested that impulsive children showed less persistence behavior (Finch, Kendall, Deardorff, Anderson, & Sitarz, 1975a), so we prepared an item that would tap observations of behavioral persistence. SCRS item 28 illustrates this: "Does the child jump or switch from activity to activity rather than sticking to one thing at a time?" We also sought teacher input and some of the items reflect their contribution. One suggested item, rumored to have been suggested by a teacher, was "If you had but one life to give for your country, it would be this child's." This item does not appear on the scale but its content does provide some information about what some individuals think about impulsive children.

Kendall, Zupan, and Braswell (1981b) found that SCRS scores were meaningfully related to classroom behavior, with higher scores associated with more disruptive behavior in the classroom setting, and Kendall and Wilcox (1979) observed the same relationship in a special testing setting. The SCRS has also been demonstrated as sensitive to the effects of cognitive–behavioral interventions (Kendall & Wilcox, 1980; Kendall & Zupan, 1981; Kendall & Braswell, 1982b) and yields score changes that parallel observed changes in classroom behavior. In addition to distinguishing between non-self-controlled children and normal controls (Kendall et al., 1981b), the mean SCRS score has been found to vary with the diagnostic category of the child (Robin, Fischel, & Brown, 1984). Hyperactives obtained the highest mean score, followed by conduct-disordered children. Children displaying more internalizing types of problems that did not involve deficits in self-control received the lowest mean ratings (Robin et al., 1984). The SCRS was originally developed for use by teachers and parents, and both were raters in the Robin et al. (1984) study, with the means for parent raters approximating those for teacher raters. More specifically, Kendall and Braswell

(1982b) had both parents and teachers complete the measure and obtained a correlation of .66 between those groups. Thus, the SCRS can be employed by both teachers and parents.

Problem-Oriented Rating Form

In addition to the structured measures described above, it is important to gather problem descriptions that are more specific to the individual child. Although such information is typically gathered via interviews with the child, parents, and/or teachers, it might be useful to employ a problem-oriented referral form to obtain some information prior to the interview or to use when extensive interviews are not possible. An example of such a form (Urbain, 1982) is presented in Figure 4-2. The information provided by such forms could be very helpful in focusing further assessment efforts and in highlighting specific intervention targets. During the intervention or at its conclusion, the clinician could follow up with a problem-oriented feedback form, such as the one also developed by Urbain (1982) and presented in Figure 4-3.

Summary

Rating forms, in particular rating scales such as those we have described, can provide some of the most valuable information. Despite this importance, it must be remembered that such forms are communicating the rater's *perception* of the child, not an actual record of the child's behavior. In some cases, parent ratings may be particularly limited in validity owing to a lack of exposure to children other than their own. Given this situation, it is highly preferable to obtain ratings from multiple sources whose opportunities to observe the child occur in different settings.

TASK PERFORMANCE MEASURES

In this section we describe some of the task performance measures that can be used with externalizing or non-self-controlled children. Before listing these measures, however, we would like to make a few general comments applicable to the administration, use, and interpretation of all the tasks to be described. If administered mechanically with the sole

Please list, in order of importance, the social behaviors that you perceive as most problematic for this student (PLEASE BE *SPECIFIC*; i.e., give an example or two if possible).

1. _____

How severe is this problem?

1	2	3	4	5	6	7
Not severe			Moderately severe			Very severe

2. _____

How severe is this problem?

1	2	3	4	5	6	7
Not severe			Moderately severe			Very severe

3. _____

How severe is this problem?

1	2	3	4	5	6	7
Not severe			Moderately severe			Very severe

Please indicate by checking those other specific behaviors you would like to have this child work on. CIRCLE THOSE WHICH ARE MOST IMPORTANT.

_____ Taking turns, waiting his/her turn   _____ Listening and paying attention
_____ Not hitting   _____ Sharing with others
_____ Not pushing   _____ Playing fair (not cheating)
_____ Not using offensive language   _____ Not blaming others
_____ Not clowning around or showing off   _____ Not teasing or bugging others
_____ Not bragging   _____ Telling the truth
_____ Staying cool and controlling temper   _____ Not interacting with others; being
_____ Sitting still   quiet and withdrawn
_____ Communicating feelings more   _____ Not bossing and telling others what
openly   to do
_____ Compromising more with others   _____ Other (specify please) _____

FIGURE 4-2. Problem-oriented rating form.

intent of obtaining one score, most task performance measures will yield little information beyond the one score. But if the examiner is careful to observe *how* the child goes about accomplishing the task demands, information relevant to both diagnosis and treatment can be obtained. Through this type of careful observation, the clinician can attempt to learn about the child's level of metacognitive development, as well as his/her cognitive abilities.

Metacognition refers to "knowledge concerning one's own cognitive process and products" (Flavell, 1976, p. 232). People demonstrate an awareness of their own cognitive capabilities when they write down a phone number they must remember, turn off the radio while studying, or repeat to themselves the name of someone they've just met. The examiner can assess the child's metacognitive sophistication through various observations that are readily available in the standard testing situation. As Elkin (1983) noted, virtually any traditional assessment tool can serve the purposes of the cognitive–behaviorist if the examiner is asking himself/herself certain questions. When asked to remember a piece of information, does the child employ memory-enhancing strategies or even recognize that he/she needs to use such strategies? If strategies are evident, how sophisticated are they? For example, does the child simply repeat the crucial information or attempt some form of elaboration, such as mental imagery? Does the child seem to recognize the role he/she plays in directing his/her own attention (e.g., talking himself/herself through a task vs. requiring direction from an external source)? Also, does the child demonstrate an ability to isolate relevant from irrelevant information in an effort to enhance task performance? How does the child handle frustration with a task? Does he/she talk himself/herself through it? Through questions such as these the therapist can gauge, if only subjectively, the child's awareness of his/her own thought processes. Depending on the child's work style, there may be very few clues to the level of sophistication of his/her meta-

---

FIGURE 4-3. Sample from a problem-oriented feedback form. *Note.* More than one problem can be listed and the problems can be those on the initial referral form. One can also provide optional space to add any additional problems one would like to have rated.

Below are listed some of the specific problems identified at the beginning of the program. Please rate each according to (1) how severe the problem is at the present time, and (2) level of improvement at this time:

PROBLEM 1 _____

How severe is this problem now? (Please circle one.)

1	2	3	4	5	6	7
Not severe			Moderately severe			Very severe

Has there been any change in this problem since the program began?

1	2	3	4	5	6	7
Got worse	A little worse	No change, about the same	A little better	Improved	Much improved	Very much improved, not a problem anymore

cognitive activities. Discerning the degree of consciousness the child brings to bear on his/her efforts is often difficult. For example, a child who approaches a problem in a calm and systematic manner may have no conscious awareness that he/she has such an approach. When available, however, this type of information is of special relevance in the implementation of cognitive–behavioral training programs.

As emphasized by Loper (1980), the cognitive aspect of the training must be calibrated to the child's level of self-awareness. For example, some children may be surprised by the notion that talking to themselves can help them perform better in academic or social situations, while other children already recognize the potential role of self-talk. By keeping these general considerations in mind, the therapist will provide a better match between the intervention and the child. Thus observation of *how* the child does what he/she does on a task performance measure can yield data that are as informative as and perhaps more interesting than a given test score. The following discussion provides illustrations of measures of impersonal problem solving, social cognition, and interpersonal problem solving.

Impersonal Problem Solving

A large number of tests have been developed to assess children's cognitive problem-solving abilities. Our present discussion will be limited to two measures that have been widely employed and researched with the target sample of interest to us: the Porteus Maze Test and the Matching Familiar Figures Test (MFF).

The Porteus Mazes (Porteus, 1955) are a series of paper-and-pencil mazes of graded difficulty that measure aspects of planning ability, foresight, and impulsivity (alternate forms available). The Porteus results in two scores: a quantitative Test Quotient (TQ) score and a Qualitative (Q) score. The TQ score is based on the highest-level maze successfully completed and the number of trials required by the subject to solve each maze. It reflects the child's ability to solve the mazes in the allowed number of trials, independent of the quality of the solution. The Q score is based on the number of qualitative errors, such as lifting the pencil contrary to instructions, cutting across corners in the maze, and bumping into or crossing the sides of maze alleyways.

Porteus originally designed the maze test as an adjunct to early measures of intelligence (Porteus, 1933); however, the test has proved particularly sensitive in the identification of delinquency. Interest in the test as a measure of social adjustment, though fluctuating greatly over the years, has reemerged. In fact, Homatidis and Konstantareas (1981) reviewed a number of measures used to identify hyperactives and found the Porteus TQ to be one of the better discriminators.

Riddle and Roberts (1974) reported that the test showed acceptable psychometric properties and interrater reliabilities. In a more recent review, Riddle and Roberts (1977) concluded that the TQ score correlates most highly with tests of visual ability or spatial memory, whereas considerable data indicate that the Q score discriminates delinquents and criminals from normal reference groups. The Q score also discriminated between recidivist and nonrecidivist delinquent groups and is considered the score most sensitive to differences in social adjustment. Evaluations of cognitive–behavioral treatments for impulsive, hyperactive, and non-self-controlled children (e.g., Douglas *et al.*, 1976; Kendall & Wilcox, 1980; Palkes *et al.*, 1968) have used the Porteus Mazes to assess changes in the children's planning, judgment, and attentional focusing abilities.

The MFF was developed by Kagan and his colleagues (Kagan, Rosman, Day, Albert, & Phillips, 1964; Kagan, 1966) as a measure of conceptual tempo. A child's cognitive tempo could be determined to be reflective (i.e., slow and accurate) or impulsive (i.e., fast and inaccurate) based on the child's latency and error scores gathered in response to the MFF. The MFF itself is a 12-item match-to-sample task in which the child is shown a single picture of a familiar object and is instructed to select from six variants the one picture that is identical to the stimulus figure. Alternate forms are described in Egeland and Weinberg (1976).

Messer (1976) has reviewed the reliability and network of correlations associated with the test. While there are limitations to the instrument (e.g., Ault, Mitchell, & Hartmann, 1976) and some concern about the necessity of including both the latency and error measures in predictions of adjustment and achievement (e.g., Block *et al.*, 1974; Egeland *et al.*, 1980), the MFF has been helpful in early evaluations of cognitive–behavioral interventions (Bender, 1976; Kendall & Finch, 1976; Meichenbaum & Goodman, 1971). A revised version of this test, the MFF 20 developed by Cairns and Cammock (1978), is reported to have superior psychometric properties.

Certain features of both the MFF and Porteus Mazes deserve mention. First, both tests are easily administered in the clinician's office. Second, published data (for MFF norms see Messer, 1976, and Salkind, 1979; for Porteus norms see the test manual and Riddle & Roberts, 1974,

1977) allow the test user to make comparisons of an individual child's score with scores of other children of the same age and sex. Third, both tests provide a sample of the child's behavior in response to standard materials. From the behavior sample, the clinician can make judgments about the child's ability in planning ahead, taking action, and inhibiting unwanted behaviors. Fourth, improvements in these tests may be said to indicate that the child has gained some self-management ability —a more reflective problem approach and a more foresightful test-taking pattern are behavioral samples that reflect an improvement over impulsive and careless performance. Fifth, alternate forms of both tests are available for repeated testing without the unwanted effects of previous exposure to the same stimulus materials.

Social Cognition

The child's ability to recognize the thoughts and feelings of others and take the perspective of others is referred to as social cognition. Two of the measures of social cognition receiving attention in the literature merit mention: Chandler's bystander cartoons, and Selman's measure of interpersonal awareness. The bystander cartoons (Chandler, 1973) require the child to tell a series of stories based on cartoon sequences presented in picture format. The child is told to pay attention to what the main character is thinking and feeling in each story. After concluding the initial story, the child is asked to retell the story from the point of view of a bystander who arrives later on in the story and is unaware of what happened at the story's beginning. The child receives an "egocentrism" score based on the degree of privileged information ascribed to the bystander (i.e., information available to the child from the previous part of the story, but of which the bystander is unaware). Reliability data are acceptable (e.g., Kurdek, 1977), and there is some evidence indicating significant relationships between the bystander cartoons score and other measures of cognitive perspective taking (Kurdek, 1977) and teachers' ratings of self-control (Kendall et al., 1981b). The relationships among measures of social cognition are not, however, entirely consistent, and some anticipated differences, such as between hyperactive and nonhyperactive children, have not been confirmed (Paulauskas & Campbell, 1979).

Selman (1980) and his colleagues have developed a series of open-ended interpersonal dilemmas, each of which is geared toward a particular age group and is presented in audiovisual filmstrip format. For example, in one such story, a new girl in town asks Kathy to go to an ice skating show with her the next day. However, Kathy has already made plans to play with her best friend, Becky. To complicate matters further, Becky has already made it clear that she does not like the new girl. An interview follows the presentation of each dilemma. In the case of the sample story just provided, *concepts about friendship* are explored and probed in detail (e.g., how do friendships develop; what makes for good friendship; jealousy). Other dilemmas and interviews serve to examine *concepts about individuals* (e.g., how people get to be the way they are and how they can change), and *conceptions about peer group relations* (e.g., how groups are formed; what makes a good or cohesive group). Each discrete response is scored by comparing it to examples of reasoning at five stages of development. Several indices of reliability have been acceptable (e.g., Selman & Jaquette, 1978; Pellegrini, 1980; Enright, 1977). Initial data support Selman's proposed sequence of developmental stages, and clinic children evidence less mature interpersonal understanding than matched controls (controlling for IQ) (Selman, Jaquette, & Lavin, 1977). While this method of assessing social cognition is extremely interesting, its utility is limited by the extensive training required to master the system and by the questionable status of its relationship to behavior in real-life situations.

Interpersonal Problem Solving

In the last decade there has been an explosion in the number of measures developed for assessing those skills relevant for solving interpersonal dilemmas. A small number of the more widely used measures will be presented, for these measures can yield information on an individual child's thinking about social problem situations; we must note, however, that at least some data suggest that the relationship between test responses on some of these measures and behavior in interpersonal dilemmas is modest (e.g., Kendall & Fischler, 1984). The interpersonal problem-solving assessment devices to be considered are the Interpersonal Cognitive Problem Solving (ICPS) measures and the Purdue Elementary Problem-Solving Inventory (PEPSI).

Spivack and Shure (1974) and Spivack *et al.* (1976) have proposed a series of ICPS skills and developed a series of tests to assess these skills. The ICPS skills include (1) sensitivity to interpersonal problems, (2) causal thinking (i.e., spontaneously linking cause and effect), (3) readiness to consider the consequences of behavior, (4) ability to generate a list of possible solutions, and (5) the ability to generate step-by-step means for reaching specific goals.

Among the measures of these skills, means–ends thinking (assessed via the Means–Ends Problem-Solving task—MEPS) has received the bulk of research attention. The assessment of means–ends problem solving involves presenting the child with a series of stories (typically six) describing hypothetical problems of an interpersonal nature. In each instance, the examiner presents the initial situation and the final outcome, with the child's task being to fill in the middle of the story. Story responses are scored for the total number of means, elaborations of specific means, perception of potential obstacles to carrying out the means, and use of a time sequence.

Means–ends thinking as measured by the MEPS has been found to differentiate between normal controls and (1) a group of institutionalized delinquent adolescents (Platt *et al.*, 1974); and (2) a group of emotionally disturbed 10- to 12-year-olds in a special school (Platt *et al.*, 1974; Shure & Spivack, 1972). In addition to a lower number of elements of means–ends thinking, emotionally disturbed children tended to limit their responses to pragmatic, impulsive, and physically aggressive means (Shure & Spivack, 1972). The means of normals were characterized by greater planning and foresight. Urbain (1979) also reported large differences between impulsive–aggressive second and third grade children and a group of nonimpulsive children on a modified version of the MEPS procedure.

The Rochester Social Problem-Solving Group (1978–1979) developed a measure similar to the MEPS, which they refer to as the Open Middle Test (OMT). Each of the four problem stories is accompanied by a series of pictures that the tester displays while explicitly probing for the child's ability to generate multiple solutions. In addition to scoring number of solutions, solution variants, repetitions, irrelevant responses, and chained responses, the child's answer is rated on the effectiveness of the solution and the content categories included. The test authors have reported acceptable interrater reliability for the scoring of responses.

Although seen less often in the literature, tests of alternative thinking and consequential thinking have been developed. The alternative thinking test (see Shure & Spivack, 1978), originally designed for adolescents and adults, has been revised for use with children. The test asks the child to generate as many different solutions as possible to several interpersonal problems (e.g., "how to make new friends"). The Awareness of Consequences test requires the child to consider the pros and cons of an interpersonal action. The test taps more than the simple listing of alternative solutions. The procedure involves describing a story of a child who is in a tempting situation. The child being tested is then asked to "tell everything that is going on in the character's mind, and then tell what happens." Scoring consequences involves the extent to which the child describes what might happen next and the child's weighing the pros and cons before offering a decision (see Spivack et al., 1976).

There are several concerns associated with the ICPS measures and related tests. First, the scoring procedures described in the test manual are not sufficiently detailed and users often create their own additional criteria, resulting in some variability in the scoring procedures employed by different clinicians and researchers. Second, there are a limited number of MEPS stories and an absence of alternate forms, thus making it difficult to conduct both pre- and posttesting. In one treatment study, for example, MEPS scores decreased (Kendall & Zupan, 1981), since children recognizing that they had already answered these questions once, created briefer stories the second time around (and scored lower). Additional unwanted variability enters into the assessments when different researchers create different stories for the purposes of repeated measurement. Stories that are psychometrically sound for both pretesting and posttesting are needed. Third, as previously stated, there is some question regarding the evidence to support the argument that a child's MEPS score actually reflects his/her ability to solve problems in a real-life interpersonal situation (see Butler & Meichenbaum, 1981). The utility of these measures may be enhanced as more is learned about the role of qualitative differences in problem-solving skills and their relationship to adjustment.

Whereas the MEPS is a (somewhat) projective test, the PEPSI illustrates the objective approach to assessing children's problem-solving skills. A test with 49 cartoon slides, it was designed to assess problem solving among disadvantaged elementary school children (Feldhusen & Houtz, 1975; Feldhusen, Houtz, & Ringenbach, 1972). Each cartoon slide portrays the child in a different real-life problem situation. The child listens to an audio tape of directions, problem descriptions, and alternative solutions, and then responds by drawing an "X" in a text booklet over the alternative of the choice. Factor analysis of the PEPSI suggested that it reflects six social problem-solving factors: an evaluative factor, and the ability to sense problems, to define problems, to analyze critical details, to see implications, and to make unusual associations (Feldhusen et al., 1972; Speedie, Houtz, Ringenbach, & Feldhusen, 1973). These authors also report acceptable reliability and changes due to a problem-solving intervention. However, the relationship between the PEPSI and indices of behavioral adjustment has yet to be investigated. In addition, since the test uses a multiple-choice format, it precludes the child's generation of alternatives and requires only the selection of a predetermined proper solution. This attribute detracts from the testing being viewed as an idication of problem solving in actual social situations.

Summary

Performance on various tasks has been used to make inferences about children's abilities: fast inaccurate performance, indicating an absence of forethought and planning; limited generation of alternative problem solutions, indicating poor interpersonal problem solving; and interference in storytelling from different perspectives, suggesting deficits in social cognition. The large majority of these tasks have been adapted from developmental psychology. While these adaptations benefit from the developmentalist's concern with age-appropriate measurement, many of the tasks were not designed with diagnosis or intervention evaluation as the primary goals. Several of the tasks are essentially projective, and, although they do not seek to uncover intrapsychic conflict, are based solely upon storytelling responses. The movement toward more ecologically valid assessments of problem solving (see Rubin & Krasnor, 1984) and social cognition is highly desirable (see section on Analogue Assessments, this chapter).

SELF-REPORT ASSESSMENT

While the child client is rarely used as the sole source of information about himself/herself, there are self-report measures that can be quite helpful in specifying the child's areas of strength and weakness and in conveying attitudes or beliefs that may be quite relevant to treatment efforts. We see merit in using self-report measures that assess the child's expectancies, attributions, and self-concept.

Expectancies

The view that expectancies influence behavior has been a component of many theories of human learning and behavior (Bandura, 1977; Irwin, 1971; Tolman, 1932, 1951). Two types of expectations are particularly relevant to the current discussion: expectations of self-efficacy, and expectations of internal versus external locus of control.

A child's self-efficacy (Bandura, 1977) is the degree to which the child expects that he/she can successfully execute the behaviors that lead to desired outcomes. Changes in self-efficacy have been posited as the common underlying cognitive process that accounts for changes in behavior (Bandura, 1977), and assessments of self-efficacy have been called for in therapy-outcome studies (Kendall, 1982a; Kendall & Korgeski, 1979). While self-efficacy assessments have begun to appear in the adult cognitive–behavioral literature (e.g., Bandura & Adams, 1977; Kazdin, 1979), they have yet to receive much attention in child intervention research. The measurement of self-efficacy involves having subjects state whether or not they expect to be able to perform certain behaviors (tasks) and how confident they are that they could complete the tasks. Bandura suggests that such efficacy measurement should occur in fairly close proximity to the point when the child will actually be performing the behavior or task.

As an example of such measurement, Schunk (1982) assessed self-efficacy with 7- to 10-year-old children in a study demonstrating that effort attributional feedback for past achievement led to more rapid mastery of new tasks and higher percepts of self-efficacy. Importantly, children were given practice with the procedure of rating self-efficacy. A 100-point scale (10-unit intervals) was applied to a jumping task (10—not sure; 40—maybe; 70—pretty sure; 100—very sure). Jumping distances ranged from a few inches to 10 yards. Thus, children were given meaningful experience with the scale and with the notion of estimating confidence. Given that a certain level of cognitive development is necessary for understanding the concept of self-efficacy or confidence, and that children may not be familiar with the standard anchors and descriptions on rating scales, extreme care is required for assessing children's self-efficacy expectations.

Brief assessments of self-efficacy expectations could be included in a traditional testing session. For example, before administering the Porteus Mazes, the tester might ask children whether or not they expect to be able to solve the mazes and how confident they are that they will complete the task. The child's response to such questions could be quite interesting. One would draw very different conclusions about a child who had no expectation of success yet did succeed, compared to a child who voiced extreme confidence in task performance yet failed, compared to yet another child who requested additional information about the task before voicing any expectations. To return to a point made in the task performance section, this type of questioning is yet another means by which the clinician assesses the child's cognitive and metacognitive sophistication.

Assessing expectations of internal versus external locus of control may also yield useful information for the clinician. As discussed by Rotter and Hochreich (1975), persons high in internal control expect events to result from their own actions and attributes, whereas those high in external control expect chance, fate, or powerful others to determine what happens to them.

Several scales have been developed to assess the concept of locus of control specifically in children (e.g., Bialer, 1961). The Intellectual Achievement Responsibility Questionnaire (IAR) was devised by Crandall, Katkovsky, and Crandall (1965) for studying children's locus of control in academic achievement situations, thus limiting the general character of the concept. This 34-item questionnaire described both positive and negative experiences. The structure of the measure permits three scores to be derived: total self-responsibility score (I), responsibility for one's success score (I+), and a responsibility for one's failures scores (I−).

A more recent and more widely used children's locus-of-control measure is the Nowicki–Strickland Internal–External Scale for Children (Nowicki & Strickland, 1973). This scale consists of 40 yes–no items that are scored in the external direction so that a high score indicates a more external orientation. The Nowicki–Strickland measure attempts to assess locus of control in a generalized fashion, rather than assessing expectancies related to only one type of situation. Factor analysis of this scale has yielded distinct factors for emotionally disturbed, delinquent, and normal groups (Kendall, Finch, Little, Chirico, & Ollendick, 1978). This measure has been used to assess therapeutic outcomes, with the results indicating that children manifested more perceptions of internal control following problem-solving training (Allen *et al.*, 1976).

Attributions

The concept of attribution is closely related to that of expectancy; however, the two concepts are distinguishable along a temporal dimension (Kendall & Braswell, 1982a), with expectancies preceding a behavioral event or situation and attributions (i.e., causal attribution) following the event and attempting to specify or account for its cause. To the extent that an individual makes similar attributions across time and situations, he/she is said to manifest an attributional style. Such attributional styles may play an important role in cognitive–behavioral therapy since the explanations that children generate for the behavior and events they anticipate or observe may be a variable that moderates their behavior and the potential effects of treatment.

Children who attribute their behavioral improvement to personal effort may be more likely to show generalization of the improvement than children who attribute behavior change to luck, fate, chance, or anything external to themselves. For example, if the child firmly believes that the better, more self-controlled behavior he/she can display is strictly the result of taking medication, then it is less likely that this child will even attempt to display the better behavior or control himself/herself when not receiving medication. Braswell *et al.* (1982a) obtained results supportive of this hypothesis, with increasing levels of positive change on teacher ratings of classroom behavior associated with attributing positive behavior change to personal effort. Bugental and colleagues (Bugental *et al.*, 1977, 1978) employed an assessment of children's attributions as part of intervention evaluation and reported that those children who had a strong sense of personal control or who were not medicated benefited more from self-control intervention than from a social-reinforcement program.

Self-Concept

How does a child referred for evaluation and treatment feel about himself/herself? Do children experience a loss of self-esteem as a result of being "treated"? Do the response-cost procedures cut into children's self-concept? Self-report indices of self-esteem or self-concept provide information relevant to this question and provide a means of assessing any treatment-produced changes. Two measures of self-concept will be discussed as illustrations of assessments in this area: the Piers–Harris Children's Self-Concept Scale, and the Perceived Competence Scale for Children.

The Piers–Harris Children's Self-Concept Scale (Piers & Harris, 1969) involves a series of true–false or yes–no questions in which the child is asked to indicate what is true for him/her. This questionnaire contains 80 items and was designed to be unidimensional. Factor analysis of this measure has yielded six dimensions; however, the majority of the measure's variance is accounted for by one general self-esteem factor (Bentler & McClain, 1976).

The Perceived Competence Scale for Children (Harter, 1979, 1982) was designed to assess the child's view of his/her own cognitive competence, social competence, and physical competence. In addition, a fourth subscale measures the child's general self-esteem without reference to particular skills or activities. In an attempt to avoid the social desirability response set that can affect yes–no type of questionnaires, Harter devised a "structured alternative format." This response format requires the child first to select which of two alternatives is most like himself/herself (e.g., "Some kids are always doing things with a lot of kids BUT other kids usually do things by themselves."). After this choice has been made, the child is then asked to qualify his/her response by indicating if it is really true for him/her or only sort of true. Items are scored on a 4-point scale, with 1 indicating low perceived competence and 4 suggesting high perceived competence. For example, if the child indicated he was most like kids who do things by themselves and then stated this was really true for him, he would receive a score of "1." If he chose this same alternative but said it was only sort of true for him he would receive a "2," and so on.

It is perhaps obvious that these self-report measures, like the other dependent measures, can help identify treatment targets or factors that may influence treatment effectiveness. Self-reports are also important for the identification of iatrogenic effects. One would certainly want to know if being in an intervention program reduced the children's self-concept! For instance, the therapeutic experiences a child receives may be undermined by a peer context in which participation in the intervention results in a less than favorable nickname for the child. The effects of self-instructional training might be undercut by a child's being goaded, "There's the guy who has to talk to himself!" Similarly, if the child learns that some form of treatment is necessary for him/her to be acceptable, he/she could develop an external attributional preference—"I can't do it by myself." Recognition of attributional styles, low levels of self-esteem, or negative self-efficacy expectations is extremely important, particularly when one's goal is ultimately the development of healthy, autonomous individuals. We might mention here, for the sake of completeness, that our data have indicated that children's self-concepts increase as a result of cognitive–behavioral treatment (Kendall & Braswell, 1982b).

BEHAVIORAL OBSERVATION

In our concern with the effective incorporation of cognitive factors, we certainly do not intend to abandon methods of direct behavioral assessment. As a preintervention assessment, behavioral observations can help delineate the problem behavior(s) to be treated and the characteristics of the condition(s) which exacerbate the problem behavior(s). For the evaluation of interventions, behaviors chosen for naturalistic observation should be helpful in the process of specifying what did and what did not change.

Conducting behavioral observations is not without its difficulties. One must first enlist assistants to serve as observers. Training these assistants to reliably assess ongoing behavior in terms of specific codes requires time. Even with adequate training, reliability levels often drop after the initial training period unless periodic checks are conducted (Taplin & Reid, 1977). If the child's behavior is filmed for later coding, this adds the concern of potentially expensive equipment. Given these considerations it is often difficult for therapists to accomplish direct observation of the child's behavior, particularly in naturalistic settings. For the purposes of example, we will discuss behavioral observation systems designed for use in the home and school, but we will also present the less rigorous, but more practical, notion of using the child's significant others as observers. For further information the reader is referred to Karoly (1981), Atkeson and Forehand (1981), and Mash and Terdal (1981).

Home Observation

One of the most widely known and researched methods of home observation is the Behavioral Coding System (and its variations) developed by Patterson, Ray, Shaw, and Cobb (1969). Within this system, trained observers code ongoing family interaction into 29 possible behavioral categories. These 29 behaviors are classified as either responses or consequences, with the former category inducing behaviors such as command, laugh, touch, and work, and the latter including items such as ignore, approve, and noncompliance. Typically the family is observed for six to ten 1-hour sessions, with observations occurring during the hour before the evening meal. In order to facilitate these observations, the family is instructed that all members must be present and remain in two adjoining rooms without watching television or making phone calls. Each member is observed for two randomly selected 5-minute intervals within the hour. During the 5-minute period the behavior of the subject and those interacting with him/her is recorded. The format of this system does allow for the examination of the relationship between specific antecedent and consequent behaviors.

Readers interested in this type of assessment may also wish to read about a similar system developed by Wahler and his colleagues at the Child Behavior Institute in Tennessee (Wahler, House, & Stambaugh, 1976) and the response-class matrix (Mash, Terdal, & Anderson, 1973).

School Observation

A number of observational systems have been developed for use in the classroom. These systems vary their focus and complexity, but we will describe three examples that are particularly relevant for the current target population. Cobb (1972, 1973) has developed a coding system that concentrates on assessing the child's attentional focusing in structured academic tasks, such as teacher-led discussions and individual work. The 15 categories in this system include behaviors such as attending, talking to teacher (positive and negative), talking to peers (positive and negative), and looking around. One feature recommending this system is Cobb's (1972) report that it can be used reliably after only 4 hours of observer training. Abikoff and associates (Abikoff, Gittelman-Klein, & Klein, 1977; Abikoff, Gittelman, & Klein, 1980) presented validational evidence supporting a classroom observational system developed for use in diagnosing hyperactive children. Twelve of this system's 14 behavioral codes have been reported to differentiate between hyperactive and normal children. Finally Cobb and Hops (1972) developed a coding system specifically for the observation of conduct-disordered children. The 37 behavioral categories of this system fall into eight major headings: approvals and disapprovals, management questions, attention and looking at, talk academic, disruption and inappropriate locale, physical negative and punishment, commands, and miscellaneous. Unlike the two previously mentioned systems, the Cobb and Hops format includes the coding of teacher and peer behaviors that precede and follow the actions of the target child. Thus, as is the case with Patterson's system, one can examine the antecedent and consequent conditions for the behavior of the conduct-disordered child.

Observations by Significant Others

When, owing to concerns with time or expense, the use of trained, nonparticipant observers is impossible, the clinician can enlist the aid of the child's parents and/or teacher as an observer of the problematic behavior. Obviously, given the close relationship between parents or teacher and the child, this type of observation can be subject to bias. It can, however, be extremely useful when attempting to assess low-frequency target behaviors such as firesetting or stealing. Within this area, a number of options are available. Barkley (1981) suggested that parents or teachers keep a diary of a small number of selected problems for 1 to 2 weeks prior to the intervention. If a more structured assessment is desired, one could prepare a checklist of the key problem behaviors mentioned in the initial interview and ask the parents to simply note the occurrence or nonoccurrence of each problem on a daily basis (Patterson, Reid, Jones, & Conger, 1975). In an effort to gather more information, Wahler *et al.* (1976) suggest that the parents record the occurrence of, at most, two problem behaviors, but the parents are also asked to note their own behavior preceding and following the child's actions. While the parents' recording of their own behavior may be quite reactive, it is hoped that this information can be used to analyze the behavioral pattern surrounding the child's inappropriate acts (Karoly, 1981).

Whether or not one uses nonparticipant observers or the child's significant others, the point is that having some record of the child's actual problem behaviors, as well as the events that precede and follow these behaviors, can be invaluable.

ANALOGUE ASSESSMENTS

Given the difficulty of conducting observations in naturalistic settings, behaviorists and others have developed a range of analogue assessment methods (Kendall & Norton-Ford, 1982a; Nay, 1977). Analogue techniques can be particularly valuable when one wishes to assess behavior that is important but low-frequency, for in the analogue situation one can build in conflict or opportunities for problem solving.

In an effort to combine the assets of naturalistic observation with the practicality of analogue assessment, a number of investigators have developed systems for observing parent–child interactions within the clinic setting (Eyberg & Johnson, 1974; Forehand & Peed, 1979; Glogower & Sloop, 1976; Hughes & Haynes, 1978; Tavormina, 1975). According to Atkeson and Forehand (1981), this type of assessment has the advantage of efficiently eliciting the problematic parent–child interactions and providing a standard background against which the clinician can make within- and between-client comparisons. Virtually all of these structured situations are designed to occur in a playroom which can be observed through one-way mirrors. Parent–child dyads are frequently observed in both task-oriented and free-play types of activities.

An example of this method of assessment is the clinical analogue observation situation described by Barkley and Cunningham (1979). In this situation the mother and child are first escorted into the playroom and asked to play together as they might at home. After 15 minutes of such play, the mother is presented a list of three commands to give to the child. The first command is to have the child pick up all the toys and place them on a table in the back of the room. The second command involves having the child sit by his/her mother at a work table and copy a set of designs on a piece of paper. Finally the child is told to select one toy and play with it in a designated area while the mother sits on the other side of the room and reads a magazine. The child is also told not to bother the mother. While these interactions are occurring, two coders observe from behind the one-way mirror. One coder records the mother's behavior into one of seven categories (question, praise, negative, command, command–question, interaction, and no response), and the child responses to her into one of six categories (question, negative, interaction, compliance, independent play, and no response). The second coder uses the same categories but codes from the perspective of the child's actions as antecedents to the mother's responses. Barkley (1981) notes that the task or command phase of the situation is particularly sensitive to the problem behaviors associated with hyperactivity. This type of analogue assessment, like naturalistic observations, yields data that are useful in formulating treatment recommendations as well as diagnoses.

Larcen (reported in Allen *et al.*, 1976) developed the Structured Real-Life Problem Situation (SRLPS) as a means of assessing the effects of problem-solving training. This measure involves video-taping an interaction in which the tester and child approach the testing room, but when they arrive the tester tells the child the room is occupied and cannot be used. The child is then asked to help generate an alternative plan. The child's responses are scored for the number of alternatives produced.

McClure *et al.* (1978) also designed a real-life assessment situation called the Friendship Club Interaction (FCI). The FCI measure involved children in a "friendship club" contest with the following rules: (1) All six team members must agree on the best answer to the contest questions; (2) all six members must help answer the question; (3) all six members have to be club officers. A number of actual problems were present in the setting, such as five chairs for six subjects, five officer possibilities for six subjects, and the problem of distributing officer titles. The problem-solving interaction was video-taped and coded for problem-solving responses. With both the McClure et al. (1978) and Larcen measures, subjects who had received problem-solving training obtained higher scores than control subjects.

While these creative efforts at skills assessment are laudable, for the clinician, video-taping such interactions and later rating them on various dimensions could be as time-consuming and impractical as actually conducting naturalistic observations. It would be possible, however, for most clinicians to include opportunities for the child to attempt solving at least minor "real-life" problems in a standard evaluation. Finding the testing room (bathroom, drinking fountain, etc.), having too few chairs in the testing room, opening a locked cabinet or desk drawer, borrowing necessary equipment from others—these are all situations in which the clinician can informally assess the child's coping. The clinician may also want to role-play problem situations that are reported to be trouble spots for the child. Role plays can serve the purposes of both assessment and treatment. Keep in mind, however, that research by Beck, Forehand, Neeper, and Baskin (1982) suggests that role-play situations may elicit more social behaviors than are observed in similar but more naturalistic interactions. They hypothesize that interacting with an adult therapist who provides social prompts may be easier for some children than interacting with peers, so that role-play situations may present a more positive view of the child's social abilities. With this caution in mind, therapist–child role plays may still prove valuable if one is concerned with how the child can behave under optimal conditions. For example, if the child cannot generate and display some appropriate responses for, say, conflict resolution or initiating play even when interacting with the therapist, this may give some indication of the severity of the deficit.

SOCIOMETRICS

As indicated in the previous section, the child's ability to interact with his/her peers yields important information, for children are remarkable judges of their peers' adjustment (e.g., Cowen, Pederson, Babigian, Izzo, & Trost, 1973). Sociometric assessment provides some indication of the child's social standing and level of peer acceptance. Unfortunately, few clinicians are able to avail themselves of this information because of the time and out-of-office activity required to obtain it. We will, however, briefly discuss the more common methods of obtaining sociometric ratings, in hopes that the interested reader may someday be able to pursue this area.

The vast majority of sociometric assessment methods can be classified into one of three major types. The peer nominations approach is perhaps the most direct and simple method of assessing sociometric status. The type of assessment requires children to nominate their peers for inclusion into some group (e.g., Whom would you like to play with? Whom would you like to work with?). An even more direct version of this approach simply asks children to choose whom they like most and least (Busk, Ford, & Schulman, 1973; Roff, Sells, & Golden, 1972).

Rating scales have also been applied to sociometric assessment. Typically, with this approach children are provided with a list of their classmates' names and asked to rate each on some dimension of acceptability (e.g., How much do you like to play with this person at recess?). Examples of this type include the Ohio Social Acceptance Scale (Lorber, 1970).

The third approach is referred to as "descriptive matching," or type casting, for the children are asked to match up peers with various behavioral or personality descriptors. For example, with Bower's (1969) "Class Play," children are asked to assume the role of director and cast their peers for any of 20 roles in an imaginary class play. Importantly, the Class Play was developed specifically for the early identification of maladjustment in school children.

The exact nature of what is being measured by sociometrics (the characteristics of others or one's own feelings about them) and the degree of confidence one places in peer assessments remain a source of discussion (Brief, 1980; Kane & Lawler, 1978, 1980). Nevertheless, sociometric status tends to be a stable variable, in the absence of intervention, and sociometric assessments have proved sensitive to emotional maladjustment in regular schools. Bower (1969) reported that children with clinical problems, unbeknownst to teachers and classmates, tended to be chosen for negative, hostile, or inadequate roles, or not chosen at all for the Class Play.

ARCHIVAL DATA

Certain "real-world" measures that accrue in archives can provide information important to a full understanding of the child's problems, as well as convincing evidence for treatment effectiveness. The most obvious examples include information such as grades, past achievement test scores, and records of "visits to the principal," which could be obtained from the child's school record if a teacher interview is impossible and the child's parents give their permission to open the school file.

In terms of treatment evaluation, Chandler (1973) and Alexander and Parsons (1973) documented the impact of their interventions with delinquents using recidivism data. Moreover, Klein *et al.* (1977) reported reduced recidivism among treated subjects and their siblings. Similar measures can be profitable in the context of a school intervention. For example, Sarason and Sarason (1981) assessed the effectiveness of a social–cognitive intervention with adolescents at risk for dropout and delinquency by counting the rates of tardiness, absence, and referral for misbehavior in the year following the intervention. A cognitive-behavioral intervention with aggressive children might be evaluated in terms of the number of detentions or formal reprimands received during a subsequent grading period or the next year. A more academically oriented intervention could examine the child's actual grades in the treatment-relevant courses. As obvious as these types of measures seem, they have yet to be fully integrated into evaluations for cognitive-behavioral treatment.

GENERAL CONCERNS

In any intervention, one must be concerned with the levels of assessment. Two levels of assessment have been described by Kendall *et al.* (1981a): the *specifying level* and the *general impact level*. At the specifying level, the evaluator is interested in determining exactly what behaviors or processes are problematic for the child. Measurement at this level helps the professional focus on what may need to be changed and provides the data necessary to determine precisely what did or did not change as a result of any intervention efforts. What exact skills were acquired and what specific behaviors were modified? The key to the specifying level is that specific skills and specific behaviors be assessed. In contrast, general-impact-level assessments are sought not to specify what exactly needs to be changed or what did or did not change, but to determine the general impact of the child's behavior on those around him/her. How is the child perceived by peers, teachers, or parents? Is the child perceived differently as a result of treatment? Appropriate assessments at the specifying level include behavioral observations, task performance measures, and indices of specific cognitive processes. Teacher and parent ratings, sociometric assessments, and archival data are examples of general-impact-level assessments. Use of *both* specifying and impact-level assessments, and measuring both cognitive and behavioral change (Kendall, 1981c), would aid the clinician in understanding the child's specific deficits and assets and in understanding how the child is perceived in his/her social world.

At a more practical level, we realize that few therapists have the luxury of extended evaluations that include parent, teacher, and peer ratings as well as all relevant psychometric information. We believe, however, that the concepts emphasized in our discussion of these various measures could be incorporated into the format of one's standard procedures. Gathering information about the child's impersonal and interpersonal problem solving is valuable, but there are a myriad of ways in which this information could be obtained.

Once the information is in hand (or, more accurately, in mind), the clinician can then engage in his or her own information processing in order to decide if this child's difficulties are, in fact, appropriate for remediation with the cognitive–behavioral methods described in this book. If the answer is yes, then the clinician is ready to use the available data on the child (and on the relevant intervention techniques) to formulate a specific treatment plan. We strongly recommend the preparation of a treatment plan or outline for each child. We view this as an aid to the therapist's own problem solving as he/she directs or guides the activity of each session. Assessments provide data for gaining a better understanding of the person and for facilitating the individualized treatment plan.

CHAPTER 5

Treatment:
The Basic Ingredients

This chapter illustrates the separate strategies that combine to form cognitive–behavioral therapy for impulsive children. Our intent is to provide both a general description of each of the strategies and some sample transcript materials. We recommend a close reading of all of the following sections, even to the reader who may already be employing some of the suggested strategies. Why? Because our discussions of strategies and transcripts of case materials try to illustrate not only correct and successful application, but also areas where difficulties arise and where some recommended remedies may be undertaken.

The main strategies for the cognitive–behavioral self-control therapy include (1) a problem-solving approach, (2) self-instructional training, (3) behavioral contingencies, (4) modeling, (5) affective education, and (6) role-play exercises. The strategies are essentially an interwoven program, but, for the sake of description, we will present each in a separate section. Readers interested in the detailed and systematic description of the program are referred to the Appendix as well as to the audiovisual tape (50-minute training demonstration tape) which can be rented from the first author.[1]

PROBLEM-SOLVING APPROACH

Basic to the strategies we will be discussing is an underlying problem-solving theme. Unlike earlier emphases on problem-solving that focused only on cognitive or impersonal tasks, our focus is on interpersonal problems as well. What are the cues that people use to recognize interpersonal problems? What are the options available for working toward solutions to interpersonal problems? When we begin to consider

1. P. C. K., Psychology, Weiss Hall, Temple University, Philadelphia, Pennsylvania.

the features of interpersonal problem solving, we soon realize that the more accurate descriptive label for our approach is social–cognitive problem solving. It is an approach that strives to remedy deficits in cognitive functioning by teaching cognitive strategies for interpersonal problem solving.

Why Problem Solving?

Our answer is simple: because problem-solving skills are valuable to adjustment. This theoretical position was evident in Jahoda's (1953, 1958) early writings where the relationship between interpersonal problem solving and social and emotional adjustment was emphasized. Accordingly, psychological health is related to a problem-solving sequence consisting of the ability to recognize and admit a problem, to reflect on problem solutions, to make a decision, and to take action.

More recent advances in the theory and application of problem-solving approaches to treatment were made as a result of D'Zurilla and Goldfried's (1971) identification of problem solving as a component of behavior therapy. These authors defined a problem as a situation to which a person must respond in order to function effectively but for which no effective response alternative is readily available. D'Zurilla and Nezu (1982) and Rubin and Krasnor (1984) have further elaborated on the process of social problem solving, the relationship of social problem solving to psychological dysfunction, and the current status of the assessment and training of social problem-solving skills. Given that maladjustment can be viewed as ineffective responding, and that maladjustment typically involves ineffective problem solutions, the central role of problem-solving skills in adjustment is readily recognized.

Why Cognition?

The full range of possible solutions to problems typically does not materialize from thin air, nor does the single best solution necessarily pop into one's head first. Rather, successful problem solving results from an involvement in the operation of cognitive strategies which allow the person to consider possible courses of action, reflect on potential outcomes, and make decisions about options.

An important component of problem solving, whether interpersonal or impersonal, is the processing of relevant information. Information-processing theories reflect the assumption that the theory can be translated into an executable program and that there is correspondence between the temporally ordered states of the human process described by the theory. In addition, the output that is reached as a result of the input that is provided depends on the knowledge state of the information-processing system. Information-processing analyses may turn out to be valuable guides to our further understanding of that which is involved in interpersonal problem solving.

The cognitive facet is critical when children are the target sample and, as a result, developmental influences are brought to the forefront. For instance, the work of J. Piaget offers meaningful contributions to matters of intervention. Piaget's approach is very much concerned with how an individual's cognitive structures both shape and are shaped by the person's interactions with the environment. Accommodation and assimilation are concepts that illustrate this aspect of Piaget's thinking. With the presence of certain underlying cognitive structures, the person's interactions with the environment affect the cognitive structures and the person's behavior. The structures are not stagnant.

Beyond cognitive structures, developmental influences affect cognitive processing. Gal'perin (1969) described a developmental series of events leading to the eventual automaticity of cognitive processing. The importance of this theoretical model is that it outlines the steps that a therapist would want to follow to successfully teach the desired mental activity and have it become automatic. The first step involves familiarization with the task. Next, the person performs the task on the basis of its material representation. This is followed by performance acts which are related to overt speech, and subsequently the external speech is self-directed. The culmination of the process is reached when the act is completed using internal speech alone.

It seems reasonable to assert that, since there exists an indefinite number of potential problem situations and an infinite list of discrete solutions, interventions are best focused not on teaching specific responses but on *training the cognitive processes* involved in problem solving. The ability to achieve successful problem solutions across various situations is the desired therapeutic outcome.

Why Social?

The type of problem solving that is of present concern has to do with effective coping in social situations—social or interpersonal problem solving. Note that the advances in our understanding of the skills in *impersonal* problem solving (see Klahr & Robinson, 1981) may not necessarily be related to arriving at solutions to *interpersonal* or social problems. There is essentially no strong evidence to support an assumption that impersonal and interpersonal problem-solving skills tap the same cognitive structures or processes, nor that individuals who readily solve impersonal problems necessarily are similarly competent with social situations. One reason for the social focus, then, is that the problems seeking solutions are social/interpersonal ones.

While we recognize "good" social problem solvers, and while we sometimes suffer from the errors of those lacking such skills, we have not yet made substantial inroads toward understanding the process of social problem solving. Most studies assess the repertory of abilities necessary for good problem solving and several studies go on to compare distressed and nondistressed subjects' performance. Typically, the procedures used require subjects to describe potential problem solutions. What we need instead are studies of the plans that are followed, the strategies that are employed, and, especially important, the thinking processes that guide accepting or rejecting potential problem solutions. Klahr and Robinson (1981) have addressed the planning process in terms of *impersonal* problem solving, but the application of their advanced methodology to interpersonal problem solving awaits further effort.

A second reason for the emphasis on "social" is based on the apparent critical role of the social context for successful development. There exists wide agreement that satisfactory relations with peers is a crucial component of children's successful adjustment to life. Poor peer relations early in life have been reported to have serious effects on later adjustment. For instance, Robins (1966), Roff (1961), and Cowen *et al.* (1973) all provide evidence which suggests that negative social standing among peers is a critical precursor of adult psychopathology. Research with rhesus monkeys (Harlow & Mears, 1979) has demonstrated a strong relationship between negative states and a lack of social experience, leading the authors to conclude that isolation without social interaction has serious, if not disastrous, effects. Interestingly, these authors also report that social contexts (peers) are powerful factors in rehabilitation (see Hartup, 1983).

Regarding the intervention strategies per se, therapists would want to keep the training context as close as possible to real life. Since many interventions are designed to stimulate the cognitive processes associated with problem solutions, it seems reasonable to propose that they be taught in the interpersonal situations where problems arise. Social–

cognitive and interpersonal problem solving emerge as important developmental topics for it is these areas of inquiry that deal with cognitive development as most closely related to interpersonal contexts.

An additional consideration comes to the foreground when we return again to the larger question: Why social–cognitive problem solving? We are, as are many current child therapists, influenced by behavioral psychology. The result is that interventions are intended to teach abilities and/or remedy skill deficits, and it is through *performance-based* procedures that such goals are reached. We refer here also to the fact that interventions are enhanced when the proper contingencies are arranged to motivate and reinforce learning. However, behavioral strategies place too great an emphasis on training discrete observable behaviors and all too often ignore the cognitive components of effective adjustment. Social–cognitive problem solving becomes the major focus, for it is concerned with teaching component problem-solving abilities, and the cognitive processes associated with behavioral adjustment, all within the realm of the child's social environment. It is a purposeful amalgam, maintaining some of the demonstrated virtues of behavior therapy, but expanding them to envelop a larger domain of relevant cognitive and social functioning.

SELF-INSTRUCTIONAL TRAINING

It is proposed that an effective means to the solution to a problem is via the careful examination of the problem-solving process. Self-instructions are self-directed statements that provide a thinking strategy for children with deficits in this area and serve as a guide for the child to follow through the process of problem solving. Self-instructions reflect the desire of the therapist to break down the process into discrete steps, and, accordingly, each self-instruction represents one step of solving a problem.

In various research reports, discussions, and chapters, self-instructions are illustrated as in Table 5-1. As shown, the somewhat standard content of the self-instruction includes five types of statements. These self-directed statements proceed from the generation of a problem definition to stating the problem approach, focusing attention, and self-rewarding for correct responses. Following incorrect solutions, coping statements are used to help teach the child that all is not lost, that he/she can try again, and, above all, that committing an error does not necessitate a disturbing outburst.

TABLE 5-1. Content of self-instructional procedures

Problem definition:	"Let's see, what am I supposed to do?"
Problem approach:	"I have to look at all the possibilities."
Focusing of attention:	"I better concentrate and focus in, and think only of what I'm doing right now."
Choosing an answer:	"I think it's this one . . ."
Self-reinforcement:	"Hey, not bad. I really did a good job."
or	
Coping statement:	"Oh, I made a mistake. Next time I'll try and go slower and concentrate more and maybe I'll get the right answer."

Note. After Meichenbaum and Goodman (1971); Kendall (1977); Kendall and Finch (1979b).

The problem-solving self-instructions are designed to help the child (1) recognize that there is a problem and identify its features, (2) initiate a strategy that will help him/her move toward a problem solution, (3) consider the options, and (4) take action on the chosen plan. Importantly, the self-rewarding self-instruction is included to strengthen the child's "thinking" habit.

The coping statements are designed to avoid overly negative self-talk. We do not want children to try, to make a mistake, and to tell themselves, "That was really stupid; I'm dumb." What we do want is an effort, and, if the effort proves incorrect, a comparatively neutral self-stated reaction such as, "Oops, I made a mistake. I'll have to think it over again" would be much preferred.

One of the most important aspects of the self-instructional procedure is the meaningfulness of the actual sentences for the individual child. That is, saying the self-instructions the way we therapists would is *not* as crucial as having the child say them in his/her own words. The therapist and child collaborate to create (have the child discover) specific self-directive statements. Individualizing the self-directed statements far surpasses "saying what we say" as the goal of the therapist. The following transcript illustrates not only the self-instructional training procedure as outlined thus far, but also the individualizing of the actual self-statements.

Therapist: Now, when we do these tasks I am going to show you how we think out loud while doing them, OK?
Child: All right.
T: I'm going to do the first one, and you can look over and watch as I do it. Now there are five steps, and I've got them written down on these cards. Notice, when I say the first step, then I do the first step.

Now the first one is, "What am I supposed to do?" Well, I'm supposed to, according to this task, find out which one doesn't belong. Do you see what I mean?

C: Yeah.

T: OK, the next step is look at all of the possibilities. Boy, there are a whole lot of things on this page. The next thing is to focus in; I guess that means I don't need to look at these other problems on the rest of this page, I just need to look at these few. Now, that is a clock and that is a teacup and that is a clock, and that is an alarm clock. And, the task was to find which one doesn't belong. So, this one doesn't belong. That is the next step, picking the answer, OK?

C: All right.

T: There is a lot to remember, isn't there?

C: Yeah.

T: OK now, when you get the problem right, and according to this that is the right answer, when you get it right you say to yourself, "I did a good job." If you get it wrong then it is sometimes a good idea to say to yourself, "Next time I've got to go more slowly and try to think more carefully." So, those are the steps that we are going to try and learn as we do each of the problems. OK?

C: All right.

T: Seems like a lot though, doesn't it?

C: Yup. Do I have to learn them all right away?

T: We'll work on them together and take our time. You don't have to learn them all right away, but you will eventually learn them all. OK, why don't you try and do the next one, and as you do it we are going to write your own ideas down for things to say for each step.

C: All right.

T: What is the first step?

C: "What am I supposed to do."

T: OK, now how would you say that in your own words? How would you say to yourself, "What am I supposed to do?"

C: "What is the problem."

T: Good. OK, "what is the problem." Why don't you write that right on the card here. You can go ahead and do that. That will be something you can use to remind yourself later. Good. "What is the problem." OK, what is the problem for that one?

C: I've got to find the answer.

T: OK, and how is this problem defined, what is it that is the answer? Do you remember when I did it I was trying to find which picture didn't belong?

C: OK.

T: So that is the problem. The second thing you have to say is, "Look at all the possibilities." Do you know what possibilities means?

C: Choices?

T: Yeah. Good. So, how would you say that to yourself. How would you say, "Look at all the possibilities."

C: "Look at all the choices."

T: OK, why don't you write that down here. Write "choices." That will be a good way to remember to look at all the choices. Now, the next step was to focus in. You don't need to look at the ones at the bottom of the page, you might block those out. OK. Now, what would be a way to say to yourself to focus in?

C: To look at just these ones.

T: OK, good. What would be a way you'd say that to yourself? Can you think of a way you might say that? Just look at these?

C: "Focus in."

T: OK, why don't you go ahead and write that right here. That will be good. That is sort of like thinking really hard. You've got to focus in and think hard. Good. All right then, the next one is to pick an answer. So far we went through these real quick. Let's go through them again just so that you can do them when you say them. What is the problem? Now, what is the problem in this case?

C: Which one is not a dog.

T: OK. Number 2 was look at the choices, and 3 was focus in. Why don't you do both of those. Focus in and look at the choices. Now, think about each one, and which one doesn't belong. The next thing you are supposed to remember is to pick an answer. Which one do you pick?

C: The lion doesn't belong.

T: OK, let me check. That is right, that one doesn't belong. When you say "pick an answer," how do you say that to yourself?

C: "Pick the right one."

T: OK. What would be another way, maybe, to say pick an answer? Can you think of a way, maybe. . . . What do you think? Pick the. . . .

C: Choice.

T: Pick the choice, OK. Why don't you write that down. This is good. Pick the right choice, or pick the choice. OK. Now, you got that one right, and when you get it correct what are you supposed to say to yourself?

C: "I did a good job."

T: OK, now, how do you say that to yourself when you do something really well? How do you say that to yourself?

C: "I did a good job."

T: So, you say it that way pretty much anyhow?

C: Mm.

T: OK, so we'll just keep that the same. So, now we have all the five steps that you have to remember. That is a lot to learn, but we are going to practice a lot. You've got the five steps, and you've got them in your words, written right here.

One of the goals of the training is for the child to internalize the self-instructions so that he/she is able to use them to think slowly through potential solutions to problems that occur outside of therapy. Toward this end, the therapist works to aid the child to use the self-instructions covertly. Thus, use of the self-instructions by both the therapist and child fades from overt (out loud), through a whispering phase, and finally to covert (silent) speech. This sequence is described in Table 5-2, and the transition from speaking in a regular voice to speaking in a whisper is illustrated in the following transcript.

Therapist: OK, you try this one.

Child: Let's see, what am I supposed to do? (*Pause.*) Which one goes in the blank? (*Pause.*) Look at all the possibilities. And you get to look at all of them carefully. I think it's (*child points to answer*).

T: Yep, that's the right answer.

C: I did a good job.

T: OK, why don't you go ahead and do the next one.

C: Let's see what you're supposed to do on this one. OK, see what goes in the blank. (*Pause.*) Go over all the possibilities. (*Pause.*) I'll go over the problem again. (*Pause.*) OK, I think it's B.

T: B? (*Checks the answer page.*) Yes, that's the right answer.

C: I did a good job.

T: Good. Do you remember the time at the end of the last session when you started whispering so that we wouldn't disturb the people around us? So why don't we try doing that for a while. I'll do the next

TABLE 5-2. Sequence of self-instructional procedures

1. The therapist models task performance and talks out loud while the child observes.
2. The child performs the task, instructing himself/herself out loud.
3. The therapist models task performance while whispering the self-instructions.
4. The therapist performs the task using covert self-instructions with pauses and behavioral signs of thinking (e.g., stroking beard or chin).
5. The child performs the task using covert self-instructions.

Note. After Meichenbaum and Goodman (1971); Kendall (1977).

one. Let's see what it is. (*Pause.*) Look at all the possibilities. (*Pause.*) OK, go over the right answer. (*Pause.*) Yep, I can just tell.

C: (*Whispering.*) OK, let's see what you're supposed to do with this problem. (*Pause.*) Look carefully. OK, I think it's B.

T: Yep, that's right. Wanna do the next one too? Remember to whisper.

C: Let's go on to the next problem. (*Pause.*) Look at all the possibilities. (*Pause.*) Look at the problem again. (*Pause.*) OK, I'm ready. It's this one.

T: Yes, that's right.

C: I did a good job.

BEHAVIORAL CONTINGENCIES

Incentive manipulation is vital, and the use of contingencies, in our opinion, is an essential feature of the training. Recall, for a moment, that we define our program as an effort to maintain the demonstrated efficacies of behavioral therapy, but with the inclusion of cognitive training. The behavioral contingency features of the cognitive–behavioral self-control therapy for children include (1) self-reward and social reward, (2) response-cost, (3) self-evaluation, and (4) rewarded homework assignments.

Self-Reward and Social Reward

The typical behavioral contingency concerns rewards for desired responses. Indeed, the law of effect has such an established track record that it truly earns the label "law." Programs for teaching children benefit from a healthy dose of reward contingencies. Two types of rewards that are employed—systematically and generously—are self-reward and social reward. The reader will recall that one of the self-instructions taught to the child is "I did a good job." The exact wording does not concern us as much as the need for self-reward following successful task performance. As a part of the self-instructions that are rehearsed for each task, the child must pause to provide and profit from self-rewards. In addition to self-reward as part of the self-instructions, we encourage therapists to foster self-reward in any instance where it would be appropriate. The increased use of self-rewards will likely enhance the child's sense of self-concept and self-efficacy. For many children, their environment offers all too few opportunities for self-rewards, and to the extent that the therapist–child relationship can allow and aid self-reward the child will benefit.

Social reward ties in directly with the suggestion to create a rewarding environment. The therapist uses smiles, comments such as "good," "fine," and "nice job," and any of the generally socially rewarding messages appropriate with children (e.g., "all right"). These rewards set the tone of the sessions: positive, rewarding, and encouraging. Interestingly, in an analysis of therapists' verbal behavior in sessions, Braswell *et al.* (1984b) found that statements of encouragement ("Keep up the good work," "I can see you're really trying hard," etc.) but not simple confirming statements ("That's correct," "Right," "Uh-huh," etc.) were associated with more positive child outcomes.

Response-Cost

A response-cost contingency operates whereby a child is given in advance a number of reward tokens (chips) and is informed that he/she can lose a token for various reasons. Some of the reasons for enacting a response-cost include making a mistake on task instructions, answering the task question incorrectly, forgetting one of the self-instructions, misusing the self-instructions, and going too fast. In this way, response-cost is designed to assist (cue) the child to remember to stop and think before responding: It is a potent contingency, but it is not the only contingency and it is not to be construed as entirely punitive. Rather, taking the chip away, with an explanation of why, cues the child about how to improve behavior and performance next time.

Because response-cost can be misperceived as a punitive prescription, we think it worthwhile to consider some of the rationale for the inclusion of response-cost. Non-self-controlled problem children tend to respond quickly without carefully evaluating all possible alternative solutions to problems; consequently, they make many mistakes. When presented with a choice of alternative answers, impulsive children will sometimes answer correctly, conceivably obtaining the right answer by chance or because the problem was so easy that the answer was immediately apparent. If one *only* reinforces an impulsive child for right answers, which can be a matter of luck or fast guessing, one in effect spuriously rewards the child for being quick and less than fully thoughtful. In order to circumvent this problem, the cognitive–behavioral strategy uses a response-cost contingency.

The following scenario from a typical classroom demonstrates why the response-cost component carries clout. The scene is a fourth grade classroom, 20 children, one teacher, and an arithmetic lesson. The teacher assigns a question, "What is 96 divided by 12?" Hands go up almost immediately. Children excitedly wait to be called on while others call out. One impulsive child cries, "Six." A few classmates put their hands down. The child calls out again, "It's 9, the answer is 9—oh, no, it's 8, 8 times 12 is 96." The teacher, perhaps seeking no more than a renewed calm, says, "Yes, correct." The reward contingency was applied for the correct answer, but it spuriously, unwittingly, and unwantingly rewarded the fast guessing.

Now, let's rerun the scene with a response-cost procedure. Everything would proceed the same way until the child cried out, "Six." At this point, the teacher would say, "No, you're going too fast and not thinking. You lose one chip. Try and think and be sure before you answer." After a pause, the teacher asks, "OK, what is 96 divided by 12?" The child pauses and then says, "Eight." The teacher provides social praise: "Good, that's the way. Take your time and be sure you've got it right."

It is conceivable that a reward contingency could be arranged so that reward is given only if the first answer is correct. That is, after one response, others do not earn reward. Theoretically, this procedure would prevent the spurious rewarding of fast guessing. However, when a child gets the answer correct, the peer group may provide the rewards and the child receives some sense of accomplishment for a correct response. Thus, even if the teacher withholds reinforcement from all responses but the first one, other children and personal perception can nevertheless provide the reward. In addition to this argument for the merit of response-cost over direct reward, the response-cost procedure provides a cue for the child and is accompanied by an explanation for the response-cost. These features carry with them the potential to inhibit responding. A sample reward menu, and comments about our banking system, are provided in the Appendix.

Self-Evaluation

When behavioral contingencies are consistently and appropriately employed, the child will learn the desired behaviors. But what happens when the child leaves the environment in which the contingencies are applied? As we know, the behavior is often not maintained. Many of the strategies discussed thus far are intended to foster generalization, and self-evaluation is another of these.

Self-evaluation skills can be taught through the use of a "How I Did Today" chart, an example of which is shown below:

How I Did Today				
1	2	3	4	5
Not so good	OK	Good	Very good	Super extra special

The self-evaluation chart is used first by the therapist and subsequently by both the child and the therapist. For instance, at the conclusion of the first session, the therapist rates the child's performance, providing feedback on how he/she did for the day. This feedback includes a thorough explanation as to why the particular rating was chosen. For example, the therapist might tell the child, "You did pretty good today; you did the problems carefully and made very few mistakes. You also remembered the self-instructions. I think I would rate your performance a 4—'very good.' If you had made many errors, gone too fast, or forgotten the steps, I would probably rate you a 1—'not so good.' If you had done even better than today, by not making any mistakes, I probably would rate you a 5—'super extra special.'" In later sessions the child is also asked to evaluate his/her own performance, and if the child's and therapist's ratings match (exactly or within one point), the child earns additional rewards. On the transcript that follows, the interaction of the therapist and child exemplifies the beginning of teaching self-evaluation skills.

Therapist: How about this: Here's a way you can earn an extra chip. Remember we talked about using this little chart here called "How I Did Today."

Child: Yeah.

T: OK, and after every session . . .

C: Yeah.

T: I pick a number to say how you did. Remember? (*Points to chart.*) Underneath number 1 it says "not so good." Number 2 is "OK." Number 3 is "good." Number 4 is "very good." Number 5 is "super extra special." OK, so . . . after every session, I'm going to pick a number that tells how good you did, and I want you to pick a number to tell me how good you think you did. And if your number is the same number as mine . . .

C: Yeah.

T: Or one on either side of it . . .

C: Yeah.

T: Then I'll give you an extra bonus chip.

C: What if it's the same one?

T: If it's the same one, you get an extra bonus chip. OK?

C: Oh.

T: But if you pick one that's just one away from the number I pick, you still get an extra chip. How do you think you did today?

C: Ummm.

T: Think about how hard you worked, how many chips you got to keep, how many times I had to correct you. Then, you can pick a number to tell me how you think you did today.

C: Five.

T: You think you did 5?

C: Yeah.

T: I think you did very good. I think you did number 4 because you got two wrong, OK, and a few times you forgot to do all the steps.

C: Yeah.

T: And sometimes you skipped ahead a little bit so you weren't "extra super special"—I think I'll give you a "very good"—number 4. OK.

C: Now that's 5 and that's 4. Just one away.

T: It's on that side by only 1 so you got an extra chip. 'Cause it was only 1 away from the one I picked.

C: I earned my chips then. (*Smiles.*)

Homework Assignments

Given the desirability of having the child stop and think outside as well as inside the therapy session, homework assignments are included as part of the training. The assignments are "graded" in two ways. First, they are graded according to acceptability—if the assignment is completed in an acceptable fashion, then the child earns a bonus chip. Second, they are graded in terms of a hierarchy of difficulty.

Early assignments are less complex and easier than later assignments. For example, at the end of one of the early therapy sessions, the child is encouraged to use the self-instructions in the classroom. A contingency is established: The child can earn an extra chip at the start of the next session if he/she can describe an instance where he/she *could have used* the self-instructions. This task is designed to simply get the child to identify instances where using the steps would be appropriate. In later sessions, the child must describe an instance where he/she *actually used* the self-instructions in the classroom or at home. Here the emphasis is on actual deployment of self-instructions outside the specific therapy sessions.

It is, of course, possible for the child to tell a story about using the self-instructions that is not in fact true. For instance, when asked how he/she used the self-instructions last week, the child might respond, "When doing my homework." Although we have no way of knowing for certain that this is an accurate report, we reward the response since it is an instance where the self-instructions could be quite helpful. Often, we will inquire further: "Oh, how did you use the steps when doing your homework?" If the child doesn't know or says "Well, I really didn't," we state that it would be a good time to use self-instructions but that he/she only gets the reward when he/she actually uses the steps. We add, however, that next session will be another chance. "If you can tell me when you actually used the self-instructions in class or at home, you can earn the bonus reward, OK?" Children's responses are rapidly shaped so that they soon learn to describe how they used the steps. The veridicality of the event cannot be checked so we reward the child for providing an apt description of when to use the steps.

Therapist: Remember, you can earn an extra reward today. You can earn it by telling me how you used the self-instructions in class or at home. Remember, this was your homework assignment.

Child: Yeah.

T: So, can you tell me of an instance?

C: When we were doing math. I thought about the answer.

T: (*Pause.*) And . . .

C: You had to pick one of the answers.

T: Could you pick any answer?

C: No, just the right one. So I looked it over good and looked at all the choices. And then I picked an answer.

T: Was it right?

C: Yeah; the first answer was 5.

T: Ah huh; so you did it right.

C: Yeah.

T: Anything else?

C: Oh, then I told myself I did a good job.

T: Good, you get an extra chip because you did a really good job of remembering the extra thing to do [homework].

C: How many chips, do I have now?

T: Let's see, 21. Plus 38 in the bank—that's 59.

C: Fifty-nine.

T: Yep, 59. So you remembered a way to use the self-instructions back in class. That was good. That was a really good way.

C: I don't believe it—59.

T: Yeah.

MODELING

The therapeutic use of modeling entails the exposure of a client to an individual (or individuals) who actually demonstrates the behaviors to be learned by the client. Modeling, also referred to as observational learning, has been used to produce such diverse therapeutic and educational outcomes as the elimination of behavioral deficits, the reduction of excessive fears, and the facilitation of social behavior (Bandura, 1969, 1971; Rosenthal & Bandura, 1978). In alternating with the child task by task, the therapist demonstrates or models problem solving and the use of the self-directed self-instructions. The cognitive–behavioral approach, therefore, involves teaching via modeling with a modicum of direct orders. The therapist does not so much tell the child what to do as work with the child showing him/her one valuable way to think through problems.

The specific manners in which the model demonstrates behavior can be quite varied. Some of the formats include graduated modeling, symbolic modeling, filmed modeling, and participant modeling. Perhaps the single most important distinction concerns whether the model displays "mastery" or "coping" behavior. A mastery model demonstrates ideal behavior. For instance, the mastery model demonstrates rapid and correct performance with an absence of difficulty and frustration. In contrast, the coping model makes mistakes occasionally and shares with the child any difficulties that are encountered while completing the tasks. The coping model demonstrates coping strategies for dealing with difficulties or failures. Thus, the coping model is more like the child than the mastery model, provides a more strategic approach, and offers methods for dealing with frustration and failure. In terms of effectiveness, a coping model has been found to be superior to a mastery model (e.g., Kazdin, 1974; Meichenbaum, 1971; Sarason, 1975).

It is also important to note that a model who self-verbalizes is superior to one who does not verbalize. That is, talking out loud while modeling offers a demonstration of the thinking through of a problem to problem solution. This practice is most potent. Meichenbaum (1971) provided data to support the statement that the most effective modeling strategy includes the model's stating out loud cognitive coping strategies.

At times, such as in the early stages, the therapist performs the task correctly and focuses directly on modeling the use of the self-instructions. Later, and throughout the rest of training, the therapist more often serves as a coping model. This modeling takes place not only in relation to the tasks and training materials, but also in the therapist's routines. We would like to illustrate the application of modeling to self-instructions and the coping model. First, a transcript will illustrate modeling the steps. Next, we shall illustrate the therapist as a coping model on training tasks, and last, we shall illustrate the role of the coping model as part of routine therapy practice. In this sample, the task is a math problem.

Therapist: OK, now we're going to use the steps [self-instructions] when we do the problems on the "Little Professor" [a hand-held computer game].

Child: OK.

T: The first time I'll do a couple of problems. OK?

C: OK.

T: So I'll set it on level 2. That's not the easiest, but it's not the hardest either. 17 plus 14 . . . I think I'll copy that onto my paper. Copy it down onto the paper. (*Therapist then writes it down.*) 17 plus 14 . . . what am I supposed to do here? Well, I'm supposed to add. There's a plus sign here. I'm supposed to add these together. OK, that's what I'm supposed to do. And actually what I'm supposed to do is, I'm supposed to figure out the correct answer, right? OK, and the second step is to look at all the possible things we could do with it. Remember when we do a math problem, the step we're supposed to do is to look at the sign. And see if it's adding or subtracting, or multiplying, or dividing.

C: OK, but you can't look at any answers.

T: That's right. There aren't any answers to look at. So we look at the plus or minus or times or divide signs.

C: That's the only signs you can look at!

T: So now I'll do the next step and that's focus in and try and solve the problem. So 17 plus 14 equals . . . I think I know what the answer is. 17 plus 14 is 31. So I'll punch it in the Little Professor and (*pause*) I got it right because (*look*) it came up with a different problem.

C: Um huh.

T: So then I must have done a good job because I got the problem right. Let's try the next one, 7 plus 13. OK, I'll write it down on my paper and I'll go through all the steps. The first thing let's find out what I'm supposed to do. I'm supposed to figure out the answer. And the different possibilities here are plus, minus, divide . . .

C: Multiply.

T: Yeah! That's a different possibility. OK, now focus in and just think of this problem, hum? 7 plus 13. I think I know what 7 plus 13 is. 7 plus 13 is 20. Did I do it right?

C: Yep.

T: I did it right. I took my time and I did a good job. OK, why don't you do a couple of them just like I did.

C: OK. [Display reads 13 plus 13.]

T: OK.

C: Find out what I'm supposed to do.

T: Uh-huh.

C: Yeah, find the answer. Step 2. Um, look at the sign and focus in. Then pick the answer.

T: Pick the answer?

C: Yeah, figure it out. (*Pause.*) OK.

T: OK, let's check it out. Oh good, 26 is correct.

C: I did a good job.

T: Now let's try a problem that's a little harder 'cause these were pretty easy.

With a minimum of direct commands, the therapist was able to get the child to use the steps to work on the math problem. Modeling was the key strategy. In the next transcript, which follows directly from the one above, the therapist serves as the *coping* model:

Therapist: I'll set the Little Professor to the highest level.
Child: OK.

T: How about this one, 84 divided by 7? What's the first thing we're going to do?

C: Write it down on paper.

T: OK, now what? (*Pause.*) Gee, it's been a long time since I've done this type problem. Some of the others have been so easy I could have just said the answer; now I've really got to think.

C: Write it down on paper.

T: OK, but then what?

C: Start the problem.

T: Yeah, but I'm not sure exactly. (*Pause.*) Wait. (*Pause.*) OK, I think you do this one number at a time. If I take my time I can get it.

C: The first one is 1.

T: Let me think. OK, 7 goes into 8 once. Then 7 doesn't go into 4. This isn't right. Wait. There's no hurry; let me think more. What about the one 1 left over. That makes this 14. OK, then you do 7 goes into 14.

C: Yeah.

T: Now I think I've got it. 7 goes into 14 twice. Put the 2 here and the answer is 12.

C: Yeah.

T: I almost muffed that one. But I caught myself before I gave up. I did a good job.

By serving as a coping model, the therapist demonstrates not only the use of the self-instructions in the performance of the task, but also the use of coping strategies when problem solutions are not readily available. Since it is inevitable that the child will run into problems that are not readily soluble, having coping responses available will reduce the likelihood that the child will throw up his/her arms and quit, or turn against the environment and act out. As we noted earlier, coping statements are built into the self-instructions for use after the incorrect response and are designed to replace overly negative self-statements such as, "I'm dumb" with more acceptable statements such as, "I'll have to be more careful."

The last of our transcripts in this section evidence the use of coping modeling in the therapist's routine. Recall that we are not telling the children what to do, but that we are showing them one way to work out solutions. The tasks provide opportunities for many learning trials, but the therapist's routine activities provide additional, and possibly more potent, examples. Numerous examples come to mind, but the following "briefcase" and "room key and chairs" illustrations are perhaps the most informative.

The tasks used for training are typically transported in a briefcase. The case is often stuffed with materials, and the beginning of each session provides the therapist with the challenge of locating the task for that particular session. Most adults, if not all, can solve this trivial problem with ease.

> *Therapist:* How's your soccer team doing? (*Puts briefcase on top of desk.*)
> *Child:* Pretty good; we won our last game. I scored a goal, too.
> *T:* Great. (*Opens briefcase upside down and materials spill out onto the desk and floor.*) Heck, why am I dumb? (*Short pause.*) No, wait. I'm not dumb; I just didn't think.
> *C:* Huh?
> *T:* I didn't think . . . I didn't remember which is the top and which is the bottom of the briefcase.
> *C:* Oh.
> *T:* Let's see; how can you tell which is the top? (*Examines case; child looks also.*) Here, this little label is on only one side; it's on the top. If I can remember that this goes on top, then I won't spill all these things next time. (*Pause.*) The label goes on top. (*Pause.*) The label goes on top. (*Whispered.*)

Yet another example of the therapist serving as a cognitive coping model on routine jobs concerns finding the key to the office (therapy room) and arranging for the correct number of chairs to be in the room. We will assume that the therapist in this case uses a room other than his/her office for the individual sessions, and that this room is also used for other purposes. The therapist and child approach the therapy room:

> *Therapist:* Here we are. (*Turns door knob.*) It's locked!
> *Child:* Locked? (*Turns door knob.*)
> *T:* Do I have the key? I don't know. Let me look in my purse. (*Opens purse, and while searching, things fall out and onto the floor.*)
> *C:* (*Laughs.*)
> *T:* Where did that key go? I always misplace it. If I could only keep it in one place. Wait, there's no hurry. I better take a look in each part of this pocketbook. First, I'll check this pocket; no, it's not there. Not here, either. Ah, here it is.
> *C:* Can we go in now?
> *T:* As soon as I put these things back in. (*Whispers.*) Maybe I can put this key on a special hook and put it in this part of my purse. Then I'll know where it is next time. (*After entering room and getting set up.*) Just a minute, Jeff. (*Goes into briefcase and removes a large*

paper clip.) I'll put this key here and then clip it in a special spot in my purse. Then I won't misplace it. I'll have to remember next time that I clipped it right here.

Both examples would be followed up at the next session, when, for instance, the therapist goes to open the briefcase and stops, pauses, and thinks out loud, "The label goes on top." After pausing and saying the above statement, the therapist then opens the case and says, "Good, I got the top on top—good job." As you might suspect, the examples here are only samples and there are many instances where routine jobs provide opportunities for coping modeling. It is desirable to use these opportunities regularly and to pause at the proper time to allow the child to provide the reminder. Experience suggests that the child will sometimes chime in, "This *(pointing)* goes on top." Such an event is a perfect opportunity to smile and provide verbal social rewards for being thoughtful.

AFFECTIVE EDUCATION

Improving the child's ability to accurately recognize and label his/her own emotional experiences, as well as the emotions of others, may be a necessary step for improved interpersonal problem solving. Toward this end, the training program includes tasks that require the child to label the emotions associated with various facial expressions, bodily postures, or problematic interpersonal situations. The actual materials used to generate such discussions are less important than the process of making the child more conscious of the nature of his/her own emotions, the association between certain emotions and certain situations, and the effect of self-talk in the mediation of emotional experiences.

The training program also addresses the child's emotional responses in the context of the role-playing exercises. While the manner in which these exercises are conducted is addressed in the next section, it should be noted that one reason for even including role-play tasks is to heighten the child's level of emotional involvement and arousal. Thus, the child has an opportunity to practice the self-instructional skills while grappling with problematic situations that may "pull for" a more impulsive, emotional type of responding. Clearly when a child is working one to one with a therapist, it may be difficult for their role plays to produce the level of affective response that might typify the same interaction if it occurred with a family member or peer. Within appropriate limits, however, the therapist should work toward such realism. When the treatment is conducted with groups of children, it may be quite possible to generate very realistic levels of emotional arousal. For example, Goodwin and Mahoney (1975) had their elementary-school-aged subjects practice displaying self-control in the face of verbal taunts by having the children play a game in which they actually called each other names. When the training situation includes opportunities for utilizing the self-instructions in emotionally arousing situations, one is, in effect, training for generalization.

ROLE PLAYS

Role playing, in conjunction with thinking through the problem situation, offers an opportunity to act out the behavior and provides a performance base for the intervention. Role plays can be arranged for either hypothetical situations or situations that are actually problems for the child. Typically, both types of problem situations are employed in a sequence that facilitates the child's involvement, reduces the likelihood of resistance, and enlivens the activity of treatment. Toward these ends, role plays of hypothetical problem situations best precede "real" problem situations. Sample hypothetical situations include:

- "You are watching television, and your mother/sister changes the channel."
- "You tear your pants at recess and someone is making fun of you."
- "You are having trouble with a worksheet and your friend is already finished."
- "You are playing a new game and your friend starts to cheat."

Each situation can be written on an index card in advance and, once the child understands what is involved in a role-play task, one index card can be selected from a deck of cards that becomes the situation for the next role play. While it may be the case that one or several of these "hypothetical" situations may be a real problem situation for the child, they are quite general and likely to be problems for many children so that the specific child is not likely to feel directly targeted.

After the child and therapist have gained experience with the hypothetical role plays, real problem situations can be performed. One suggested way to introduce real problem situations into the session is to write the situation on a new index card and include it among the cards for which role plays will be chosen. If one or two cards among three or four choices are real problem situations, then it is quite likely that at least one will be chosen. We have found teachers to be valuable sources of descriptions of the problem situations for children in their classes. Via individual consultation with a child's teacher, accurate and properly worded real situations for role plays can be acquired. Proper wording is important. For instance, a child is reported by the teacher as getting in trouble for "visiting." Not "out-of-seat" behavior, and not "talking." "Visiting" had a special meaning, and when the child selected the card for role playing that read "You are in class and the teacher singles you out for visiting—you get in trouble for visiting," the child knew exactly what was meant.

Once the child has become accustomed to the role-play format, each new situation can easily be acted out. Since the first few role plays may feel somewhat awkward for both the therapist and child, special attention can be paid to the transition. In an effort to overcome the initial difficulties moving from just talking about situations to acting them out, we have found the following format to be quite helpful.

First, just as in previous sessions, the child is asked to state the problem. For example, after the child has selected one of the situation cards, the following interaction might ensue.

Therapist: OK, what does your card say?

Child: It says, "You are watching television but your little brother keeps changing the channel."

T: So what is your problem? Or, to use our "step-words," what are you supposed to do?

C: Well, I guess I'm supposed to figure out how to handle that situation with my brother.

T: Right.

In the second step of problem solving the child knows he/she is supposed to look at all the possibilities. The therapist's role at this point is to help the child understand that in social problem situations, he/she has to generate or create his/her own possibilities for action while taking into account the practical limits of the situation. In our work, we typically urge the child to think of at least three or four different alternatives for coping with each situation. During step 2, the emphasis is clearly on generating the alternatives, with evaluation of the quality of each possibility being held until step 3. While in step 2, the therapist–child interaction might resemble the following.

Therapist: Now that you know what the problem is, what are some different things you could do about it?

Child: I could hit my brother, but then my mom would really be mad.

T: We will think about which things would be best to do in just a moment. One possibility you thought of would be to hit your brother. What would be another thing you could do? Let's see if you can think of at least two more possibilities.

C: Uh . . . I could tell my mom!

T: Yes, you could tell your mother. What's another idea?

C: I could *try* to work out a deal with my brother, but I don't know about that one . . .

T: Good. That's three different possibilities. You could hit your brother, or you could tell your mom, or you could try to work out a deal with your brother.

The therapist can translate the third step—think hard or focus in—into a process of evaluating the relative merits of each alternative. We recommend attempting to evaluate the possibilities in terms of their behavioral and emotional consequences for the child and for the other people involved in the situation. Such an evaluation process might resemble the following interchange.

Therapist: All right. You've thought of three different choices or possibilities. Now let's think hard about each one. What would happen if you decided to hit your little brother?

Child: Well, he'd get mad and start crying. Then he'd probably go tell mom and I'd get in trouble.

T: Would hitting your brother mean you would get to watch your TV program?

C: No. I'd probably get sent to my room.

T: And how would everyone feel after you hit your brother?

C: Well, my brother and mother would be mad. It might feel good to hit my brother (*pause*), but it wouldn't feel good to have to go to my room.

T: Let's think about the next choice—telling your mom. What would happen if you did that?

C: Well, my brother would probably get mad, but if mom took my side, I might get to watch my show. Of course, mom doesn't really like it when we tattle on each other.

T: So that choice has some good things about it and some bad things. What about the last one?

C: What was it? . . . Oh, yeah, try to work out a deal with my brother. I don't know, but maybe my brother and I could decide that I get to keep watching my show but he could pick what we watch next. Then he'd be happy and I'd be happy and mom wouldn't know anything about it. I guess if I couldn't make a deal with him, then I could go tell mom.

T: OK. You've done some careful thinking about your three choices.

The fourth step still involves picking an answer. With social problems the therapist can tell the child that sometimes there will be more than one good answer or good way to solve a problem. With more cognitively sophisticated children, the therapist may also wish to add that in other, more difficult situations, none of the choices may seem very good and that in those cases one has to try to pick the least bad solution. With regard to the child's actual choice, if the therapist is satisfied that the child has evaluated each possibility, then the actual response the child selects is of less importance. To use the current example, if, after examining the consequences, the child decides that it still might be worth it to hit his/her little brother, then he/she should be allowed to select this choice without receiving a response-cost. After all, it is the thinking process that we are teaching—not what to think, but how to think. The therapist should feel free to state why he/she thinks another alternative would be more optimal, but the child's choice should be respected.

Step 5 can be handled much as it is with impersonal problem-solving tasks. The child should be encouraged to use a self-reinforcing statement to reward his/her good problem solving or, if he/she has gone too fast or forgotten a step, a coping statement should be used.

When the child has a clearer understanding of how the steps can be used to solve social problems, one need not rigidly adhere to the five-step model outlined in the last examples. The following transcript contains a description of the therapist and child working or defining the role-play task and then using the steps in a more informal manner.

In this case, the therapist and child talk about the problem and then act it out.

Therapist: You want to call your friend Sam, but your mom is on the phone. OK. Do you need to think to figure that one out?
Child: Yeah. What are we supposed to do with these problems? Act them out?
T: OK, yeah, we'll act out this one.
C: You know about this; just say, "Get off the phone."
T: OK, but then what would happen?
C: Trouble.
T: Probably.
C: Could ask her to get off.
T: What would be the consequences of that?
C: Huh?
T: What would be the consequences of telling her to get off? That means, what would happen then?
C: I don't know.
T: Would your mom get off the phone if you asked her to get off? (*Child nods yes.*) Would she? That's a good possibility then.
C: I could just walk over to Sam's house.
T: That's a possibility.

Once the therapist and child have become accustomed to role plays, problems that are specific to the child are introduced as the content of the role plays, and the response-cost contingency would be reapplied to errors, and so on. The therapist can begin to expect generally more thoughtful and successful behaviors within the role plays.

While it is important for the therapist to play an active role in the acting out of problem situations, the child's suggestions and input regarding the setup of each role-play situation are extremely important. The therapist would be wise to encourage the child's participation by getting the child to fill in the details of the problem situation (Where is it happening? Who else is there? What are they doing?). The therapist can also get the child's feedback about aspects of the dialogue (Would your mom really say that like I just did? What would she say?).

Some children may become quite excitable during role playing. An increase in emotional arousal is actually quite desirable; however, this arousal may occasionally take the form of giddiness or silliness that actually impedes the conduct of meaningful role plays. At such times, or any other point at which the child's behavior appears to be out of control, the therapist could hold up a stop sign or ask the child to "freeze" as though he/she were a statue. After having captured the child's attention in this manner, the therapist can focus attention on the child's current behavior and ask the child to problem-solve about what other ways he/she might handle this situation.

Our experience suggests that if the therapist initiates the role plays with enthusiasm and a willingness to share his/her own awkwardness about having to "be an actor" with the child, these sessions can be an involving and enjoyable learning experience for the child. The therapist can use the initiation of the role playing as yet another opportunity to be a coping model.

TRAINING TASKS

We write this section with trepidation, for we have emphasized, in this book and elsewhere, that the actual tasks used in training are quite unimportant relative to the method of task approach that is being taught. While we cannot overemphasize the truth of this statement, we would like to describe those aspects of the nature and sequence of the tasks that do appear to contribute to the effectiveness of training. We describe the sequence using a 12-session format, yet this is merely an illustration of a sequence that would apply to lengthier interventions as well.

We recommend a progression from impersonal, cognitive tasks to more interpersonal, emotionally laden material. Beginning with a simple cognitive task allows the child to devote more of his/her attention to the new method of problem approach without becoming bogged down in the actual mechanics of the task or his/her personal problems. The training program we have researched begins with a simple pattern-matching task ("Which One Comes Next?"), which most children find totally nonthreatening. This emphasis is continued in sessions 2 and 3 via the use of tasks from Barnell-Loft's Specific Skill Series.[2] This series includes tasks that focus on skills such as following directions and using the context more effectively.

Sessions 4, 5, and 6 employ psychoeducational games that provide a transition between the purely impersonal cognitive problems and

2. These pamphlets are available from Barnell-Loft Publishers, Baldwin, New York. Having these particular pamphlets is not crucial to the intervention. They are merely illustrative of the types of tasks that might be used.

more socially oriented games. We have found that children respond well to the "Little Professor" math toy and the games that have been developed to be used in conjunction with it. Tangram puzzles are another example of a pattern-matching task that combines elements of a cognitive problem and a game.

Next, it is appropriate to introduce more typical games, such as checkers. This allows the child to practice the application of the steps with more common activities. The game-type interaction also provides an opportunity for the therapist to begin asking the child more about his/her opinion of what types of situations are most troublesome for him/her. In the current training programs, the therapist and child play checkers in session 7, and a new game, Cat and Mouse, is introduced in session 8. Applying the steps with a totally new game provides an interesting opportunity for transfer of the self-instructional skills for both the therapist and the child.

In session 9, the material becomes more relevant to interpersonal problem solving, for it focuses on the accurate recognition and labeling of emotions. This allows the child to begin to think about the role of emotion in his/her behavioral responses and what types of emotions are produced in various interpersonal situations. Session 10 carries the discussion of interpersonal situations even further by asking the child to think of alternative responses in problematic situations and the possible emotional and behavioral consequences of each alternative. Finally, in sessions 11 and 12 the child is assisted in role playing the various alternatives for problematic situations, with the primary focus being on situations that are particularly difficult for that child.

Applied experience and research (e.g., Kendall & Braswell, 1982b) indicate that the procedures reviewed in this chapter are effective methods of intervention with impulsive children. A more detailed training format as utilized in applied settings and outcome studies, including a summary "therapy checklist" (Table A-9), is presented in the Appendix.

CHAPTER 6

Optimizing Treatment Impact

Confidence in the chosen therapeutic strategy, enthusiasm for the therapist–child interaction, and knowledge of the treatment program all contribute to a rewarding and effective intervention. But even when confidence, enthusiasm, and knowledge are high, there are no guarantees that the desired gains will be forthcoming. Indeed, monitoring of progress and adjusting the implementation of the program will facilitate optimal gains.

In an effort to provide some guideposts that will enhance the implementation of the cognitive–behavioral program, we describe and discuss several factors that offer promise as means of enhancing effectiveness and generalization. Second, the discussion turns to the pitfalls, or potential pitfalls, that can undermine the provision of an effective intervention and suggestions on how to avoid them. Lastly, we remind the reader of the individual difference factors, such as age and intellectual ability, that were examined in Chapter 2 as possible moderators of the effectiveness of the procedures. Whether stressing the things "to do," the things "not to do," or the features of children to whom things "should be done," this chapter emphasizes the various factors that contribute to an optimally effective intervention.

ASSESSMENT AND SELECTION

Perhaps more than any other suggestion for optimizing treatment gains, the careful assessment and proper selection of children deserve special emphasis. Assessment and selection are required for the matching of the type of behavior problem with the intervention of choice. We have already discussed in earlier chapters both the nature of the deficit and assessment strategies for selection and evaluation, so we needn't restate any of the details. The reemergence of these topics at this time is nevertheless justified because of their importance.

Consider the following case. June, we will call her, was a 9-year-old girl referred from a child psychiatry service in a university medical center. She had been diagnosed as hyperactive and was receiving methylphenidate, but she was still reportedly getting in serious trouble at home for impulsive behavior. Her mother had reported that she was out of control and very mischievous—"She just doesn't think." At first blush, the referral seemed appropriate.

A subsequent interview with June's mother revealed that she had an idiosyncratic perspective on impulsive behavior. For instance, June's mother had decided that June could not wear jeans to school. Since the school permitted jeans and many of June's peers wore them, the no-jeans rule was a point of contention. One day June packed a pair of jeans with her school supplies and once at school changed clothes. Because June had to take her medications, she had to report to the school office routinely. On this particular day she forgot and June's mother was notified. In an effort to take action, June's mom went to pick June up from school and, as the reader anticipated, caught her wearing the jeans.

The incident is not uncommon among youngsters. What is uncommon, however, is the perception of this type of rule breaking as impulsive. June planned to wear the jeans, arranged to have a way to get them to school, and was planning a change of clothes before going home. A great deal of forethought, planning, and scheming went into the event. Hardly an impulsive child.

As it turned out, June's problems were largely related to her mother's personality and her mother's sense of ambivalence about the child. With regard to personality, the mother was a rigid, religious, absolutistic, and perfectionistic woman. She was employed part time as a proofreader and prided herself on not missing a single error! If she said no jeans, then it was to be no jeans! Never! Absolutely never. Not even for a special picnic day at school. And, when June and her mom were baking cookies, if it was to be two dozen, then it would be 24 cookies. Not 25, and not 23. When doing dishes, you did silverware first, glasses second, dishes third. That was the order.

The fact that June was a foster child and that her "mother" was a foster mother created ambivalence: "Do I adopt her as my own? No, she's a problem child. . . . Yes, I must care for her." The verbalized ambivalence was also evident in behavior. Sometimes, "mother and daughter" were close, other times "foster mother" threatened "foster child" with being sent to an institution.

Was June an appropriate referral for cognitive–behavioral training? Apparently not. Without careful assessment and selection, June might have been an unsuccessful case, causing frustration for parent and child and mistakenly leading the therapist to conclude that the procedures were ineffective. Forethought and planning on the part of the interviewer, in the form of assessment and selection, cannot be ignored.

COOPERATION AND COLLABORATION

Children are not known for their willingness to cooperate with adults. When the presence of the adults is imposed on the child, as opposed to being self-selected, relationship difficulties can be exacerbated and it is not rare that certain teachers, coaches, or therapists have difficulties interacting with children—especially problem children. An effective therapeutic relationship must overcome these inherent drawbacks and the therapist must make a conscious effort to achieve cooperation and collaboration.

Regarding the cognitive–behavioral training, we cannot emphasize enough the need to work toward and with collaboration. That is, both the end goal and the process require the therapist and child to work together. For example, the therapist and child take turns when rehearsing the self-instructional steps. Turn taking not only enhances the relationship and friendship between therapist and child, but also requires collaboration. Collaborating in the initial sessions, even if as elementary as sharing the use of the training task sheets, sets the foundation for collaboration during later sessions involving more complicated and sophisticated problems.

Role playing the resolution to problem situations requires collaboration. Therapist and child have to work together to determine the roles to be played, how the scene will be set, what problem solutions will be role-played, and what if any props will be used. It is this decision-making process that requires collaboration, for without it the therapist would be merely dictating what paces through which the child should step. As we know, involvement in the therapeutic process contributes to the achievement of desired gains (Braswell *et al.*, 1984b) and the therapist must encourage collaboration as a part of involving the child in the treatment process. In role plays, asking the child "What do you think" and following through on some of the suggestions is one concrete method of involving the child. Similarly, recognizing when the child is involved, such as when a suggestion is offered, and rewarding it must be a part of the therapist's awareness throughout the program.

Cooperation and collaboration also refer to enlisting the support of significant others in the child's environment. Teachers and parents come to mind first since they often create and control the environments in which children spend most of their time, and in the following chapter we describe some strategies for working with these important groups.

TRAINING FOR RELAPSE PREVENTION

The process of learning a new behavior pattern contains both dramatic advances and select setbacks. Indeed, the setbacks are a part of learning. Given the inevitability of setbacks or of a resurgence of a problem situation where the trained skills were inappropriately applied, forgotten, or ineffective, paying direct attention to the management of setbacks is encouraged. We are recommending, not unlike what Marlatt (1979) has encouraged in the treatment of alcohol problems, that a part of the initial remedial intervention address the methods and skills and the desired cognitive interpretations for overcoming relapse and failure experiences.

Assume for the moment that child and therapist have progressed approximately three-quarters of the way through the program and that, until now, the child has succeeded in learning the self-talk, controlling impulsive behavior, and implementing the skills in the classroom context. Assume also that the child is now involved in the school carnival and that he/she has $3 to spend on the various activities. Starting at one booth, he/she spends $2.75 and, when seeing a later, more appealing booth, is short of funds for other activities. The child thinks:

I'm out of money; where can I get more. Oh, no one will give me their money cause they want it. Darn it, I wanted to try shooting baskets [game at the booth]. Heck. (*Pause.*) I guess I should have saved some money or maybe not spent so much on the waterpistol game. If I'd only thought to look at all the booths first. I'm an idiot. I'll never learn to stop and think.

Left uncorrected, this type of thinking can leave marked negative effects. First, the child is making an internal and global attribution for his/her failure. Second, the child is abandoning hope. Third, the child has discounted the self-talk program—not by saying it doesn't or can't work, but by saying he/she can't do it. The entire monologue depicts a loss of self-confidence, a drop in self-efficacy and self-mastery, and a "why not give up" attitude.

Training for relapse involves the specific targeting of failure experiences as part of the initial training program. During the training, the child routinely makes some errors. The "handling" of these error experiences provides the basis for the therapist's assisting the child to manage failure. Therapist modeling, particularly the coping and verbalizing form of modeling, serves to initiate relapse training. The following examples illustrate the procedure during different stages of the program.

Any of the initial sessions offer opportunities for coping with failures to recall the separate self-instructions. Recall that as part of the self-instructional steps, the child is taught to use a coping statement after an error. For instance:

Child: Oops, I goofed. I'll have to remember to go more slowly, be careful, and think ahead.

The therapist, following an error and the related response-cost, can also think out loud in a coping fashion.

Therapist: Oh, was that one too difficult? Maybe. But he did go too fast and that may have been the reason. I know he can do better when he takes his time. We have to practice going slower.

Also, as illustrated in the earlier discussion of the intervention (Chapter 5) and in the subsequent manual (Appendix), the therapist is to be sure to make errors himself/herself and to be a coping and verbalizing model in response to these errors.

While playing a game, such as one of the math-related board games that accompany the Little Professor, it is likely that both child and therapist will have unwanted experiences: landing on a square that requires you lose a turn, for instance. If the contest is close and the child is truly trying to win, such a setback can seriously undermine the progress that has been made. Such occurrences provide opportunities for the therapist to address the fact that they are chance occurrences and not due to anything the child might have done or said. Parts of some games are skill—and one can work to improve these parts, but other parts are chance and no one can control chance. When it is the therapist's turn and something negative results from chance, the therapist might think aloud:

Heck, that sets me back a lot. You're gonna win. Darn. I was trying hard too! (*Pause.*) Well, all I can do is answer the questions—I can't control the roll of the dice. That wasn't my fault, it was just bad luck. (*Pause.*) I'll keep trying, so when my luck is good I can maybe win the game.

Both the homework assignments and the role-play sessions provide further instances for training for relapse. In fact, it is in these contexts that the notion of relapse training is dealt with most directly.

Therapist: Do you remember last time we met I said you could earn some extra chips if you could tell me about a time when you used the steps? Can you tell me a time?
Child: No, I forgot.
T: Oh, well. Let's take some time and think.
C: I can't think of anything.
T: Last week you told me about how you used the steps to think about making your lunch for the bike ride. That was a terrific example. This week you don't have one, but maybe next week you will. I'll remind you at the end of today's meeting. You did well last time so I'm sure you can do it again. This one time doesn't mean you can't do it later on.

Experiencing difficulty with the self-instructional steps and their application to real problem behaviors can be seen in the role-play sessions. Occasionally, a child will throw up his/her hands and give up.

Child: Are we done yet? I want to go back to my class. I just can't do this stuff.
Therapist: Gee, does this one mistake mean you can't do it at all? What do you think?
C: I don't know.
T: Let's take a short break. You know, you did well at this last week. Maybe you're tired, or just don't feel like trying today. We all have ups and downs. We can talk about other stuff for a minute, if you like.

C: What stuff?

T: Well, how's your dog doing?

C: OK, except he got loose yesterday.

T: Did you help find him?

C: Yeah.

(*One minute later.*)

T: OK, let's try another one [referring to role plays]. You know we did several of these very well before we ran into a problem. Let's try and do several more again without a problem. Problems come up, and that's OK; we just have to keep trying and, well, try to have fewer of them. Let's see if we can go on for the rest of today.

The main idea behind training for relapse must be obvious at this point. Accept a failure or an error, label it as a failure or error, but rebound back with a new goal. Also, do not allow the child to attribute the failure experiences to global and internal features. Failures happen to people, and bouncing back is what it takes.

TRAINING FOR GENERALIZATION

The early promise of cognitive–behavioral therapy was that it would overcome the limited generalization produced by pristine behavior modification. Improvements that were evident during and at posttreatment were not being transferred to other contexts. By implementing cognitive training, it was argued, a child would acquire skills that are transsituational: By learning to stop and think on his/her own, the chances for generalization beyond the treatment situations would be greater. While this is true (the chances are greater), we cannot assume that the generalization process is that simple. Rather, generalization may itself require training.

One way to help ensure that learned behaviors in one context will transfer to a second context is to provide some training in the second context. If you desire self-control in the home, then some of the training must include thinking through problems that occur in the home situation. If you desire less impulsive classroom behavior, then training tasks must parallel tasks in the classroom. Generalization is less a magical process and more a trainable goal. Specific sessions focusing on how to use forethought and planning in new and different contexts are encouraged. Working together to answer the question, "Would thinking about this problem help us solve it and how would I have to adjust what I've learned to make it apply?" fosters generalization.

TERMINATION

To the novice, termination means no more than discontinuing the sessions that have been ongoing since treatment was initiated. Quite the contrary is true. Termination is the first effort to determine if the child has learned and can apply the skills to problem situations on his/her own. Not all first efforts are successful, and readdressing certain facets of the problem may be necessary. Thus, termination does not mean the end of contact.

Follow-ups and booster sessions are a part of the posttermination responsibilities of the therapist. How is the child doing in the new classroom? How has he/she adjusted to the new family member? What happened when the child's mother and father fought? Checking up on the child's activities since the formal sessions ended provides the opportunity to remind the child of the thinking strategies, to encourage the child toward higher levels of control, and to reestablish the direct link between real problems and the problem-solving skills.

Booster sessions are recommended in two instances. First, and most obviously, booster sessions are appropriate whenever the child has experienced a difficult situation with an unsuccessful outcome. This type of booster session would involve retracing the problem through its stages and rethinking the various actions along the way. Second, booster sessions can be conceptualized as preventive. If the therapist is aware that a child will be shifted to a new classroom, will be receiving a new family member, or is exposed to parental conflict, then booster sessions can be scheduled for these events before they become problematic. In either case, reliable follow-ups and timely booster sessions contribute meaningfully to the quality and quantity of the eventual gains that are achieved.

SPECIFIC PITFALLS TO AVOID

Murphy's Law states that "if anything can go wrong, it will." As any coordinator of people, schedules, or activities is aware, things typically do not go as planned. Child therapy is not immune. Children do not attend "key" sessions, parents counter therapeutic recommendations, peer pressures undo long sought after gains, and therapists recognize helpful strategies only upon retrospection. The seasoned clinician is all too aware of the vicissitudes of behavior change.

Cognitive–behavioral strategies are subject to the potential difficulties of all therapies and then some. In an effort to prevent unnecessary frustrations when implementing the self-control therapy, and in an effort to provide helpful hints, we discuss several pitfalls that one tries to avoid. These potential pitfalls are specific to the intervention strategy outlined thus far, and must be added to the already long list that pertains to all therapies.

Intensive Task Focus

Becoming overly tied to the specific tasks used within each session for teaching and practicing the self-instructions is a mistake commonly made by novice researchers and practitioners of self-instructional training. Although difficult, the therapist must remain cognizant that the emphasis of this intervention is on teaching thinking *strategies* or processes and not on teaching performance of specific tasks. Obviously, task performance is learned in the process of acquiring these thinking strategies, but the task is a means to an end, *not* the end itself. In other words, whether or not the child becomes a real whiz at math problems, tangram puzzles, or even role plays, is not nearly as important as is the learning of the process of self-talk and problem solving. Written correspondence that we have received from practitioners and researchers suggests that some implementations of the cognitive–behavioral training are perhaps too focused on exact replication of our efforts. That is, some have expressed a desire to copy the exact tasks and implement the use of the tasks in an identical manner. Replications are encouraged, but exact replications are less impressive than conceptual ones. Specifically, if desired gains are evident following cognitive–behavioral training when different tasks are used, we can be more confident of the efficacy of the training than when the tasks are identical. One of the jobs of the practitioner is to identify and select the optimal training tasks for the child or children to be treated.

Even after having determined the specific training tasks, the therapist must still be cautious to prevent an overemphasis on the tasks. For instance, some of the tasks can have multiple answers—two of four choices could be considered correct. In a task requiring the child to pick which picture doesn't belong there are four pictures: (1) a child sleeping; (2) a man sleeping in a chair; (3) a man walking; and (4) a man sleeping on a bed. The text states that (3) is correct—the others are pictures of people sleeping but (3) is of a man walking. Let us assume that the child states that (1) was the picture that didn't belong. A rigid adherence to the tasks might mistakingly lead the therapist to evoke a response-cost for an incorrect response. But was the response incorrect? The goal is to practice and improve the thinking process and a response-cost, if contingent upon careful thinking, would unwittingly detract from the desired goals. Therefore, it would be desirable to inquire of the child the reasoning for his/her choice. "So, you say (1) is different; why did you pick (1)?" The child responds, "All the others are men and this one is a child." While not strictly the best answer, and certainly not the answer indicated in the answer key, the child did think about the task and produced a reasonable answer. Flexible training would provide social reward for careful thinking and point to the other possible answer. However, a response-cost would not be enacted. The task, and the specific task demands and answers, are again less important than the thinking process. Being eyewitness to thinking deserves, if not requires, encouragement, and the task itself can be sidelined for this higher goal.

The therapist should make explicit statements that draw the child's attention to the transsituational or, in this case, transtask, nature of the self-instructions. How readily the child actually grasps this notion will be highly dependent on his/her age and cognitive level, but it is still important for the therapist to, in essence, "preach" generalization of the thinking processes or strategies.

Mechanized Self-Instructions

Mechanical or rote use of the self-instructions by either the therapist or the child is an easy trap. In learning how to slow down and not answer automatically, the repetitive nature of the self-instructions may render the self-instructions themselves overly automatic. Although it is important that the child has rehearsed the self-statements in order to use them consistently, at the same time, different task situations necessitate variations in the exact wording of the self-instructions. Repeated use of the same catch words or phrases is important during the child's initial commitment of the steps to memory, but once the child has a basic knowledge of the steps in the problem-solving process, the therapist should try to think about using variations in his/her verbalizations of the steps. As discussed earlier, the therapist should help the child translate the self-instructions into his/her own words. The child may nevertheless begin to use the personal phrases in an overly mechanistic fashion. The therapist may then need to coax the child to try out new words and phrases. This may be accomplished by simply asking, "What's another way to say that step?" or "What does the second step mean?" It may also be useful for the therapist to "catch" himself/herself being too mechanical in his/her own use of the self-instructions and then model the use of new variations of the old statements. For example, one might state, "Man, I'm starting to sound like a broken record every time I use these steps. I wonder what I could do. . . . I think I'll come up with a new way to say some of these; it will be good to know a lot of different ways to say them. . . ." In this way the therapist can communicate to the child that not only is it all right to use different words, but, in fact, it is considered a good idea to do so.

Tension and Upset

Some children may be upset or tense when they come to the therapy session, or if and when they encounter difficulties with the tasks. In this case, the therapist might try playing a brief game with the child called "Tense–Relax." The game is intended to help relax the child and is played by demonstrating and asking the child the following:

How do people look when they're tense and upset? (*Contract all muscles and squeeze up your face.*) And how do people look when they're relaxed? (*Let out all the tension suddenly and let your body go limp.*)

Let's try this together: Tense (*both you and child tense up*) and relax . . . tense . . . relax . . . tense . . . and relax.

Another game that helps children relax is "Robot–Rag Doll" where both therapist and child act first like robots (stiff and tense and walking without bending limbs) and then like rag dolls (floppy, relaxed, limp). The therapist might check the rag doll floppiness by lifting the child's arm and letting it drop and showing the child how a floppy arm just flops around when you drop it. These relaxation techniques can be employed when the child is apparently tense, but in most cases these games should be kept brief and used only when necessary. If, however, one is working with a child whose impulsivity appears to be mediated as much by anxiety as by a lack of self-control, then relaxation techniques may be made a regular part of the sessions.

In connection with these procedures, it could be explained to the child that sometimes when people get worried, tense, or anxious they don't make good choices. They may tend to pick an answer too quickly or jump ahead to another problem before they have solved the one they were working on originally. The therapist's job is to help them learn to make good choices, to teach them some ways to relax, and, therefore, to reduce the amount of tension their bodies are experiencing.

Rigid Behavioral Contingencies

Flexibility is also a part of the application of the behavioral aspects of a cognitive–behavioral intervention. In this case, flexible does *not* mean inconsistent. Once established, the behavioral contingencies are to be enforced reliably. The particular contingencies utilized with a given child should, however, be tailored or altered to fit that child's needs and should not be rigidly applied in situations where it is clear that the contingencies are not applicable for that child's behavior. The following three cases are offered as examples to illustrate this point.

In a recent study, three of our subjects were so emotionally distressed by the loss of a chip that they could not function effectively in the session. With these children, the response-cost aspects of their program were maintained, but, in addition, at the beginning of each session the children were given the opportunity to earn bonus chips by answering simple questions that reviewed the steps and the events of the previous sessions. The therapists used only questions that they felt these children could answer, for the goal of this program addition was to provide each child with a clear success experience that would set a positive emotional tone at the beginning of the session and increase the child's sense of control over the gain and loss of chips. In addition, with these children, rather than simply keeping a written record of the total number of chips they had remaining from previous sessions (see Appendix), we brought in the actual number of chips and gleefully counted them out with each child at the beginning of the session.

This program modification was effective in completely relieving the distress of two of the three children, but a third child continued to show some signs of emotional discomfort. In the face of his distress, we came up with the following modification. We suggested that his therapist should allot 20 chips to herself, as well as to the child, and when she was performing problems the child should be instructed to response-cost her according to the same rules she was using with him. This provided the therapist with a natural opportunity to model appropriate coping with mistakes, response-cost experiences, and loss situations in general. In addition, it increased the gamelike quality of the interaction between the therapist and child, which resulted in a decrease in the child's anxiety in the session. Following this alteration, the child was able to participate, accept response-cost enactments, and actually express enjoyment of the training activities.

A fourth case illustrates the potential importance of the backup reinforcers that are available on the reward menu. During a recent treatment study, one of the fifth grade girls referred for training was not responding well in the sessions. Despite valiant efforts on the part of her therapist, the girl persisted in being hostile and resistant to the procedures; she did not seem at all motivated by the potential rewards she could receive. Our standard reward menu included a wide variety of items appropriate for use in the school setting, such as pens, pencils, and folders. This array of rewards was determined to be desirable in the previous treatment studies, but it clearly was not having the intended impact on this girl's behavior. In talking with her teacher and listening to comments within the session, we hypothesized that we had failed to recognize that this fifth grader actually viewed herself more as an adolescent, and she was insulted by our perception of her as a little girl who would be motivated by the chance to earn such "little kid stuff." Our hypothesis was confirmed, for we found that once we altered her reward menu by adding items geared for adolescent females, such as teen magazines, makeup, and various grooming trinkets, she became quite engaged in the training.

Aversive Context

A final potential pitfall concerns making the therapy sessions unnecessarily aversive for the child. Handling this concern will require some special attention to scheduling. In a school-based intervention program, the therapist should avoid scheduling sessions during recess or any of the child's highly preferred activities. Achieving this goal may require some careful consultation with the child's classroom teacher, for it would also be undesirable to have the child consistently miss class time spent on content areas that are already particularly difficult for that child. Clearly, some negotiation with both the teacher and the child may be necessary, but the point is to avoid cutting the child off from reinforcing activities.

With clinic-based interventions, scheduling may also be an issue. Demanding that the child consistently miss some favored after-school activity in order to come to the sessions will not enhance the therapist–child relationship.

In order to keep the therapy from becoming aversive, it seems to be important to learn how the child's teachers and parents are labeling the intervention. If the important adults in the child's life consider the therapy a waste of time or refer to it as something the child needs because he/she is "sick and dangerous," the child is certainly less likely to develop a positive attitude about the intervention. Suggesting that parents and/or teachers refer to the treatment as a special training program that will help the child learn how to solve problems in new ways and avoid some of the difficulties or hassles he/she has been experiencing is highly desirable.

Subject Variables

The relationship between treatment outcome and certain subject variables was reviewed in Chapter 2. We want to remind the reader of that review, and to state once again that attending to the age and cognitive level of the child is extremely important. Optimizing treatment success is in large part associated with a careful examination of the features of the child client.

It is our belief that by following these recommendations regarding what features to optimize and what pitfalls to avoid, the therapist will increase the amount of variance in treatment outcome over which he/she exerts control. As indicated by the nature of the suggestions in this chapter, if it is to be successful, self-instructional training cannot be implemented as a formulaic treatment package. Rather, like any other effective intervention, it requires a sensitive therapist who can process a myriad of subtle variables, collaborate with the child client, and calibrate the intervention accordingly.

CHAPTER 7

Working with Parents, Teachers, and Groups of Children

As is true for virtually every intervention, the goal of cognitive–behavioral training is the generalization of the knowledge and skills acquired in the therapy session to the child's "real-world" environments such as the home and classroom. One of the powerful methods for programming this generalization is to prepare the child's parents or teachers to recognize and foster the child's newly developing thinking and problem-solving skills. Another means of fostering generalization is for the child to be taught these skills in the presence of other children.

We have some suggestions regarding how parents and teachers can be taught to enhance the child's cognitive and behavioral problem-solving skills, and how cognitive–behavioral children's groups could be conducted, but we must note that they really are suggestions and not research findings. Our research has addressed and answered several questions about the training procedures, but we are only beginning to systematically investigate some of the issues we will be describing in this chapter. Nevertheless, the concepts and recommendations presented are based on our years of experience and we do have confidence in them.

WORKING WITH PARENTS

One may not always have the luxury of working with both parents and the child, but it is our contention that it is highly desirable to require some form of parental involvement—for example, conducting a parent group concurrently with the child's training. A parent group, as opposed to individual parent meetings, reduces the required professional time. Parent groups also provide an opportunity for developing a cohesive effort at resolving child problems. But what is the content of the parent group?

We propose that the parent groups focus on features of the training that their children are receiving. Our goal is to try to enlist the parents in the therapy of their child—our goal is not parent therapy, though parents seem to learn and to adjust their own behavior as a result of targeting the child. The following suggestions are offered as examples of the format and content that might be utilized in a parent group. Although our preference is for an active parent group, written materials (such as the handout prepared by Braswell, Shapiro, & Kendall, 1984a) for parents can be provided in lieu of the group meeting.

Form of Parent Training

Typically, parents are not knowledgeable about the actual procedures used in the treatment of their child. They may have read a brief summary if they signed an informed consent sheet, but the anxiety and general stress of the initial meeting often cloud the parents' actual understanding of the training. To communicate to the parents the nature of the treatment provided for their child we advocate assuming a didactic stance in the initial sessions. As you might expect, these initial sessions are easily conducted in group format. However, we recommend that no more than four or five sets of parents be a part of any single group. Sharing among the group members is extremely desirable, and as groups become too large such sharing becomes psychologically more difficult for each parent and logistically difficult owing to the sheer numbers of people and the limits of time.

The initial didactic presentation may take 4 to 5 hours, and could be broken down into two to five separate sessions. Following the presentation of the basic concepts and ideas, the parents are encouraged to discuss and explore how these notions could be applied with specific situations in their home lives. Parents with special needs and concerns that they do not want to discuss in a group format might wish to have individual discussions with the therapist. To the extent that each child's behavior problems can be conceptualized as similar, however, such discussions can be more profitable and effective in the group format.

Out first task is to have the parents walk through the sessions that the child is or will be experiencing. This encounter not only informs the parents of the specifics of the training, but also demonstrates that the training takes time and patience and that a structured sequence is important. The description of the training highlights the central role of modeling and, without pointing the finger at the parents, demonstrates how the therapist models cognitive problem solving and suggests that parents could do likewise in their home environments. The tasks used in training resemble many games and materials available in the home and, once parents have been told of the training, their ideas for home tasks and how to apply the procedures would help to assure that the connection to home use has been made.

The actual length and number of these didactic sessions is open to the discretion of the therapist. We do recommend at least two sessions (or one 2-hour session) for communication of the cognitive–behavioral perspective and methods, and another two sessions or hours devoted to discussion of the application of these concepts and procedures to specific situations.

Content of Parent Training

PURPOSE

While this may seem all too obvious, we still feel the need to state that the therapist should outline the purpose of the parent training, as well as the child training, at the beginning of the first training session. We let the parents know at the outset that while it is possible to help their children learn new thinking strategies in their therapy sessions, it's up to the parents to model appropriate thinking strategies (and not to model *non*thinking) and to reinforce and encourage the use of these strategies in the home environment. In other words, the trainer explains the concept of generalization to the parents. While discussing generalization, the therapist emphasizes a collaborative "teamwork" approach to improving the child's behavior, with the parents heading up a team that includes themselves, the child, the child's therapist, and the child's teacher. It could also be explained that, in simplest terms, the purpose of the child's therapy is to help him/her learn to stop, slow down, and consider all the available behavioral alternatives when faced with a problem, and that this method must be applied and encouraged in school and at home.

THE COGNITIVE–BEHAVIORAL PERSPECTIVE

Parents may wonder if the training is "behavior modification," "play therapy," or "psychoanalysis." Some discussion of these other approaches is helpful to distinguish the cognitive–behavioral perspective.

It is our experience that parents often enjoy discovering what it means to take a cognitive–behavioral perspective. The trainer might even provide the parents with a formal (but understandable) definition, such as the following.

Cognitive–behavioral therapy represents an amalgam of the emphasis of cognitive psychology on the effects of thinking on behavior and the emphasis of behavioral psychology on the beneficial effects of performance-based training.

Or, to use less academic language, parents can be told that practice is essential to learning and that their child needs to practice thinking before acting. Other definitions of the cognitive–behavioral perspective appear in graduate texts (e.g., Kendall & Hollon, 1979), journal articles (e.g., Mahoney, 1977b), and undergraduate texts (e.g., Coleman, Butcher, & Carson, 1980).

Any definition will require some explication and discussion, but it is important to convey to the parents the joint emphasis upon thought (cognition) and action (behavior). The therapist can point out that one feature distinguishing cognitive–behavioral approaches with children from other types of child interventions is the therapeutic emphasis upon *thinking processes*. This focus on adaptive thinking processes is in contrast to the behaviorists' emphasis on teaching specific skills or discrete behaviors. It might also be noted that in stressing the need to modify thinking processes, cognitive–behavioral child therapists teach *strategies* that are designed to be aids to adjustment across a variety of settings. To allay any parental fears that the child's therapist isn't really concerned with behavior change, the trainer might add that, of course, changes in specific behaviors are considered desirable end products. Selected behaviors are shaped and rewarded throughout treatment, but an essential characteristic of the cognitive–behavioral model is the assumption that it is the training at the level of the cognitive processes that control behavior that will result in the generalization or diffusion of treatment effects to many different situations. The child's feelings during this process are also addressed.

BACKGROUND INFORMATION
Providing the parents with some information on the background of the intervention can build acceptance and respect for this particular approach. Such a presentation might include a review of the background literature (appropriately modified for a nonprofessional audience), as well as a discussion of the factors that led mental health professionals to become interested in adopting the cognitive–behavioral perspective.

In our minds these factors include discontent with previously established treatments for externalizing children, such as psychostimulant medication and strict behavioral interventions, and a growing concern that treatment should enhance the child's sense of internal control and responsibility with regard to his/her behavior.

MAJOR COGNITIVE-BEHAVIORAL CONCEPTS

Following the presentation of background information, the trainer is ready to begin introducing the parents to some cognitive–behavioral concepts. While it is our intent that the understanding of these concepts will help them better understand and explain their child's behavior, it is also possible that learning about these notions may help them understand and, if necessary, change *their own* attitudes and behavior toward their child. While there are a number of concepts that could be discussed, we have opted to limit our discussion to what a trainer might say regarding the concepts of expectancies, attributions, and self-statements.

It may be advisable to begin the discussion of cognitive–behavioral concepts by talking about *expectancies*, for most lay people have some general understanding of an expectancy. They may also have a general acceptance of the notion that what an individual expects or anticipates may have some bearing on what that individual does. The parents, however, are not likely to be familiar with the idea that expectancies can be general or global, as well as rather specific.

An example of a generalized expectancy that may hold across a range of situations is the notion of locus of control. We recognize that this concept may be aptly referred to as the "locust" of control, for there has been an infestation of studies (and it continues) devoted to the exploration of this concept. Despite its pervasiveness, or perhaps because of it, the concept deserves consideration. Indeed, evidence supports the merits of this concept as a generalized expectancy.

As proposed by Rotter (1966), someone with an internal locus of control expects events to result from his/her own actions and abilities, whereas someone with an external locus of control expects chance, fate, or powerful others to determine what happens to him/her. Considering this concept in light of the two purposes we previously enumerated, the parents could be asked to think about whether their child seems to expect that what happens to him/her is controlled by his/her own actions or whether the child expects that the events that happen to him/her are always the result of something external to himself/herself, such as luck or powerful others. In addition, the parents could be asked to reflect upon their own behavior, particularly their behavior in relation to the child. Do they expect that the nature and quality of their interactions with their child will be determined by their own actions, or do they consider it to be a matter of luck or something else external to themselves?

The trainer can also point out that expectancies can be much more specific or related to a particular issue or activity. For example, the kind of expectancy one has for the effectiveness of therapy may have a very real influence on just how effective the therapy actually is, and there is a significant body of literature to support this conclusion, although this research is not without its methodological problems (Bootzin & Lick, 1979; Kazdin, 1979b; Lick & Bootzin, 1975; Wilkins, 1973, 1979). Another type of specific expectancy worth mentioning to the parents concerns the concept of self-efficacy expectations (Bandura, 1977). It can be explained that self-efficacy expectations refer to the person's expectation that he/she is capable of successfully performing the act or acts necessary to achieve a certain goal or outcome. The parents can be asked to think about what kinds of self-efficacy expectations they believe their child may have regarding his/her ability to accomplish various tasks, such as getting a good grade on a math test, keeping his/her cool when angered by siblings, or successfully playing a game with peers. In addition, the parents could be encouraged to disclose and discuss their self-efficacy expectations regarding their own abilities to handle a variety of parenting tasks such as helping their child with his/her homework, resolving sibling conflicts, and clearly expressing their affection for their child. Moreover, parents may be holding expectations for their child that are beyond the child's developmental level. Providing some developmental education to parents would help to place their expectations in a more realistic framework.

The concept of *attributions* is clearly related to the concept of expectancies. The therapist could explain to the parents that attributions are beliefs that people develop to explain their behavior and why events happen as they do. While attributions are similar to expectancies, attributions *follow* a behavioral event and are attempts to explain its cause, whereas expectancies *precede* a behavioral event (see Kendall & Braswell, 1982a). For our purposes the literature with which we are most interested concerns the elucidation of different dimensions of attributions (e.g., Weiner, Frieze, Kukla, Reed, Rest, & Rosenbaum, 1971) and their relation to psychopathology (e.g., Abramson, Seligman, & Teasdale, 1978). In a paper on the application of cognitive–behavioral strategies in the treatment of marital discord, Baucom (1981) discussed how the consideration of attributions and their various dimensions may have relevance for marital therapy. In a similar vein, we believe the discussion of attributions and their dimensions can play a role in child-management (parent) training.

One dimension described by Abramson *et al.* (1978) is the tendency to attribute problems or events to internal (within the person) factors versus external (outside the person) factors. This is very similar to the generalized expectancy of locus of control mentioned previously. To provide an example, parents may attribute their child's problematic behavior to factors outside the child (e.g., a poorly structured environment), or factors inside the child (e.g., neurological impairment). In explaining this notion, the therapist may want to emphasize that it is unlikely that one or the other factor is "right"; rather, as Baucom (1981) noted, the point is to highlight the multiple causation of problems. Parents can also be encouraged to discuss this notion with regard to their parenting abilities. Their unsuccessful parenting efforts could be the result of their own lack of skill (internal factor) or the severity of their child's problem (external factor), and it is most likely to be the result of some combination of these factors.

Another relevant dimension of attributions concerns their global versus specific nature. Global attributions are those that could apply across a range of different situations, such as attributing difficulties to the severity of the child's impulsivity. Specific attributions, on the other hand, are those that affect only a limited number of situations, such as the child's failure to read each answer on a multiple-choice test before he/she responds. The trainer can point out to the parents that global attributions, although they may occasionally be true, are, for several reasons, likely to be less productive explanatory concepts than specific attributions. Global attributions are typically stated in vague and unclear terms, whereas specific attributions are stated in clear, behavioral terms. Also, global attributions can have a derogatory quality and may be anger-producing in the child, whereas specific attributions are less inflammatory. In addition, global attributions are often stated in terms that make the problem seem unchangeable while specific attributions almost provide the prescription for change. After explaining this notion, the therapist can help parents translate their global attributions about their child and/or themselves into more specific behavioral terms.

Attributions can also be characterized as stable versus unstable. Stable attributions are those that are less likely to be altered, such as the child's general lack of self-control. Unstable attributions are those that, in the right circumstances, allow for the possibility of change, such as the child's frequency of jumping up out of his/her seat in a specific situation. The trainer might explain to parents that although, as was the case with global attributions, there may be some truth to the stable nature of certain causes of their child's behavior, it may be much more productive (not to mention more hopeful) to focus their attention on those more specific aspects of the child's behavior that can legitimately be viewed as unstable or changeable.

Self-statements are another cognitive–behavioral concept that require some discussion with parents. The therapist might explain that "internal dialogues," "automatic thought," "internal sentences," and "self-statements" are all phrases that have been employed to refer to those things that people say to themselves. The therapist could also note that, clearly, self-statements are not independent of the constructs previously discussed. Attributions and expectancies are manifested, at least in part, via self-statements, but self-statements can be many different things, including statements of strategies and plans. The introduction of the topic of self-statements and the effort to underscore their universality can be accomplished in a lighthearted manner. The group leader might begin by asking, "How many people talk to themselves?" Most audience members raise their hands, but some will not. The group leader then comments, "Those of you who didn't raise your hands are saying to yourselves, 'I don't talk to myself.'" The routine reaction is laughter as participants recognize the paradox.

To further explain this concept to the parents, the trainer might make the following statements:

To clarify this notion of self-statements or self-instructions, it is important to realize that we all engage in self-talk at various times. One clear example is when you are learning to perform some new type of activity. Perhaps you can remember when you first learned to drive a car. Most of us began by driving while our parents or driving teacher talked to us and told us what to do. Then we began to talk ourselves through even the most basic maneuvers: "Let's see . . . I have to turn the key in the ignition . . . then I push in the clutch with my left foot and pull the stick back into reverse . . . OK, now I'm ready to back up. . . ." Eventually this self-talk went from being overt to being covert. That is, we quit talking out loud and began to think the instructions to ourselves. Finally, the actions involved in driving became so automatic that we didn't need to consciously talk ourselves through them each time. To cite another common example, many of us consciously talk to ourselves when we are dancing or at least when we are learning to dance. First we may say the steps aloud and use the words to direct our physical behavior. As we practice more we just count or say cue words quietly to ourselves and, eventually, we don't have to consciously talk ourselves through each step. If we do not practice regularly, however, we may find that each time we dance we must talk to ourselves again, as we attempt to recall the steps or actions that once were automatic. With regard to parenting tasks, both mothers and fathers may have had to talk themselves through the first few diapers they changed, but this process quickly became automatic!

After introducing the parents to the cognitive–behavioral concepts of expectancies, attributions, and self-statements and encouraging extensive discussion directed at helping the parents see how these constructs are relevant to their thinking about their child *and* their own parenting ability, the trainer can describe the cognitive–behavioral procedures being utilized with the child in his/her individual training sessions. For descriptions of most of these procedures the reader is referred to Chapter 5. A specific example of what the therapist might say when explaining self-instructional training to a group of parents is presented in Braswell *et al.* (1984a).

When a discussion of the cognitive–behavioral training procedures has been completed, the trainer is then ready to begin helping the parents recognize what they can do at a behavioral level to encourage the development and maintenance of improved problem solving in the home.

WHAT CAN THE PARENT DO TO IMPROVE TREATMENT EFFECTIVENESS?

Modeling in the Home

The therapist can share with the parents that you don't have to be a psychologist to know that all children learn by seeing things done. Children with attentional difficulties or learning problems often have an even greater need to watch someone model appropriate task performance. The therapist can then explain that just as verbal self-instructional training emphasizes teaching the child *how* to do a task, the best type of modeling a parent can provide also emphasizes *how* a given behavioral goal is to be accomplished. Often it is simply not enough for parents just to tell the child what they want him/her to do. It is necessary for the parents to show the child what they want him/her to do *and* how they want him/her to accomplish it.

To illustrate this point, the trainer might share the example of the mother who had a difficult time getting her son to put his belongings away in the correct places when he arrived home from school. She tried reminding him to put his things away when he walked in, but this didn't seem to help. Then it occurred to her that her son might not have a clear idea or plan for what it meant to put his belongings in their appropriate places, so for the next 2 days she greeted him at the door when he returned home and actually walked him through the actions required to accomplish this task. She showed him how he could first place his snowboots by the door and hang his coat in the nearby closet after placing his mittens in the coat pockets. Then he was to set his lunch box in the appropriate place on the kitchen counter and take his book bag to his room. She emphasized the advantages of this method by showing him it took only 1 minute to put his belongings away in an orderly fashion right after school, whereas it sometimes took him much longer to put them away after he had already strewn them all over the house.

In addition, the therapist can point out that not only do we know that modeling is an effective way to teach children what we want them to learn, but we also know some factors that increase the chance or likelihood that the child will actually perform the behaviors or actions they have seen modeled.

First of all, the type of relationship the child has with the person doing the modeling is an influential factor. If the model is someone the child looks up to and feels warmly about, then the child is more likely to imitate the model. Thus, all other considerations aside, a child is more likely to imitate a given behavior if it is modeled by a loved and respected parent than if it is modeled by someone who is disliked or not close to the child. The therapist might admit that, granted, there are times when it probably seems as though children would purposefully do the opposite of whatever they saw their parent do, but for the most part parents are powerful models for their children, particularly elementary-school-aged children. If the parents are skeptical of this notion, ask them to think for a moment about how many of their "bad habits" they've seen their child imitate! The trainer can then emphasize that parents can help their children by realizing what extremely important models they are, and by letting this realization help them control and direct their own behavior.

Another thing that might be beneficial to point out about modeling is that children are more likely to imitate the behavior of a verbalizing model. As discussed in Chapter 5, kids are more likely to copy a model who talks about or describes what it is that he/she is doing. Perhaps this is because it gives the child a chance to not only *see* the right thing to do but to also *hear* the right thing to do. To illustrate this point, the therapist could state something like "Your child might learn what to do by watching you correctly solve a math problem or watching you correctly set the dinner table, but he/she is likely to learn more if you also describe your actions as you are actually doing them. In a way, you could think of it as sharing your own self-instructions with the child."

Finally, the trainer could reaffirm that research indicates that children are more likely to imitate what is referred to as a *coping* model than they are to imitate a *mastery* model. As indicated in Chapter 5, the advantage of the coping model may be that it gives the child more information about *how* to do a given task or *how* to overcome the emotional or behavioral problems he/she has that potentially interfere with correct task performance. Of course, it would be silly for the parent to constantly "play dumb" so he/she can be a coping model for his/her child. Nevertheless, each day presents natural opportunities for the parent to be a coping model. The therapist could then state, "For example, say your child is having a hard time fitting everything he/she needs to take to school into his/her book bag. You have a choice: You could be a mastery model and quickly fit everything into the bag as soon as you see how it needs to be arranged, or you could be a coping model and take a more trial-and-error approach in which you tested out different ways of fitting all the objects into the bag." Again, the coping model seems to be more powerful as a learning tool because it gives the child more information about the *process* or "how-to" part of problem solving.

Behavioral Contingencies

In an effort to further enhance treatment generalization, the therapist may also wish to discuss how parents can arrange the contingencies within the home environment to reinforce reflective problem solving.

Children with externalizing behavior problems are often in need of greater structure in their environments than is the case for other children. One method parents can use to increase the structure in the home environment is to be very clear and consistent about what is acceptable and unacceptable behavior. It is equally important for parents to be clear and consistent about the consequences for the acceptable and unacceptable behavior. Depending on the skill level of the parents and the interests of the therapist, some of the group time could be devoted to discussion of basic contingency management procedures, or the parents could be referred to one of the therapist's favorite books on this topic. In some cases where the parents appear to be in need of more intensive training in the area of behavioral management, they might be referred to other parent education programs.

Of relevance to the current topic is the issue of how parents might use behavioral contingencies to enhance the treatment effectiveness of verbal self-instructional thinking. Toward this end, the trainer could encourage the parents to provide social recognition—in the form of a smile or words of praise and encouragement—whenever the child is observed to be making an effort at reasoning through some type of problem. The therapist might remind the parent that a child is unlikely to produce sophisticated reasoning as a part of problem formulations, but fledgling efforts at reflective problem solving should be rewarded. One could then help the parents identify situations in which they might be able to "catch" their child being a careful thinker. One class of such opportunities involves any situation in which the child has to pause and consider a number of alternatives. For example, the trainer might say, "The next time you allow your child to select a treat at the grocery store, try to fight against the tendency to tell him/her to hurry and, instead, comment that you can see he/she is thinking slowly and carefully in order to make the best choice." Or the trainer could encourage the parents to take notice the next time their child is puzzling over the rules of a new game and make a remark such as, "I can see you're trying to figure out the right way to play. That's great."

In some situations it will be necessary for the parents to use punishment or response-cost types of contingencies with their children. The therapist can help the parents learn to handle such situations in a manner that might ultimately enhance the child's self-control by emphasizing that the usefulness of such contingencies may hinge upon the manner in which they are employed and explained to the child (as well as the extent to which they are consistent). Using the example of "grounding," the therapist might point out that a brief period of time out, such as a few minutes away from a play area, will be sufficiently potent to be a deterrent for young children. Using threats such as "I'll ground you for a month" will only undermine the effectiveness of the contingency, since, almost without exception, parents do not follow through on such grandiose threats. One doesn't need a shotgun to swat a mosquito.

Time out can also be introduced as a period of time when the child can calm himself/herself down and rethink the problem situation. The therapist might ask the parents which of the following methods of enacting a time out is most likely to foster better problem solving in the child.

> A. "Jim, I've told you 100 times that you shouldn't hit your little brother. You stupid kid. Why can't you act right? Go to your room and stay there until I say to come out."
>
> B. "Jim, you are hitting your little brother and that is against the rules in our house. I think you need some time to calm yourself down and get back in control of your own behavior. Go to your room and stay there until you have gotten yourself under control."

In both examples, the unacceptable behavior is labeled; however, Example A also contains insults that may only serve to further hurt and anger Jim. Example B contains no insults and presents the time out not only as a negative consequence for a negative behavior (hitting) but also as an opportunity for the child to "pull himself together" and reflect more on his behavior in order to do a better job. The use of such examples is almost sure to spark further discussion.

In Summary

We propose that providing the parents with new conceptual tools and suggestions on how to think through their own home behaviors will foster improvement in their child's problem solving. Methods of enhancing generalizations of behavioral improvements to the home environment require parent involvement and support.

WORKING WITH TEACHERS

All the concepts and procedures discussed in the parent education program would certainly be relevant and appropriate for presentation to the teachers of non-self-controlled children who are in cognitive–behavioral treatment. Having 4 to 6 hours per week of teacher time is unlikely, so unless one is fortunate enough to present a workshop or is working with an exceptionally dedicated teacher, one may not be able to communicate all the concepts discussed in the parent section. Accordingly, we have suggestions about what information is most important to communicate given limited teacher contact.

As with parents, it is essential that the clinician tell the teacher the purpose of the intervention with the child. While the therapist will be helping the child learn new skills, the generalization of these skills to the home and school settings requires a team approach, with the parents, teacher, and therapist all considering themselves members of the intervention team. After sharing this, the therapist should reassure the teacher that he/she is not expected to actually become a therapist in the classroom, for he or she is responsible for many children, but that nevertheless, an informed teacher is the key to the generalization of treatment effects.

In addition to some specific suggestions that will be presented shortly, the two general concepts worth communicating to the teacher are the notions of self-instructions and modeling. The therapist should describe the actual self-instructional sequence the child is learning and how these steps are applied to different types of tasks. Then he/she might explain that while the child is explicitly taught the steps, much of the learning is the result of the therapist's modeling of the use of self-instructions. At that point, the clinician might also share the distinction between mastery and coping modeling, emphasizing how coping modeling seems most effective with these children for it teaches them strategies for overcoming frustrations and obstacles to problem solutions. Some curious teachers might question why children would learn more from a display of difficulty in problem solving versus a superior performance in solving the same problem. If such a question occurs, the therapist emphasizes that, ideally, both types of models eventually produce the "correct" answer, but that the coping model also indirectly communicates what one can do when things are not going smoothly or when one is feeling fearful or anxious. Thus, the coping model may be more reflective of what the child's own experience would be if he/she were trying to solve a given problem.

The therapist can also offer some direct suggestions for how the teacher can aid generalization of treatment effects. One obvious suggestion is for the teacher to accept and perhaps even encourage the child's quiet self-talk if the child appears to be using such verbalizations as a means of guiding and directing his/her own behavior in an appropriate manner. If the child becomes an object of ridicule by peers for this self-talk, the teacher might make a general statement to the class that reframes talking to oneself as a desirable thing to do if it is done quietly and results in better-quality work. Since singling out a child in this manner can have unwanted effects, it is best to have the child self-instruct silently when in the classroom. The teacher might also label the attack strategies he/she presents for solving math problems or decoding words as just more specific examples of self-instructions that we can use to help ourselves solve those particular types of problems. When the teacher is willing to assume a slightly more active role, he/she can help the child implement strategies that result in a better work focus. For example, Parsons (1972) found that if children were required to both name the operation required for a specific math problem (plus vs. minus) and circle the sign of each problem as they began to solve it, their performance on addition and subtraction problems was significantly improved. In our terminology, the tasks of naming the operation and circling the sign made the children truly answer the question of "What am I supposed to do?"

In a similar vein, the teacher might be able to help an individual child develop a short checklist that he/she can use to improve the quality of his/her work in a given type of assignment. For example, questions on a writing assignment checklist might include "Did I begin each sentence with a capital letter?," "Did I put a punctuation mark at the end of each sentence?," "Did I indent at the beginning of each new paragraph?" As the child's assignments show that he/she has mastered the initial problem areas, new and more sophisticated questions are included on the checklist (e.g., "Does each sentence have a subject and a verb?," "Did I start a new paragraph whenever I began a new topic or idea?"). Ideally, the teacher and student can work together to develop the checklist, with the teacher first asking the child what he/she thinks should be on the checklist. The teacher can refer to this list as a special set of self-instructions, designed to help with writing (or whatever the assignment).

If the classroom curriculum includes materials related to social problem solving, such as affective programs like Toward Affective Development (TAD) or Developing Understanding of Self and Others (DUSO),[1] then the teacher could be urged to be explicit about the relationship between these materials and what the child is learning in his/her individual sessions. In such a situation the teacher might point out that learning to recognize feelings is an important part of interacting with others. Being able to identify and label feelings accurately also helps us to identify the emotional consequences that our behavior has, for ourselves as well as for others. Finally, with the parents' and child's permission, it would be appropriate to share with the teacher the

1. TAD and DUSO are published by the American Guidance Service, Circle Pines, Minnesota.

special problem areas the child has agreed to work on or the therapist plans to have the child work on, so that the teacher can be particularly attuned to offer social praise and reinforcement for any positive behavior changes in those areas.

WORKING WITH CHILDREN IN GROUPS

While most of our research and clinical experiences have involved an individual therapist working with an individual child, we believe many of the cognitive–behavioral procedures can be effectively applied in a group setting. The ideal treatment plan for any given child certainly depends on the nature of that child's strengths and deficits, but for many of the non-self-controlled children we have observed an optimal plan might include 12 to 16 individual sessions followed by participation in a group that incorporates some of the principles and procedures we will be describing. The one-to-one work would help the child establish some initial controls and introduce him/her to the notions of self-instructions and problem solving, and the group format would provide supervised practice of social problem solving in a setting with peers.

As discussed in Chapter 2, Kendall and Zupan (1981) examined the effectiveness of self-instructional training conducted in a group format and obtained some positive gains. As our thinking has evolved, however, we do not believe that the structure and format applied in the Kendall and Zupan study actually capitalized on the richness of the group experience, for it basically involved the therapist interacting with three or four children in the same manner as he/she interacted with children in the individual sessions: child by child, taking turns. The group procedures we have chosen to describe were developed (and continue to be elaborated) by Urbain (1982). These procedures make an active effort to incorporate the behavior occurring within the group as a part of the child's learning experience. The cognitive–behavioral training builds, nurtures, and utilizes the group process.

In this section we will describe the major concepts and the specific format of our recommended groups. Many of the cognitive–behavioral concepts and procedures come from our earlier work with individuals and have been described in greater detail in Chapter 5. They will receive only brief discussion here to illustrate their application with groups. Readers desiring a more detailed description of a related cognitive–behavioral group program might consult the Urbain manual (1982).

Major Concepts

Urbain's group program, as is true for the individual program also, could best be described as a cognitive–affective–behavioral approach for it incorporates content and procedures from the domain of interpersonal cognitive problem solving, affective education, and traditional behavioral management. In the group context, spontaneous emotionality can be triggered by the peer interactions such that the affective component can be real and genuine for that moment and provides "affective content" for the training program.

Within the area of interpersonal cognitive problem solving, a number of discrete, yet related, interpersonal problem-solving skills have been delineated by various investigators (see reviews by Butler & Meichenbaum, 1981; Kendall *et al.*, 1981a). Spivack, Platt, Shure, and their associates propose that interpersonal cognitive problem-solving skills include problem sensitivity, generation of alternatives, consequential thinking, causal thinking, and means–ends thinking (Spivack *et al.*, 1976). In a similar vein, D'Zurilla and Goldfried (1971) outlined five stages of problem solving, including general orientation, problem definition and formulation, generation of alternatives, decision making, and verification. Clearly, these systems evidence a great deal of similarity and reflect the beginning of a consensus on the nature of problem solving. Cognitive–behavioral training incorporates these notions with a great deal of explicit attention in groups devoted both to the concepts of problem identification and generation of alternative solutions and to the practice of identifying problems and generating alternatives.

Problem identification involves helping the child (1) recognize that a problem or opportunity for problem solving exists, and (2) identify what the specific problem is. This is equivalent to the first step in the five-step self-instructional sequence described earlier. Urbain (1982) refers to this with the catch phrase "STOP AND THINK." This phrase becomes the cue that a problem exists and that group members should focus their attention on identifying the problem that needs solving. The group is given some formal instruction regarding what it means to "STOP AND THINK," and the group leader may hold up a "STOP AND THINK" sign during ongoing group activities as a signal that some problem exists involving the behavior of the group members.

Generating alternatives or thinking of different ideas to solve a problem is a second focus of group training. The emphasis at this point is on the process of generating ideas, *not* on the quality of each alternative. An example of a brainstorming exercise to help the children develop their ability to think of different alternatives to selected problem situations involves a picture game in which a problem situation is depicted and the group must generate as many different alternatives as possible. Each group member could be required to generate at least one of the alternatives. If the leader senses that the group has difficulty with the basic concept of generating alternatives—independent of the problem situation—then it might be wise to back up a step and devote some time to exercises that convey the notion of alternatives. In one such exercise, the leader could hold up a simple object, such as a stick, and explain that he/she wants the group members to use their imaginations to come up with three different things this stick could represent (e.g., a golf club, a sword, a baton, a fishing pole). The children could then be asked to act out their choices and have the other group members guess their alternatives. A variation on this type of exercise involves having each child pick a special movement of his/her arms and legs and perform this for the group. The group then has to come up with three different alternative explanations of this movement (he/she is sawing wood; or dancing; or playing tug-of-war).

The affective education aspect of the program emphasizes notions from the domain of social cognition such as perspective taking, as well as the recognition, identification, and appropriate labeling of "feelings." Perspective taking is introduced via the phrase, "Put yourself in the other guy's shoes." This act is explained to the children as a way in which they can learn to understand the feelings of another person by pretending or imagining that they are that other person. Role playing is the chief procedure used to dramatize this notion. Group time is also spent discussing what a feeling or emotion is and how feelings are communicated or expressed in different ways. The children can be helped in developing an "emotions vocabulary" via activities such as creating a "feelings dictionary." This activity involves taking a piece of posterboard and writing the headings POSITIVE, NEUTRAL, and NEGATIVE at the top. The children are then asked to generate "feelings words" that could be listed under each heading. Children often need some assistance in generating positive and negative emotions, and the therapist may have to assist them in identifying more neutral emotions such as "calm" or "bored." Activities such as drawing faces expressive of different emotions, having the children act out different emotions via bodily gestures and facial expressions, or having them guess what feeling the therapist is modeling are all methods of helping them recognize and label feelings.

The behavioral aspect of the program appears primarily through the use of a token economy or point-incentive system. The particular system utilized can vary, but we, along with Urbain, recommend positive reinforcement (points earned) for specified prosocial group behaviors and response-cost (points paid) for certain disruptive behaviors. We also encourage the frequent use of verbal praise and recommend rewarding or response-costing those behaviors the leader actually sees. Not letting children "tell" on the behavior, good or bad, of other children works to assure that the group leader maintains control of the contingencies.

The procedures used to implement the cognitive–behavioral training discussed throughout this book are relevant in a group context. However, two group procedures, (1) relaxation and imagery and (2) role-play exercises, deserve some elaboration.

As a means of helping the children calm down and separate themselves from whatever events or frustrations occurred prior to group, the group leader begins the session with relaxation and guided imagery exercises. These techniques are explained to the children as being a means whereby they can find a quiet place inside themselves when they are experiencing strong or uncomfortable emotions. In preparation for the actual muscle relaxation exercises, the relaxation rules of "keeping your space" (not touching others) and "controlling your body" (not moving around too much) are introduced and explained. These rules may be incorporated into the point system as necessary. Fairly traditional progressive relaxation procedures are then implemented.

The Robot–Rag Doll game is a quick method of relaxation in which the children are told first to act and move like robots (with very tense, tight muscles) and then, when given the special signal, to act like rag dolls and go very limp. The children are told that to be a rag doll their arms and legs must be able to swing free and be very flexible.

After the children have mastered the basic relaxation sequence, imagery techniques can be introduced. The leader may choose to elaborate relaxing real-world images (sitting in your favorite chair, floating in water, lying in cool grass, etc.), or lead the group on a guided fantasy experiences (riding a magic carpet, walking in space, etc.). As the group becomes skilled at these exercises, the leader may recognize that some of the group members are capable of leading a guided fantasy experience. When possible, this use of the children as exercise leaders is strongly encouraged.

Role playing was discussed in Chapter 5, but role-play exercises in a group setting provide a unique and powerful opportunity for learning about social problem solving. Specific skill or content areas for role playing include making friends, learning to help and/or support others, developing assertiveness and anger control, and learning cooperation and compromise. Situations selected for role plays need to be age-appropriate, and initial role plays can be based on sources that are recognizable and appealing to the children. For example, problem sequences involving favorite TV, motion picture, or cartoon characters could be created. Eventually, it is important to build situations that relate to specific problem areas of the group members and to include situations that have been actual problems within the group. The group represents a microcosm of children not unlike the clusters in which the group members have difficulties. Practice among other children adds to the ecological validity of the role plays.

Once the group becomes accustomed to the role-playing procedures, it is suggested that when a problem develops during group time, the leader should have the group members "freeze," identify what is happening, generate other behavioral alternatives, and then act out these alternatives. The group leader calls for the freeze, but, once the group has become accustomed to this activity, children can be given the role of calling a freeze—thus providing practice at the identification of problems.

Following selected role plays, the group leader could have the participants switch roles, as a very concrete exercise in perspective taking. In addition, in order to involve more group members without increasing the actual "cast of characters" in the role play, each "actor" can be assigned a "coach" in the audience who has the job of helping the actor recognize and identify feelings and generate behavioral alternatives. In this manner, the leader can maintain the involvement and attention of the nonacting members.

Group Format

Following Urbain, there are some specific guidelines for the actual organization of each session. The first two sessions are primarily devoted to the introduction of group members, discussion of the purpose of the group, setting up ground rules, introducing the notion of individual differences to the children, and establishing what each child's behavioral contract with the group will be. The next four sessions involve establishing the basic activity structure of the group and presenting the cognitive problem-solving and affective education concepts. As time progresses, the group activities begin with an initial checking-in phase and rating of the previous week in terms of how well each child thinks he/she is doing on his/her behavioral contract, relaxation exercises, discussion of current problems or reporting of successful problem-solving efforts, presentation of new concepts, sharing of compliments and suggestions for feedback, point totaling, and specific reminders on how each child can try out his/her problem-solving skills at home and school. After approximately session 6, few new concepts are introduced and the time previously devoted to teaching the problem-solving and affective education notions is devoted to discussion and actual role playing of problem situations.

Group sessions typically last 90 minutes, including an informal snack or fun time at the end, and groups meet for approximately 4 to 6 months. While more research is needed to document the cognitive and behavioral changes resulting from this type of group intervention, our informed experience with and knowledge of this approach suggests that it can be a powerful method with children, and it clearly makes effective use of many of the central concepts of cognitive–behavior therapy with children.

Developing Self-Control in Children: The Manual

PHILIP C. KENDALL, WENDY PADAWER, BRIAN ZUPAN, AND LAUREN BRASWELL

This appendix is designed to present the essentials of the intervention within a session-by-session program. While we have tried to offer practical suggestions throughout, this is the most detailed "how-to" portion of the work.

The manual presents the training exercises in a 12-session format. While this 12-session format has been used in research and been found to be efficacious, we recommended an extended format when providing the intervention in most clinical situations. The inevitable difficulties associated with multiple-problem clinical cases may require the clinician to have multiple treatment foci, which results in longer treatment than is the case when working with less disturbed children. In both research and clinical applications, the sessions are designed to last approximately 50 minutes.

As the reader will recall, each session involves the therapist teaching the child to use the self-instructional procedures via modeling while working on a variety of impersonal and interpersonal problem-solving tasks. The initial tasks are psychoeducational and are similar to tasks required in the classroom. The central purpose of these tasks is to foster the acquisition of the self-instructions. Thus, they are designed to be simple and nonstressful. Gradually, the sessions shift emphasis to interpersonal play situations and the appropriate use of self-instructions in these cases. The final series of sessions deal with the child's particular behavior problems and involve the role playing of specific problematic situations. This gradual build-up to the role playing of difficult interactions is designed to assure that the child understands the use of the self-instructions before having to apply them in emotionally arousing situations. Response-cost contingencies for violations of the agreed upon "therapy rules" operate throughout each session. In addition, social reinforcement, as well as self-reward, for successful performance and appropriate behavior are actually encouraged.

TABLE A-1. Sample reward menu

Little paper clip	2 chips	Big paper clip	20 chips
Lead pencil	5 chips	Pencil sharpener	20 chips
Pencil crayon	8 chips	Ruler	25 chips
Key ring	10 chips	Paper folder	30 chips
Large plastic clip	12 chips	Ball-point pen	37 chips
Scratch pad	15 chips	Flair pen	45 chips
Desk eraser	15 chips	Puzzle/reading books	75 chips
		Guinness Book of World Records	100 chips

As applied for research and clinical purposes, the children are able to use the chips they have accummulated to select prizes from the "Reward Menu," illustrated in Table A-1. The child must buy *one* prize at the end of each session, but many choose to "bank" or save some chips in order to buy a more expensive prize after a future session. Appropriate rewards will vary from child to child and therefore a wide variety of rewards is advisable. A variety of "costs" for different rewards is also desirable, with some rewards available for as few as two or three chips. This guarantees that each child will be able to earn some type of reward, and also allows for the purchase of inexpensive prizes when in the process of saving chips for a more expensive prize. The acceptability of the rewards, when taken back to the classroom or to the home, should be checked in advance. The sample reward menu presented in Table A-1 emphasizes school-related materials that are popular with children and are typically allowable within the classroom.

The present manual describes the content of each session by stating its purpose, describing the tasks (keep in mind that similar tasks will be equally helpful), illustrating the application of the procedures, and, in several sections, providing sample transcripts. If readers have suggestions that might be incorporated into the manual, they should not hesitate to correspond with us. Session 1 might actually occur after one or more meetings with the child; therefore some rapport may already be established.

SESSION 1: WHICH ONE COMES NEXT?

Purpose

The tasks in the first session are simple and straightforward, with the intent of aiding in the child's thorough acquisition of the verbal self-instructions. Thus, the purpose of this session is for the child to be given an initial exposure to the self-instructions that will enable the child to see how the self-statements can be used to stop and think before attempting to solve problems, to cope with mistakes, and to provide self-reinforcement for thinking and reflecting as a problem-solving strategy. The first session also acquaints the child with the reward chips, reward menu, and the contingencies.

Task Description

The task consists of pictures that are placed in a certain sequence, as presented in Figure A-1. The child must study the sequence and pick from three possible choices the one that would come next in the sequence. There are numerous task items, beginning with easy sequences and progressing to more difficult items.

Application of the Procedures

The following section provides a detailed outline of two topics: (1) introducing the therapy to the child, and (2) a general example of the modeling procedures and dialogue as they occur most frequently. A somewhat lengthy yet crucial discussion is given which stresses the importance of these first examples, as they create the foundation of the self-control therapy. Subsequent examples appearing throughout this appendix indicate problem areas particular to each session that may arise and include ways in which the therapist may handle these situations.

Because a great deal of material is presented to the child in the first session, the therapist must be careful to calibrate his/her speed of presentation to the child's apparent speed of acquisition, and stop and review the information just introduced as often as is necessary for each child.

Introducing Therapy to the Children

Therapist: My name is _____, and we'll be working together for 6 weeks. We'll meet twice a week and do different tasks together [point to or flip through

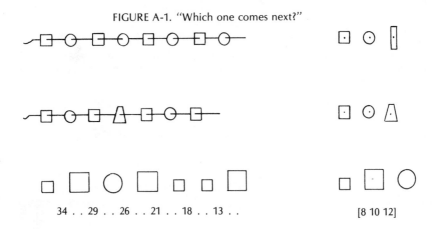

FIGURE A-1. "Which one comes next?"

34 . . 29 . . 26 . . 21 . . 18 . . 13 . .   [8 10 12]

tasks]. Now, that might look like a lot to finish. But it doesn't matter how many we get done. We're going to try and go very slowly and do a good job, even if we only finish a few tasks.

When we do each task, we're going to talk out loud, and say five [show five fingers] things, or steps, every time we do a task. I'll do the five steps with you in just a moment.

See these chips? When we start each meeting together, I'll give you 20 chips. They are yours to keep for the whole meeting. But when you make a mistake, you will lose a chip. There are three kinds of mistakes or three ways to lose a chip:

> 1. Going too fast. I want you to do all the work slowly and carefully. If you go too fast, you lose one chip.
> 2. We will be saying several steps for each task. If you don't say a step, that's a mistake, and you lose a chip.
> 3. The third mistake is the easiest to understand. If you get the wrong answer, that's a mistake so you lose a chip.

OK, there's a lot to know—but let's see if we can restate the three ways you can lose a chip. The first one is "going too fast." What are the other two ways? [Therapist coaches child in recalling the rules.]

Now don't worry, you won't lose all your chips. At the end of each meeting you'll have some chips left for buying a prize. There are lots of prizes [show menu and prize samples], and they cost different amounts of chips. See . . . [go through prize menu and show prizes].

Also, there are two other ways to earn extra chips that I will describe to you later.

There's one rule about prizes. Each time we meet, you *must* buy one prize, and you can buy only *one* prize. But, you can also put some chips in the bank, and save up for a more expensive prize another day. For example, here are 20 chips. If one day you lose five chips [take away five chips] you have 15 chips to buy a prize. You could buy a desk eraser for 15 chips, or you could, for example, buy a pencil for five chips and put ten chips in the bank. Then, if you save some each week, you could buy a puzzle book for 75 chips later. See, the puzzle book costs 75 chips, and you only start with 20 chips each time we meet. But if you decide to save chips, then you might have enough to buy the puzzle book. The chips are yours to spend as you like as long as you follow one rule: Each time we meet, you *must* buy one prize, and you can buy only *one* prize.

Introduction of Verbal Self-Instructions

Therapist: Now let's talk about the five things or steps that we shall be saying out loud each time we do a task or problem. At first it may be hard to remember them all, but we shall practice them together so you will know what to say.

The first thing to say to yourself is, "What am I supposed to do?" We say that so we can be sure we are doing the right problem in the right way.

The second thing we say is, "Look at all the possibilities." That means be sure to look at all the different answers so we can find the best possible one.

Next, we'll be telling ourselves to "focus in." That way we remind ourselves to really concentrate or think hard about just the problem we are working on right now. We don't need to look at or think about anything else.

The fourth step is to pick an answer after studying the different choices or possibilities.

And, finally, the fifth step is to check out our answer and if we got it right we tell ourselves that we did a good job. If we didn't get it right, we don't have to put ourselves down, but we could remind ourselves to be more careful or go more slowly on the next task.

Let's do a few tasks to practice the steps. I'll do the first one. Listen carefully so you'll be able to do a task using the steps. Watch how when I *say* the first step, I then *do* the first step. Then I will *say* the second step, and then *do* the second step. If we would only say the steps and then not do them, they wouldn't help us with the tasks as much as saying *and* doing the steps together will.

[The therapist gets set, focuses on the task, and begins modeling the self-statements, raising one finger with each step to represent which step he/she is on.]

Well, the first step is to find out what I'm supposed to do. [Point to specific "Which One Comes Next?" task.]

Second, I need to look at all the possibilities or all the different answers. [Point to three possible answers and examine carefully.]

Next, I have to "focus in"—think only about what I'm doing right now. [Cover the remaining tasks with hand and arm.]

[The therapist thinks out loud while solving the problem.] OK. I think this is the one that comes next. [Point to your answer and check the answer sheet.]

All right! That *is* the one that comes next. I did a pretty good job.

Let's do the second task together. Do you remember the first step? No? OK. Let's repeat it together. I have to find out what I'm supposed to do. [Continue with remaining steps in similar fashion.]

Now I'd like us to think about putting these steps or statements into your own words. We can write your words down on these little notecards and you can use them like cue cards to help you remember each step. The first step is, "Find out what I'm supposed to do." What's the way you might say the same thing? [Continue creating cue cards using the child's own words for the remaining steps. Don't require your own words, but rather let the child, within the bounds of the concepts in question, employ his/her own words.]

All right. I'll do this next one, and then you can do one by yourself; listen and watch carefully. Here goes. . . .

Coping Statement

[The therapist may at this point intentionally choose a wrong answer and model a coping statement as a substitution for self-reward.]

Therapist: Hmmm. . . . I guess I made a mistake. I'd like to toss these papers—this stinks! But wait, I can do these, but I'll have to remember to go slower and think harder next time. Let's see now . . . I think the right answer is. . . . OK. focus in now . . . I think it's this one [pointing to the correct answer]. There! I did better this time. I did a good job.

OK. Your turn now. It doesn't matter if you use the exact same words I did. But I want you to say the steps that mean the same thing. Don't worry about losing a chip this time. Even if you make a mistake, you won't lose a chip yet. Just remember to go slowly and say *and* do the five steps. All right, let's see you do this one. [One or two more "free" trials may be allowed. However, the response-cost contingency should be started as soon as the child has the basic ideas of the steps.]

[Upon completion of the free trial(s), the response-cost contingency can be reintroduced as follows:] I think you know the steps pretty well, even though you made a few mistakes. Now we'll start to use the chips. [In a matter-of-fact, *nonpunitive* voice] If you make a mistake, you lose one chip. Remember the three kinds of mistakes? (1) Going too fast. (2) Forgetting one of the five steps. (3) Getting the wrong answer.

Let's start. I'll do one first, then it'll be your turn. Listen carefully to the steps so you don't lose a chip when it's your turn!

Response-Cost

[In the event of a mistake by the child, a response-cost is enacted as follows:]

Therapist: No, that's not correct. You lose a chip for not choosing _____, which is the right answer. [*Or:*] Well, you chose the right answer, but you lose a chip for forgetting to say the second step: "I have to look at all the possibilities."

[Note that this is concrete labeling as compared to the conceptual labeling to be used in later sessions.]

Introduction of Self-Evaluation

Therapist: Before we finish I'm going to show you how to earn extra "bonus chips." [The therapist shows the child the "How I Did Today" chart (see Chapter 5, p. 127) and describes the differences between each level.] Today I am going to pick one number which I think tells us how you did today. Let's see, I have five possibilities here. . . . OK. I'd say number 3, "Good," tells us how you did today. You lost five chips for forgetting the steps and getting a wrong answer, but you did a good job on the other tasks and remembered to use the steps most of the time. Later on I'll be asking you to rate how you did. If we both pick the same number or if you pick the number next to mine you will earn one bonus chip. You can practice rating yourself at the end of the next two sessions. One last thing, I'd like you to look for a time when it would be a good idea to use the steps on your work in class. Next session, if you can tell me about one time that it would be a good idea to use the steps, you will earn one extra chip. Try not to forget the steps and try to remember at least one time when using the steps might be a good idea so you can earn a chip at the start of our next session.

[At the end of the session the child's chips are counted and the child purchases one prize from the reward menu. Any chips remaining after the purchase are recorded on paper and referred to as the "bank."]

SESSION 2: FOLLOWING DIRECTIONS

Purpose

The second session consists of the "Following Directions"[1] task. Accurately following directions plays an essential role in problem solving, and non-self-controlled children typically have deficits in this specific area. The "Following Directions" booklets are ideally suited for the early stages of therapy as the skills acquired in this session can be effectively utilized in problem-solving strategies during future training sessions. Thus, the purpose of the second session is twofold: (1) to provide practice materials that directly attack the target area of correct following of directions, and (2) to serve as a foundation for later sessions as the child learns to self-instruct or self-direct himself/herself to "stop and think."

Task Description

The "Following Directions" booklets span 14 levels (Picture Level, Preparatory Level, and A to L) which provide ample variance when selecting task level. Booklet A is suitable for children on a first grade *level*, booklet B is suitable for pupils on a second grade *level*, and so forth. (*Note:* It is wise to consult the child's teacher beforehand to obtain an accurate reading level estimate.) Each booklet contains 50 units and each unit consists of a set of directions followed by three or four task-relevant questions. The child is taught to apply the verbal self-instructions to the task questions in each unit (see sample in Table A-2).

1. These tasks are grade-level-sequenced manuals that teach the specific skill of following directions. (Available from Barnell-Loft Publishers, Baldwin, New York.)

TABLE A-2. Following directions

DIRECTIONS:

Here is a way to show that the strength of air pressure is the same in all directions.

EXPERIMENT:

Fill a glass of water to the very top. Cover the glass with a thick piece of cardboard. Hold the cardboard in place with one hand, and slowly turn the glass upside down. Remove your hand from the cardboard. The cardboard now holds the water in the glass.

1. You are to find out whether air pressure is the same in
   a. one direction only
   b. all directions
   c. some directions only

2. You are asked to cover the glass with
   a. a lid
   b. a piece of cardboard
   c. your hand

3. You must fill the glass with
   a. water
   b. bubbles
   c. air

4. To prove the strength of the air pressure, take away
   a. your hand
   b. the water
   c. the cardboard

Application of the Procedures

The therapist reviews the self-statements at the onset of the session as a "warm-up" for the child and as an indicator for the therapist of the child's retention of the verbal self-instructions. This "check" is best carried out before introducing the "Following Directions" booklets so as to curb the distractions provided by the booklets. Some children may have problems remembering the steps, and they can use the previously mentioned cue card(s) as an aid in the recollection process. If difficulties in recalling the self-statements persist even after viewing the cue card(s), the tasks may be introduced and the training may proceed in a fashion similar to Session 1 examples. Often the response-cost contingency is needed to promote thoughtful attention to the self-instructions.

The therapist also asks if the child noticed an instance in class that may have provided an opportunity to use the steps. If the child did, the therapist should reward him/her with one extra chip and suggest how the steps might have worked. If the child fails to provide an instance, the therapist can describe a few cases that children typically relate as good chances to use the steps and see if any occurred for the child.

Spoken, or overt, verbal self-instructions will constitute the major portion of this session. During the last two or three tasks the therapist may begin the verbal self-instructions fading process by modeling whispered self-statements:

Therapist: We've been saying the steps out loud for awhile, and you seem to be catching on pretty well.

Child: [typical response] I'm doing a good job!

T: That's right, you are doing a good job in our sessions! And the steps are useful in other places too. But if you wanted to use them while working in the classroom, you probably couldn't say them out loud. That might disturb the other kids and your teacher might be upset with you for talking. Now you could use the steps in class if you whispered them or if you said them silently to yourself. So what we're going to do now is [therapist starts whispering] practice whispering the steps while we take turns doing the problems. OK? I'll do the next task, whispering the steps . . . making sure I still say all the steps, even though I'll be whispering them now.

Fading should only be introduced, however, if the therapist has a clear sense that the child has fully learned the self-instructions. Coping statements are modeled by the therapist whenever a response-cost has been enacted on the previous task. If the child is making only occasional, or no errors, coping statements are still modeled via the therapist by either (1) making a purposeful mistake (being a good actor isn't required, but it helps, as the children pick up on contrived mistakes very quickly), or (2) modifying Step 3. For example:

I need to think about what I'm doing right now. . . . If I make a mistake I'll have to remember to take more time and look at *all* the possibilities next time.

Concrete labeling of errors is continued throughout this session, as are the reward and "bank" systems, and the self-evaluation ("How I Did Today") chart. The following is an example of a typical "bank account":

Name: Charlie Brown

Session number	Chips left today	Chips to spend	Prize	Chips in bank
1	19	19	Pencil (5 chips)	14
2	18	32	Ruler (25 chips)	7
3				

The child is encouraged to recognize times when using the steps would help to solve a problem and is reminded that he/she can earn an extra chip for describing a "stop and think" time at the start of the next session.

SESSION 3: SPECIFIC SKILLS SERIES

Purpose

Each child undergoing the training procedures will undoubtedly exhibit his/her own areas(s) of deficit (e.g., poor reading skills, low verbal ability). The third session provides an opportunity for the application of the verbal self-instructions to each child's specific weakness by utilizing the "Specific Skills Series" (Barnell-Loft). This session attempts to illustrate to the child the usefulness of the self-instructions as a tool in solving idiosyncratic problem areas.

Task Description

The complete "Specific Skills Series" contains eight booklets with topics ranging from "Getting the Facts" to "Drawing Conclusions" (see list in Table A-3). For a more detailed example of a particular skill booklet, refer back to the "Following Directions" description in Session 2.

Application of the Procedures

A brief review of the verbal self-instructions and an inquiry to see if the child noticed a time when the steps would help to solve a problem once again precede work on the day's task. By now, many children will have a reasonable grasp of the self-instructions; however, some children may still be having difficulties with the system. To remedy this problem, additional work with cue cards or verbal prompts (e.g., a key word from each statement) is suggested.

The verbal self-instruction fading process continues in Session 3, with the majority of self-instructions practiced at the whispered stage rather than out loud. The first two or three tasks are modeled overtly, with subsequent self-statements primarily whispered.

If the child is handling the self-statements with relative ease, the therapist and child need not alternate after each task. Rather, the therapist models

TABLE A-3. Specific Skills Series

1. Working with Sounds
2. Following Directions
3. Using the Context
4. Locating the Answer
5. Getting the Facts
6. Getting the Main Idea
7. Drawing Conclusions
8. Detecting the Sequence

occasionally, perhaps after the child has completed three or four tasks. The therapist is reminded, however, to supply a sufficient amount of direct and indirect coping statements (at least 3 to 5, partially dictated by the number of errors made by the child) during the course of the session.

Session 3 marks the beginning of the response-cost labeling fading process. If enough errors are committed, the final one or two mistakes are labeled as follows: (1) "You lose one chip for not taking your time and not getting the right answer," *or* (2) "You lose one chip for not using all of the steps."

Notice how each response labeling (both concrete and conceptual) begins with the phrase "you lose" rather than the more punitive "I'm going to take one chip for. . . ." The former phrasing also encourages the child's experiencing internal control of the consequences (i.e., while "you lose" indicates that "I" [the child] "made a mistake," it also implies, "I have control in keeping my chips if I don't make a mistake").

SESSION 4: THE LITTLE PROFESSOR MATH SKILLS

Purpose

In the fourth session, the child uses the self-instructions to solve arithmetic problems. The therapist chooses a level of problems that is suitable to the child's classroom arithmetic level. The use of flashcards, multiplication tables, and repetitive drilling often encourages children to throw out answers as fast as they can. While one important step of solving a problem does involve a quick and automatic response (e.g., $2 \times 2 = 4$), it is important that the child understand that a more complicated problem may require a series of steps completed slowly and in an appropriate order. The purpose of this session is for the child to learn to apply the self-statements to grade-appropriate mathematical equations and thus to solve them in a logical and reflective manner. In addition, the cooperative efforts of therapist and child that are required when using the "Little Professor" should enhance the developing relationship. Like the conch in *Lord of the Flies*, the manipulation of the hand-held game serves to provide order to the turn-taking and an opportunity for cooperative efforts.

Task Description

This session uses the Little Professor,[2] an electronic game that generates arithmetic equations. It looks very much like a calculator and includes multiplication, division, addition, and subtraction problems on four levels of

---

2. Made by Texas Instruments, Incorporated, and available where most Texas Instruments calculators are found. Similar and/or related tasks are equally useful.

mathematical difficulty. A "Fun with Math Facts" booklet containing many learning games and activities is also included with the Little Professor. To operate the Little Professor one must:

1. Turn it on.
2. Select the level of difficulty located on the right side.
3. Press the "Set" key.
4. Select the desired math operation by pressing one of the four keys.
5. Press the "Go" key. The Little Professor will generate the first problem to which the child must punch in the answer. If the child chooses the correct answer the Little Professor will generate the next problem. On the other hand, if the child chooses the wrong answer, the letters "EEE" will momentarily appear, indicating an error. The same problem will return after a few seconds, allowing the child to redo the problem. The child has three tries at each problem before the Little Professor gives the correct answer.

Note: After an equation is presented on the Little Professor screen, it will remain visible for approximately 45 to 60 seconds. Since some problems take much longer to solve, it is advisable to incorporate "copying the equation" into the first self-instruction. After 45 to 60 seconds the problem disappears from the screen. However, the calculator will function normally. Not all versions of the calculator function identically—check yours in advance.

Application of the Procedures

The introduction of a new task creates an ideal setting for (1) rephrasing of the verbal self-instructions, and (2) inclusion of additional steps to better suit the problem-solving approach necessary for a new task. Rewording the self-statements is important, as often children develop the habit of saying the statements mechanically, without actually *using* them. Rephrasing encourages the children to think carefully about the meaning of the verbal self-instructions. The self-instructions may be rephrased as follows:

Therapist: First of all, I need to find out what I'm to do. Let's see, I'm supposed to use the steps in solving this problem.

Next, I need to look at all the possibilities. Hmm . . . what are the possibilities? Well, I guess the possibilities are adding, subtracting, multiplying, or dividing.

Now I have to concentrate hard [pause].

OK, my answer is _____.

All right! I'm doing quite well.

An additional step may be inserted as follows:

Therapist: OK. I think I know the answer, but first I'll check my work to make sure I've done the problem correctly. [This step was suggested by a child for use with mathematical computations.]

In this session, whispered self-instructions and conceptual labeling continue as previously described. Note also that conceptual labeling of errors will be used throughout the remaining sessions.

Recall that during the self-evaluation the child will now do the evaluation himself/herself and attempt to match the therapist exactly or within one point in order to earn the bonus point. Again the child is encouraged to identify a time when the steps would help to solve a problem and instructed to use the steps at that time. That is, the child is now required to bring to the next session an example of when he/she *actually used* the self-instructions in class or at home. As before, he/she can earn one extra chip for bringing such an example to the next session. The self-evaluations and "homework assignments" are continued throughout the remaining therapy sessions.

SESSION 5: THE LITTLE PROFESSOR MATH GAMES

Purpose

Throughout the first four sessions, the verbal self-instructions have been applied strictly to psychoeducational/academic tasks. The "Little Professor Math Games" mark the beginning of the application of self-statements to an interpersonal task. The math games serve as initial exposure to the self-instructions as employed in game and related play activities. The pairing of familiar material from the previous session (Little Professor calculator) with new math games helps provide a smooth transition to the interpersonal situations of future sessions.

Task Description

The math games used in Session 5 are found in the booklet accompanying the Little Professor entitled *Fun with Math Facts: 18 Learning Games and Activities.* The various math problems generated by the Little Professor are incorporated into the rules of the appropriate age-level game.

Application of the Procedures

At this time, the therapist may proceed with the final stage of the fading process (whispered to covert verbal self-instructions) as determined by the child's proficiency with the self-instructions.

Because the final objectives of the self-control therapy are the internalization and generalization of the self-statements, the decision as to when to enter the covert phase of the self-instructions is considered one of the key variables in the therapy procedures. In covert self-statements, only the amount of time taken to solve the task is directly observable. Therefore, opportunities for enacting a response-cost for what may be incomplete or incorrect verbal self-instructions are minimal. Entering the covert phase too early may deprive the child of adequate supervision in his/her use of the self-statements. On the other hand, because therapy may be time-limited, entering the covert phase too late might not allow sufficient exposure to the covert verbal self-instructions and thus might reduce the amount of internalization and generalization achieved with the self-statements.

As a general rule, the best time to introduce the covert verbal self-instructions is when the child has demonstrated reasonable competence with the self-statements and is able to *rephrase* his/her five steps with little difficulty. The following dialogue is a sample introduction to the covert stage of verbal self-instructions.

Therapist: OK, Charlie, nice job on that problem. Let's see, I guess it's my turn, but before I take my turn let's stop and think about what we've been doing with the steps. What *have* we been doing with the steps? [Pause.]

Child: Well, we've been slowing down when doing tasks.

T: That's right. And we've also been saying the steps different ways. When we first began using the steps we said them out loud. Then we started whispering the steps. What might be another way of doing the steps?

C: Hmmm . . .

T: Let's see . . . talking out loud . . . whispering quietly . . . what might come next?

C: How about not saying them out loud *or* whispering?

T: You mean doing the steps silently?

C: Yes.

T: That's a great idea. You say the steps to yourself, without talking out loud or without whispering. Even though other people won't hear you saying the steps, you'll still be saying them to yourself, just like you've been doing all along.

C: You mean I'll say them in my head.

T: Exactly. And why might it be important to say the steps in your head rather than out loud?

C: So I don't bother anyone.

T: Yes. By saying the steps to yourself, you won't disturb the other kids in class or the teacher, like you might if you say the steps out loud.

C: Are you going to say them that way too?

T: I sure will. In fact, I'll do the next task right now, still using the steps, but this time saying them silently to myself.

The therapist and child continue to alternate tasks for the remainder of the session. If when beginning the covert phase, the therapist has been modeling, for example, every third task rather than every other task, it might be wise to return to alternating every other task for a short time. In addition, the therapist and child frequently take turns performing a task overtly or whispering to ensure retention and use of the verbal self-instructions.

When modeling, the therapist includes numerous nonverbal cues that emphasize careful, reflective thinking. The continued use of the "raising a finger for each step" procedure as previously mentioned provides an excellent means of signaling that you are using the steps and, if the child does likewise, checking whether the child is still using the self-instructions.

SESSION 6: TANGRAM PUZZLES

Purpose

This session provides experience for the child in using the cognitive–behavioral strategy as a tool in the problem approach and the problem solving of more abstract puzzles. The self-instructions are implemented to facilitate and improve the "choice" element that is embedded in abstract problem solving by reducing the haphazard, fast, trial-and-error approach and practicing the well-thought-out, systematic approach.

Task Description

The tangrams consist of seven geometric figures (five triangles of three different sizes, one square, and one parallelogram) which are used to construct various puzzle designs (information in Table A-4). The puzzle designs to be duplicated range in degree of complexity, and also differ in the way they are presented, as either an *actual* scale-size or a *reduced* scale-size puzzle. Thus, actual scale-size puzzles are geared for the younger child and are used by simply instructing the child to place the appropriate geometric figures directly over the puzzle design. In contrast, the reduced-size puzzles may be used for the older child, requiring him/her to construct the figure by comparing the reduced puzzle design to the one he/she is building.

Application of the Procedures

Throughout Session 6 the therapist continues the final phase of the fading process (whispered to covert verbal self-instructions). While the majority of tasks at this time are performed covertly, a few puzzles are solved using

TABLE A-4. Tangram puzzles: Starting tangram levels for children grades 1–6

Grade	Degree of complexity when using *actual* scale-size puzzle	Degree of complexity when using *reduced* scale-size puzzle
1–2	Low and medium	—
3–4	Medium and high	Low
5–6	High—modified	Medium and high

Degree of complexity	Number of tangrams used
Low	1–3
Medium	4–5
High	6–7
High—modified	7 (with 2 or more tangrams *not* drawn in on design)

Tangram samples (reduced scale size)

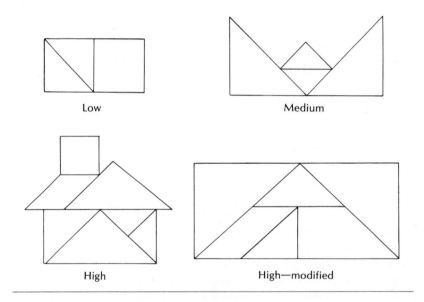

Low   Medium

High   High—modified

whispered self-instructions. In addition, the therapist models a coping statement via whispered self-statements at least once or twice during the session, and *always* after the child makes a mistake. In the latter instance, the child follows the therapist's model with overt or whispered self-instructions until correctly solving a puzzle.

If the child is solving the puzzles without making any mistakes, the therapist need not hesitate in allowing the child to do three or four tasks to every one puzzle modeled by the therapist. In this session, as in previous sessions, the therapist is cautioned with regard to task appropriateness. If the child is solving puzzles that are too easy, the child may believe the steps are not necessary (and rightly so). Thus, an adequate supply of mildly frustrating tasks (i.e., tasks in which the answer and steps in obtaining the answer are not readily apparent) which remain within the child's conceptual level is imperative if the therapy process is to continue properly and effectively.

The following example illustrates one way of modeling a coping statement when working with the tangram puzzles. Note that the coping statements used earlier were at the end of the task or after the final solution. In comparison, the following coping statement is modeled while the puzzle is still being solved.

Therapist: Let's see. The first thing is to make sure I know what I'm supposed to do. I have to use these tangrams to build this puzzle. [Point to tangram figures and appropriate design.]

Hmmm. . . . I must make sure I look at all the possibilities. [Move hand above each tangram and think about each shape.] I must look at all the ways I can put these tangrams together to build this puzzle. [Point to design.]

I should only think about what I'm doing right now, and not about making other figures. [Carefully examine tangrams, fitting two or three in place with pauses inserted between placements. After several correct placements, *misplace* one tangram.] Oops, I think I made a mistake. Yes, I made a mistake. I'll have to try another piece and remember to go slow and think hard. Let's see now . . . looking at *all* the possible ways these pieces could fit . . . I think it goes like this. [Place tangram in correct place on design after pausing and thinking.] OK. I'm doing better now.

I must think about what I'm doing right now. [Proceed with reflective placement of tangrams and correctly solve puzzle.]

There! I did it. I built the tangram puzzle. I'm doing just fine.

SESSION 7: CHECKERS

Purpose

The purpose of including a session of playing checkers in the therapy is to give the child an enjoyable task, to enhance the development of a positive therapist–child relationship, and to employ the use of self-instructions in a more social situation. The main thrust of this session is on applying the self-instructions to a situation bridging the workbook-type task and the social situation. In addition, as the therapist–child relationship develops, the therapist begins to inquire about the personal dilemmas in which the child finds himself/herself. For example, "What gets you in trouble in class?," or "When does Ms./Mr. _____ yell at you?" These inquiries are not an interrogation, but rather a conversational search for the specifics (as seen by the child) of several classroom and interpersonal problems. (See the section on interviewing in Chapter 4 for additional ideas about discussing the child's problem behaviors.)

Adherence to the rules should be accomplished via the modeling of self-instructions, and breaking the rules can result in a response-cost contingency.

Task Description

Standard checkers and checkerboard are used.

Application of the Procedures

The child's typical impulsive enthusiasm displayed with the introduction of a fun game coupled with the immediate confusion often created by the notion of applying the self-instructional steps to checkers can serve as an ideal setting for (1) an effective practice of the generalization of the self-instructions, and (2) inquiry into specific classroom or school-related problems.

Therapist: I'm glad to see you like today's task. You must have played checkers before.

Child: I sure have. And I'm pretty good at this game, except my sister almost always beats me.

T: Why do you think your sister almost always wins when the two of you play checkers? Is it because she's a much better player or do you often make mistakes?

C: I usually lose because I make a dumb move and she jumps my checkers.

T: Sometimes when we play a game, we can get so excited about playing that we don't stop and think, and then we make careless mistakes. I bet if you used the steps when playing checkers, you'd probably be a better player.

C: Use the steps? In playing a game? I don't get it.

T: Well, let me show you. In fact, you can use the steps to help you in many other games and situations. I'll make my first move using the steps. I will say them out loud at first. Okay, first thing is to know what I'm to do . . . and that's move my pieces over here [point to opposite side of board] to get kings, but also watch out so you don't jump me. Hmmm . . . I have quite a few possibilities . . . they all look like pretty safe moves so far. All right, this is my move, and I'm doing just fine.

Note how the therapist has blended the self-instructional steps into a more natural dialogue, and yet the statements still remain distinct and serve their intended functions. Use of the steps becomes much more beneficial as the game progresses, as the options for "good" and "bad" moves become more numerous and the final decision more crucial. The therapist can inform the child of this fact (again with the aim of curbing any early conclusions that the steps aren't needed for playing checkers). In addition, a new rule can be applied whereby a player may move a piece in the desired direction and consider the consequences of such a move as long as his/her finger remains in contact with that checker. Only when the finger is lifted from the checker is the pending move considered an actual move. This rule enables the child to begin to evaluate consequences in a concrete manner and may aid in the child's planning ahead two or more moves.

Session 7 also marks the onset of the therapist's inquiry into specific classroom or school-related problems. For an example of a dialogue covering this issue, see the "Application of the Procedures" section in Session 8.

SESSION 8: CAT AND MOUSE

Purpose

The inclusion of another enjoyable board game task facilitates in the transition of the training to interpersonal situations. This session also provides additional time in which the therapist may continue inquiring about the different ways the child sees himself/herself encountering home or classroom problems.

"Cat and Mouse" requires virtually all children to learn new rules to a new game. It is actually ideal if the game is also new to the therapist, for this creates a very realistic situation in which the therapist can model how one can systematically approach a new task. As in Session 7, learning the rules and adherence to the rules is accomplished through the modeling of the self-statements and a response-cost is enacted when a rule is broken.

Task Description

A standard checkerboard and five checkers (one red and four black) are used. Briefly, the lone red checker (the mouse) tries to evade the four black checkers (the cats) as it advances across the checker board. Further instructions are given in Table A-5.

Application of the Procedures

Before inquiry into the child's personal problems begins, we assume that a comfortable therapist–child relationship exists. In most cases, by the seventh or eighth meeting such a relationship is already well established. However, in

TABLE A-5. "Cat and Mouse" instructions

OK [child's name], today we're going to play a game called Cat and Mouse. We will use these five checkers and checkerboard [point to one red and four black checkers] in playing the game. See this red checker? It's the mouse. And these four black checkers are the four cats. In Cat and Mouse, the four cats try to "catch" the mouse, and the mouse tries to "get away" from the cats [point to respective checkers while explaining]. Let me show you how to play:

1. [Place checkers on board.] Both the cats and the mouse can only move on the black squares [demonstrate].
2. The cats may only move forward, like this [demonstrate]. But the mouse can move both forward and backward, like this [again demonstrate]. [The therapist should make sure child has sufficiently grasped the movement aspect of the game.]
3. Cat and Mouse is different from checkers because the pieces *do not* jump each other. They just slide along like this [demonstrate], OK?
4. Play begins with the mouse on either of the two center dark squares at one end of the board. The cats are lined up on the four dark squares at the other end of the board. Remember, the mouse can move diagonally in any direction, while the cats can move diagonally only in the forward direction.
5. The mouse attempts to evade the cats and reach the other side of the board. The cats attempt to "surround" the mouse by occupying all possible spaces where the mouse might move.
6. The game is "won" when either the mouse has successfully evaded the cats or the cats have surrounded the mouse.
7. Do you understand how Cat and Mouse is played? Good. Let's start. Here, you be the cats and I'll be the mouse. You try to "catch" me. All right, the mouse moves first, so . . .

some situations the child may respond a bit uneasily to the initial inquiry. The therapist is advised not to push the questioning, which might disturb the child, but rather to probe gently in the following manner:

Therapist: Gee . . . I got a little too excited for a few seconds and made a bad move. I guess sometimes I get a little too excited when doing other things too. I forget to stop and think and then I get in trouble or make a mistake.

Child: What kind of trouble?

T: Oh, I might say something I shouldn't have said and I might make someone angry with me. Things that wouldn't have happened if I would have remembered to stop and think first. Does anything like that ever happen to you?

C: Uh . . . ummm . . . no, not really, I don't know.

T: There's nothing terribly bad about maybe saying the wrong thing or doing the wrong thing. But it would be better if we could remember to think first. Everyone gets into trouble once in a while. Maybe if some people used the steps they'd get in trouble less often. Can you think of a time when using the steps or stopping and thinking in school might have kept you out of trouble?

C: Well, once I ran across the parking lot to get a ball and the teacher made me go to the principal's office.

T: How could the steps have helped you?

C: I guess I wouldn't have run after the ball so soon. I forgot running on the parking lot was against the rules. Just like when I always talk to my friend in class and the teacher yells at me . . . I forget about the rules. . . .

At this time, the therapist tells the child he/she can earn an extra chip during the next session by being able to recall an instance where self-instructions were used in a social/interpersonal situation. The child is encouraged to use the steps in the course of the day and to remember when he/she "stopped and thought" for the next session.

SESSION 9: IDENTIFYING EMOTIONS

Purpose

This session deals with problem solving in the area of interpersonal behaviors. It is suggested that for a child to adequately solve an interpersonal problem involving the modification of his/her behavior, he/she must be able to identify the emotions involved in the interaction. After the child has identified these emotions he/she may then be able to understand why these emotions may be occurring. The purpose of this session is for the child to learn to use the self-statements to (1) identify the emotion present in a situation such as "Vern is laughing" or "Michael yelled at Margo," and (2) generate alternatives as to what Vern is laughing about or why Michael yelled at Margo. The therapist should view this session as a minicourse in affective education.

Task Description

The tasks selected for use in this session will vary in accordance with the cognitive and developmental levels of each child. In general, the therapist presents a set of stimuli (e.g., pictures, short stories, sentences describing a picture) in which a character is behaviorally portraying an emotion. Examples of such are given in Table A-6.

Prior to presenting these stimuli, however, it will be helpful to spend time generating a "feelings dictionary" so the child will have a ready fund of different emotional descriptions to use when describing the pictures or stories. An example of a feelings dictionary is presented in Table A-7. As suggested by the layout of this table, the therapist can help the child generate "feelings words" by asking, "What are some emotions or feelings that we like to have because they feel good?" The therapist can then ask about negative emotions and then later introduce the concept of more neutral or "in-between" feelings.

TABLE A-6 Identifying emotions

1. When I get home, Barry calls to tell me that he can't come over. I have no one to play with.
2. This week I try out for the school band. I make it!
3. During the holidays, Aunt Sally comes to visit us. She brings a big toy for my brother and a little one for me.
4. It's Friday after school and I have no homework. Soon I'll be going out with Jon, who's lots of fun. We'll ride our bikes.
5. The teacher calls on me. My answer is wrong. All the children laugh.
6. This morning I wanted to buy a present for Mother's Day. I was scared to ask Mr. Thompson for help. My friends told me he doesn't like kids. But when I finally asked for help, he was very friendly. He said, "How about a box of candy? I'll bet your mother would like that." How would Mr. Thompson feel if I told him what my friends said?

Application of the Procedures

As outlined above, the child's task is to use the verbal self-instructions as an aid in identifying the feelings of the characters and subsequently producing several reasonable explanations as to why the characters feel as they do.

Failure to identify an emotion correctly results, of course, in a response-cost. After the response-cost, it is essential for the therapist to question the child about his/her erroneous answer. One of two things may be happening: (1) In retrospect, the child understands what the correct emotion should be, but originally answered impulsively and incorrectly, or (2) the child does not understand the particular feeling exhibited by the character. Instances of the latter case tend to appear in younger children and the tasks may need to be limited to a few basic feelings that the child understands, particularly if he/she displays difficulty even after generating the feelings dictionary. For each task, after the therapist thoroughly describes a new feeling to the child, the response-cost contingency is reinstated for the second stage of the task—generating alternatives to explain why the character feels as he/she does. The therapist can make it a rule that the child generate at least three different alternatives.

TABLE A-7. Feelings dictionary

Feel good	In-between	Feel bad
Happy	Surprised	Scared
Excited	Bored	Sad
Proud	Shy	Mad
Pleased	Calm	Upset
Content		Embarrassed
Joyful		Angry
		Bitter
		Mean

Most children have no problem correctly labeling an emotion but initially display some difficulty in generating alternatives. If such a situation arises the therapist may help the child by asking questions that guide the child toward a plausible explanation. To help clarify this matter, consider the following therapist–child interchange (this excerpt consists of overt self-instructions).

Child: First, I have to find out what I'm doing. I need to read the sentence and look at the picture and then tell what they're feeling. . . . "When I get home, Barry calls to tell me that he can't come over. I have no one to play with." Next, think about different ways to feel . . . think hard . . . probably I'd feel sad.

Therapist: [Nodding approvingly.] You'd feel sad. Would you feel any other way?

C: [Silence.]

T: How do you feel when you have no one to play with and you're all by yourself?

C: Sad and . . . lonely, I guess.

T: Uh-huh. When we have no one to play with we might feel sad and lonely. When else might someone feel sad or lonely?

C: Ummm . . . when they're all alone.

T: OK, when they're alone or maybe when something sad happens like . . .

C: Like their dog getting sick or something.

T: Exactly, and they might feel lonely when . . .

C: Well . . . when their dog is in the pet hospital or . . . their father's on a business trip.

T: Or they might feel sad if someone picks on them in school or they might feel lonely if no one plays with them at recess.

C: Uh-huh. I think I did a good job.

If the child continues to fail to generate three or more emotions or explanations, the ultimatum of "think of another feeling (alternative) or you'll lose one chip" has been successfully employed.

Finally, a few extra turns of overt or whispered self-instructions by both therapist and child are advisable to ensure proper utilization of the self-statements.

SESSION 10: HYPOTHETICAL SITUATIONS— WHAT WOULD HAPPEN IF?

Purpose

In this session the child learns to generate alternative ways to handle a hypothetical social situation. Many of these situations involve a problem that is not immediately soluble. The purposes of this session are to encourage the child to cope with problems or situations which involve the inhibition of impulses, to help the child examine ways he/she could modify his/her behavior in a social situation, to help the child to consider the consequences of his/her actions, and to help the child to approach interpersonal situations in a self-controlled manner.

Task Description

As in Session 9, the tasks used in this session correspond to each child's developmental and cognitive level. The tasks simply consist of hypothetical social situations (which can be printed on index cards) that require "stopping and thinking" as part of the coping process and ultimate problem resolution. Samples of typical hypothetical situations used in therapy are provided in Table A-8. Pictures of problematic social situations could also be used.

Application of the Procedures

Each hypothetical situation is drawn randomly from a stack containing many possibilities. The intent is to add a "surprise" or "fun" element into the session. Of course, if specific social situations seem especially well suited for the individual, the therapist includes such possibilities in the selection process.

The therapist then models the process of applying the steps to the problem situation and explains what activities are necessary at each step. The first step (identifying the problem) is presented in virtually the same manner as it has been in all previous sessions, and it still involves basically just a clear statement of the problem at hand. With the second step (looking at the possibilities) the therapist should emphasize that the child now has to generate his/her own possible solutions or choices for solving the problem. As in Session 9, it is advisable that the child be required to produce at least three alternatives. In the third step (focusing in), the therapist explains that when concentrating on

---

TABLE A-8. Hypothetical situations

1. You are working on your schoolwork and your friend starts talking to you.
2. You are watching television and your little brother changes the channel.
3. You tear your pants at recess and someone makes fun of you.
4. You are playing checkers and your opponent is cheating.
5. You are having trouble with a worksheet and your friend has already finished.
6. You promised your friend something, but later you can't give it to him/her.
7. You say the wrong answer in class and the person behind you starts to laugh.

interpersonal problems it is important to examine the emotional and behavioral consequences of each alternative: "How will a given response make others feel? How will it make you feel? What will it make others do?" Thinking about the consequences yields the information necessary to pick the best response. After a response has been selected (step 4), the child can then congratulate himself/herself for thinking through the situation and picking the best answer. For example, the therapist might provide the following model.

Therapist: Number 1, I must remember to find out exactly what my problem is. [Reading from the card.] "You have promised to mow the lawn, a job that takes 2 hours. What would happen if your friends came by as you were about to begin mowing and asked you to go to the circus for a few hours?" Okay, I need to think of different ways to solve this problem. Hmm . . . it's a tough one. I'll need to think a minute. . . . Well, I could go to the circus with my friends . . . or . . . umm . . . I could just say, "No way, I can't go." Let's see . . . I need to think of at least three different things I could do. Oh! I guess I could also tell them that I have to work first but I could meet them there later. Hmm . . . Let me concentrate on these. If I just go with my friends, I'll be happy and they'll be happy, but the lawn won't get mowed and I promised my mom I'd do that. If I don't go to the circus at all I'll be pretty unhappy, but if I go after the lawn is mowed then I won't feel so bad and my mom won't be irritated with me. I like that last choice. I guess I did a pretty good job of figuring out that problem.

A common occurrence in Sessions 9 through 12 involves a moderate protest from the child in response to using the steps with the interpersonal situations (e.g., "Do we have to use the steps today?" "I don't know how to use the steps to do these problems." "I think I'll do these situations without the steps."). This dilemma can usually be avoided by (1) preparing the child in earlier sessions for the time when "we'll be using the steps to solve different kinds of problems, like when we're playing with other people," and (2) assigning homework probjects in one session and discussing them during the next meeting.

Often a child will initially respond with the "best" solution to the problem. In this situation, the therapist acknowledges the sensible response but also encourages the child to consider many solutions to the predicament, even those that seem like poor solutions. The therapist can state that no harm is done looking into another solution as long as it's evaluated properly. In fact, many times what at first appears as a "poor" solution may, after stopping, thinking about and modifying it, result in a "good" solution.

Working with interpersonal problem situations rather than psychoeducational tasks necessitates some change in the response-cost contingencies. While at this phase of the training it is still appropriate to response-cost the child for going too fast or for failing to utilize the steps in problem solving, it is less appropriate to response-cost for picking the "wrong" answer or solutions to an interpersonal problem. Ultimately, the emphasis of the training is of teaching kids *how* to think, not *what* to think. In other words, while it isn't ideal, if Johnny decides, after generating other alternatives and considering the emotional and behavioral consequences, that it is still worth it to him to hit Billy for stealing his pencil, that is Johnny's choice.

SESSION 11: HYPOTHETICAL SITUATIONS—ROLE PLAYING

Purpose

In this session the child works to find the best solution to a role-played social problem or situation. The role playing is included so the child will actually have a chance at physically "acting out" what he/she would do in a situation. The purpose of this session is to further generalize the use of the self-instructions to increasingly more real-life interpersonal situations.

Task Description

The hypothetical situations (both "created" and "real") used in Session 11 closely parallel the ones used in Session 10. However, the therapist must make sure the items selected for this session are appropriate for role-playing behaviors (e.g., the sample situation detailed in Session 10 would be less desirable for use in the present session). Examples of better-suited role-playing situations include patiently waiting in line, choosing fair teams, or problems encountered when walking to school.

Application of the Procedures

The session is introduced in the following manner:

Therapist: Today we will work on some tasks that are a lot like the ones we did last time, except today we'll *act* out the situations. We will use the steps again, sometimes saying them out loud, other times just saying them silently in our head just like we've been doing all along. Remember to *do* what you *say* when using the steps. Remember how last time we made up different solutions to each situation? Well, today we will think about the situation, come up with our choices, and think about the consequences of each choice. Then we will act out each one and pick the one we think is best. For each situation, you will pretend to be one character or person and I will pretend to be the other person. You will lose a chip if you go too fast or forget a step.

The procedures for engaging in the self-instructions in this session are similar to those of Session 10 with the exception of physically "acting out" rather than just verbalizing each choice. It is important to let the child be maximally involved in specifying the details of each role-play sequence, for this increases the possible similarity between the role play in the therapy setting and what the child experiences outside the session. An illustration of the use of the cognitive–behavior therapy in this context is a part of the training videotape (Kendall & Braswell, 1982c; available from the first author).

Quite frequently it becomes apparent that the child is giving socially desirable answers and possibly wouldn't respond as thoughtfully in a real-life situation. It is helpful for the therapist to talk to the child about how he/she might respond differently (i.e., quickly) in *real life* (where no chips are involved and where "saving face" commonly outweighs staying out of trouble) and the consequences associated with impulsive–reflective responses.

SESSION 12: REAL-LIFE SITUATIONS—ROLE PLAYING

Purpose

In Session 12 the child uses the self-instructions to solve any interpersonal problems he/she may be having or could have in the classroom or at home. The purpose of this session is to aid the child in generalizing the use of self-instructions by applying them to "real" problems he/she is experiencing. If the therapy is administered at the school, dealing with problems in the classroom environment can be emphasized. If administered in a different setting, other problems can be given major emphasis.

Task Description

The tasks in the final session concern target behaviors or situations that are specifically relevant to the individual child. These real-life situations are obtained over the course of the treatment or by simply asking the child what areas in school and home present problems. In anticipation of few offerings from the child, the therapist also may request a list of actual dilemmas that the child's parents or teacher may have witnessed.

Application of the Procedures

The therapist begins the session by modeling self-instructions while introducing a real-life situation of his/her own, examining alternate paths to a solution, and thoroughly considering the consequences of each available resolution. The session continues with the presentation of a problem to the child. Ideally, the therapist plays as active a role as possible in the acting out of the problem. At the same time, the therapist will probably need to assist the child initially in modifying the self-instructions and generating possible solutions.

Therapist: OK, here's your situation. "While walking into the classroom you accidentally stumble over Ann's [real classmate's name] notebook which is lying on the floor. Dave, a boy you don't especially like, calls you clumsy and tells you you're a dummy. You feel yourself getting very embarrassed about stumbling and very mad at Dave for calling you a name." Now I'll pretend to be Dave and you be yourself. We'll try to make this situation as real as possible. So pretend you're walking into the room and pretend to stumble on this notebook [place notebook on floor] but don't hurt yourself. Try and use the steps to find the best way to solve the problem. This is your first try, so it doesn't have to be perfect—but try your best.

Child: I don't know if I can use the steps to do this.

T: Well, let's give it a try and see what happens. I think it will be a lot easier than you think. Ready?

C: Yup. [Child acts out entering room and stumbling.]

T: Hey, look at [child's name]! He almost fell over that notebook. Boy, how clumsy. You're always tripping over something. What a dummy!

C: What do I do now? Say the first step?

T: Yes, or something that means the same thing as the first step.

C: I have to make sure I know what I'm supposed to do.

T: Or, "I need to stop and think about this problem before doing anything."

C: Next I have to look at all the possibilities.

T: What are the possibilities?

C: Well, I can punch Dave [child laughs].

T: Uh-huh. What might happen then?

C: I'd get in trouble for hitting Dave. He might hit me back, too.

T: What else could you do?

C: I could tell the teacher.

T: That's another way to solve the problem. What might happen if you tell the teacher?

C: The other kids would call me a tattletale.

T: What would happen to Dave if you told the teacher?

C: He might get in trouble, but he'd probably get back at me on the playground. And the other kids would *still* call me a tattletale.

T: So those solutions might not be the best ones for you.

C: No, but I'd probably hit him.

T: Well think ahead, what might happen if you didn't hit Dave and you didn't tell the teacher? What if you just didn't pay any attention to Dave?

C: I'd still be mad.

T: You could tell yourself, "Just because Dave called me clumsy doesn't mean I am always clumsy or I'm a dummy. In fact, I do quite well in gym class and soccer." It might also be a good idea to ask Ann if she could put her notebook someplace else so other people won't trip over it. Sometimes it's smart thinking not to get into a fight.

As the session progresses, the therapist's involvement in modifying the steps and generating alternatives for the child decreases. Some situations are solved covertly but often the major portion of the therapist–child interchange involves discussions as detailed above and the self-instructions naturally become part of the conversation. In such cases, productive overt problem solving takes precedence over ineffective covert self-instructions.

A few minutes at the end of the session are reserved to have the child tell the therapist specifically what has been learned over the meetings. The child also pretends to teach the steps to a new child (role-played by the therapist). Finally, all of the remaining chips can be used to purchase several prizes. This last session, as is true for almost any of the sessions, can easily be extended over many sessions. As acceptable for individual cases, we encourage an extended intervention. Indeed, extending Sessions 9 through 12 over much longer periods of time is highly recommended.

SUMMARY: IMPORTANT CONCERNS

The following summary is offered as a reminder of the processes and activities that should be occurring within each session and across sessions. In addition, Table A-9 presents a checklist that can be used to guide the therapist's behavior in each session.

TABLE A-9. Therapy checklist

---

1. Begin each session by checking that the child remembers the self-instructions and has an example of when and how they can be used.
2. Fade from overt to covert speech over the course of the treatment and occasionally during each session.
3. Enact a response-cost when the child:
   a. forgets a self-instruction
   b. solves the task incorrectly
   c. goes too fast
4. Label each response-cost. Be specific in the very beginning, but emphasize conceptual labeling in latter sessions.
5. Teach self-evaluation and give bonus chips for accurate self-evaluation.
6. Model the task immediately following a response-cost. Highlight the *coping statement* when you model a task following a response-cost.
7. Watch for mechanical use of the self-instructions.
8. Banking; reward menu.

Alternating Tasks with the Child

Alternate task by task with the child in each of the therapy sessions, in each case until you are confident that the child has a good grasp of the self-instructions. Then let the child do the majority of the tasks for that session. When the child loses a chip, model the next task for him/her, making sure to include coping statements where appropriate.

Fading from Overt to Covert Speech

Begin the therapy procedures using the self-instructions out loud. Gradually change your modeling to a whisper (and ask the child to whisper) and then to go covert speech. When modeling the self-statements silently, "look like" you're thinking carefully by using "thinking gestures and facial expressions," such as pointing to each possibility you are considering as a problem solution.

Fading from Concrete to Conceptual Labeling of Response-Cost over the Course of Therapy

When the child loses a chip in the early therapy sessions, give him/her concrete, specific explanations for the loss. Make the explanations more conceptual or general in later sessions. Take a moment now to reread the examples given in several of the therapy session descriptions and notice the differences between concrete and conceptual labeling of response-costs.

Beginning and Ending Each Session

At the start of each session check on the child's level of acquisition of the self-instructions by asking him/her to recite the different statements. Exact wording is *not* important; in fact, personalized statements are desired.

At the end of each session, tell the child to use the self-instructions outside of the therapy sessions, and to remember one instance where he/she used the self-instructions and to bring the example to the next session. At the beginning of subsequent sessions, ask the child to provide an example of the use of self-instructions. Self-evaluations, using the "How I Did Today" chart, and the spending and banking of chips close each session.

In General

Talk out loud to yourself as you shuffle papers or look for directions and such, so that the child sees variations of the use of self-instructions in situations other than the prescribed therapy tasks. You might have the child do the necessary arithmetic at the end of the therapy session when he/she figures out how many chips he/she has, how many he/she spends for a prize, and how many are left to bank. Encourage him/her to talk out loud and "use the steps."

Remember to mention to the child that although "there are lots of tasks here, we don't have to do them all. In fact, it doesn't matter how many we do. The main thing is to go *slowly* and be careful, and do a good job."

Involvement is essential: Encourage the child's participation by rewarding his/her suggestions for role plays or other forms of input. Being an active, alive, and animated therapist also generates an involved child.

References

Abikoff, H. Cognitive training interventions in children: Review of a new approach. *Journal of Learning Disabilities*, 1979, *12*, 123–135.

Abikoff, H., Gittelman, R., & Klein, D. F. Classroom observation code for hyperactive children: A replication of validity. *Journal of Consulting and Clinical Psychology*, 1980, *48*, 555–565.

Abikoff, H., Gittelman-Klein, R., & Klein, D. Validation of a classroom observation code for hyperactive children. *Journal of Consulting and Clinical Psychology*, 1977, *45*, 772–783.

Abikoff, H., & Ramsey, P. P. A critical comment on Kendall and Finch's cognitive–behavioral group comparison study. *Journal of Consulting and Clinical Psychology*, 1979, *47*, 1104–1106.

Abramson, L. Y., Seligman, M. E. P., & Teasdale, J. D. Learned helplessness in humans: Critique and reformulation. *Journal of Abnormal Psychology*, 1978, *87*, 49–74.

Achenbach, T. M. The classification of children's psychiatric symptoms: A factor analytic study. *Psychological Monographs*, 1966, *80* (Whole No. 615).

Achenbach, T. M. The Child Behavior Profile: I. Boys aged 6–11. *Journal of Consulting and Clinical Psychology*, 1978, *46*, 478–488.

Achenbach, T. M., & Edelbrock, C. S. The classification of child psychopathology: A review and analysis of empirical efforts. *Psychological Bulletin*, 1978, *85*, 1275–1301.

Alexander, J. F., & Parsons, B. V. Short-term behavioral intervention with delinquent families. *Journal of Abnormal Psychology*, 1973, *81*, 219–225.

Allen, G., Chinsky, J., Larcen, S., Lochman, J. E., & Selinger, H. *Community psychology and the schools: A behaviorally oriented multi-level preventive approach*. Hillsdale, N.J.: Erlbaum, 1976.

Arnold, S. C., & Forehand, R. A comparison of cognitive training and response-cost procedures in modifying cognitive styles of impulsive children. *Cognitive Therapy and Research*, 1978, *2*, 183–187.

Atkeson, B. M., & Forehand, R. Conduct disorders. In E. J. Mash & L. G. Terdal (Eds.), *Behavioral assessment of childhood disorders*. New York: Guilford, 1981.

Ault, R. L., Mitchell, C., & Hartmann, D. P. Some methodological problems in reflection–impulsivity research. *Child Development*, 1976, *47*, 227–231.

Baker, H. J., & Leland, B. *Detroit Tests of Learning Aptitude*. Indianapolis: Bobbs Merrill, 1967.

Bakwin, H., & Bakwin, R. M. *Clinical management of behavior disorders in children*. Philadelphia: Saunders, 1966.

Bandura, A. *Principles of behavior modification*. New York: Holt, Rinehart & Winston, 1969.

Bandura, A. Psychotherapy based upon modeling procedures. In A. Bergin & S. Garfield (Eds.), *Handbook of psychotherapy and behavior change*. New York: Wiley, 1971.

Bandura, A. Self-efficacy: Toward a unifying theory of behavioral change. *Psychological Review*, 1977, *84*, 191–215.

Bandura, A. Self-efficacy mechanism in human agency. *American Psychologist*, 1982, *37*, 122–147.

Bandura, A., & Adams, N. E. Analysis of self-efficacy theory of behavioral change. *Cognitive Therapy and Research*, 1977, *1*, 287–308.

Barkley, R. A. Predicting the response of hyperkinetic children to stimulant drugs: A review. *Journal of Abnormal Child Psychology*, 1977, *5*, 351–369.

Barkley, R. A. Hyperactivity. In E. J. Mash & L. G. Terdal (Eds.), *Behavioral assessment of childhood disorders*. New York: Guilford, 1981.

Barkley, R. A. Guidelines for defining hyperactivity in children: Attention deficit disorder with hyperactivity. In B. Lahey & A. Kazdin (Eds.), *Advances in child clinical psychology* (Vol. 5). New York: Plenum, 1982.

Barkley, R. A., & Cunningham, C. E. The parent–child interactions of hyperactive children and their modification by stimulant drugs. In R. Knights & D. Bakker (Eds.), *Treatment of hyperactive and learning disordered children*. Baltimore: University Park, 1979.

Baucom, D. *A cognitive–behavioral approach to marital therapy*. Paper presented at the meeting of the Association for Advancement of Behavior Therapy, Toronto, 1981.

Beck, A. T. Cognitive therapy: Nature and relation to behavior therapy. *Behavior Therapy*, 1970, *1*, 184–200.

Beck, A. T. *Cognitive therapy and the emotional disorders*. New York: International Universities Press, 1976.

Beck, S., Forehand, R., Neeper, R., & Baskin, C. H. A comparison of two analogue strategies for assessing children's social skills. *Journal of Consulting and Clinical Psychology*, 1982, *50*, 596–597.

Bem, S. Verbal self-control: The establishment of effective self-instruction. *Journal of Experimental Psychology*, 1967, *74*, 485–491.

Bender, L. *A visual–motor gestalt test and its clinical use*. New York: American Psychiatric Association, 1938.

Bender, N. Self-verbalization versus tutor verbalization in modifying impulsivity. *Journal of Educational Psychology*, 1976, *68*, 347–354.

Bentler, P. M., & McClain, J. A multitrait–multimethod analysis of reflection–impulsivity. *Child Development*, 1976, *47*, 218–226.

Bialer, I. Conceptualization of success and failure in mentally retarded and normal children. *Journal of Personality*, 1961, *29*, 303–320.

Blechman, E., Olson, D., & Hellman, I. Stimulus control over family problem-solving behavior: The family contract game. *Behavior Therapy*, 1976, *7*, 686–692. (a)

Blechman, E., Olson, D., Schornagel, C., Halsdorf, M., & Turner, A. The family contract game: Technique and case study. *Journal of Consulting and Clinical Psychology*, 1976, *44*, 449–455. (b)

Block, J., Block, J., & Harrington, D. Some misgivings about the Matching Familiar Figures test as a measure of reflection–impulsivity. *Developmental Psychology*, 1974, *10*, 611–632.

Bobbitt, B. L., & Keating, D. P. A cognitive–developmental perspective for clinical research and practice. In P. C. Kendall (Ed.), *Advances in cognitive–behavioral research and therapy* (Vol. 2). New York: Academic Press, 1983.

Bolstad, O. D., & Johnson, S. M. Self-regulation in the modification of disruptive classroom behavior. *Journal of Applied Behavior Analysis*, 1972, *5*, 443–454.

Bootzin, R. R., & Lick, J. R. Expectancies in therapy research: Interpretive artifact or mediating mechanism? *Journal of Consulting and Clinical Psychology*, 1979, *47*, 852–855.

Bornstein, P., & Quevillon, R. The effects of a self-instructional package with overactive preschool boys. *Journal of Applied Behavioral Analysis*, 1976, *9*, 179-188.

Bower, E. M. *The early identification of emotionally handicapped children in school* (2nd ed.). Springfield, Ill.: Thomas, 1969.

Bradley, C. Characteristics and management of children with behavior problems associated with brain damage. *Pediatric Clinics of North America*, 1957, *4*, 1049-1060.

Brandon, S. Overactivity in childhood. *Journal of Psychosomatic Research*, 1971, *15*, 411-415.

Braswell, L., Shapiro, E., & Kendall, P. C. *Verbal self-instructional training: A parent's guide*. Unpublished manuscript, University of Minnesota, 1984. (a)

Braswell, L., Kendall, P. C., Braith, J., Carey, M., & Vye, C. "Involvement" in cognitive-behavioral therapy with children: Process and its relationship to outcome. *Cognitive Therapy and Research*, 1984, in press. (b)

Braswell, L., Kendall, P. C., & Koehler, C. *Children's attributions of behavior change: Patterns associated with positive outcome*. Paper presented at the meeting of the Association for Advancement of Behavior Therapy, Los Angeles, November 1982. (a)

Braswell, L., Kendall, P. C., & Urbain, E. S. A multistudy analysis of the role of socio-economic status (SES) in cognitive-behavioral treatments with children. *Journal of Abnormal Child Psychology*, 1982, *10*, 443-449. (b)

Brief, A. P. Peer assessment revisited: A brief comment on Kane and Lawler. *Psychological Bulletin*, 1980, *88*, 78-79.

Broden, M., Hall, R. V., & Mitts, B. The effect of self-recording on the classroom behavior of two eighth grade students. *Journal of Applied Behavior Analysis*, 1979, *4*, 191-199.

Brown, A. L. The development of memory: Knowing, knowing about knowing, and knowing how to know. In H. W. Reese (Ed.), *Advances in child development and behavior* (Vol. 10). New York: Academic Press, 1975.

Bugental, D. B., Collins, S., Collins, L., & Chaney, L. A. Attributional and behavioral changes following two behavior management interventions with hyperactive boys: A follow-up study. *Child Development*, 1978, *49*, 247-250.

Bugental, D. B., Whalen, C. K., & Henker, B. Causal attributions of hyperactive children and motivational assumptions of two behavior-change approaches: Evidence for an interactionist position. *Child Development*, 1977, *48*, 874-884.

Burns, H. F. The effect of self-directed verbal commands on arithmetic performance and activity level. *Dissertation Abstracts International*, 1972, 33, 1782B. (University Microfilms No. 72-22, 884)

Busk, P. L., Ford, R. C., & Schulman, J. L. Stability of sociometric responses in classrooms. *Journal of Genetic Psychology*, 1973, *123*, 69-84.

Buss, A. H., & Plomin, R. A. *Temperament theory of personality development*. New York: Wiley, 1975.

Butler, L., & Meichenbaum, D. The assessment of interpersonal problem-solving skills. In P. C. Kendall & S. D. Hollon (Eds.), *Assessment strategies for cognitive-behavioral interventions*. New York: Academic Press, 1981.

Cairns, E., & Cammock, T. Development of a more reliable version of the Matching Familiar Figures test. *Developmental Psychology*, 1978, *5*, 555-560.

Cameron, M. I., & Robinson, V. M. J. Effects of cognitive training on academic and on-task behavior of hyperactive children. *Journal of Abnormal Child Psychology*, 1980, *8*, 405-419.

Cameron, R. *Source of problem solving inefficiency in relation to conceptual tempo.* Paper presented at the biennial meeting of the Society for Research Development in Child Development, New Orleans, 1977.

Camp, B. W. Verbal mediation in young aggressive boys. *Journal of Abnormal Psychology*, 1977, *86*, 145–153.

Camp, B. W., Blom, G., Herbert, F., & van Doorninck, W. "Think Aloud": A program for developing self-control in young aggressive boys. *Journal of Abnormal Child Psychology*, 1977, *5*, 157–168.

Cantwell, D. P. Psychiatric illness in the families of hyperactive children. *Archives of General Psychiatry*, 1972, 27, 414–417.

Cantwell, D. Hyperkinetic syndrome. In M. Rutter & L. Hersov (Eds.), *Child psychiatry: Modern approaches*. London: Blackwell, 1977.

Chandler, M. Egocentrism and antisocial behavior: The assessment and training of social perspective-taking skills. *Developmental Psychology*, 1973, *9*, 326–332.

Chess, S., Thomas, A., & Birch, H. G. Behavior problems revisited. In S. Chess & T. Buch (Eds.), *Annual progress in child psychiatry and child development*. New York: Brunner/Mazel, 1968.

Chittenden, G. E. An experimental study in measuring and modifying assertive behavior in young children. *Monographs of the Society for Research in Child Development*, 1942, 7 (1, Ser. No. 31).

Christophersen, E. R., Barnard, J. D., Ford, D., & Wolf, M. M. The family training program: Improving parent–child interaction patterns. In E. J. Mash, L. C. Handy, & L. A. Hamerlynck (Eds.), *Behavior modification approaches to parenting*. New York: Brunner/Mazel, 1976.

Ciminero, A. R., & Drabman, R. S. Current developments in the behavioral assessment of children. In B. B. Lahey & A. E. Kazdin (Eds.), *Advances in clinical child psychology* (Vol. 1). New York: Plenum, 1977.

Coats, K. I. Cognitive self-instructional training approach for reducing disruptive behavior of young children. *Psychological Reports*, 1979, *44*, 127–134.

Cobb, J. A. Relationship of discrete classroom behaviors to fourth grade academic achievement. *Journal of Educational Psychology*, 1972, *63*, 74–80.

Cobb, J. A. Effects of academic survival skill training on low-achieving first graders. *Journal of Education Research*, 1973, *67*, 108–113.

Cobb, J. A., & Hops, H. *Coding manual for continuous observation of interactions by single subjects in an academic setting* (Report No. 9). Eugene, Ore.: Center at Oregon for Research in the Behavioral Education of the Hanidcapped, University of Oregon, 1972.

Cohen, R., Meyers, A., Schlesser, R., & Rodick, J. D. *Generalization of self-instructions: Effects of cognitive level and training procedures*. Unpublished manuscript, Memphis State University, 1982.

Cole, P. M., & Kazdin, A. E. Critical issues in self-instructional training with children. *Child Behavior Therapy*, 1980, *2*, 1–23.

Coleman, J. C., Butcher, J. N., & Carson, R. C. *Abnormal psychology and modern life* (6th ed.). Glenview, Ill.: Scott, Foresman, 1980.

Combs, M. L., & Slaby, D. A. Social-skills training with children. In B. B. Lahey & A. E. Kazdin (Eds.), *Advances in clinical child psychology* (Vol. 1). New York: Plenum, 1977.

Conners, C. K. A teacher rating scale for use in drug studies with children. *American Journal of Psychiatry*, 1969, *126*, 884–888.

Conners, C. K. Symptom patterns in hyperkinetic, neurotic, and normal children. *Child Development*, 1970, *41*, 667–682.

Conners, C. K. What parents need to know about stimulant drugs and special education. *Journal of Learning Disabilities*, 1973, *6*, 13–15.

Conners, C. K. *Food additives and hyperactive children*. New York: Plenum, 1980.

Conrad, W., & Insel, J. Anticipating the response to amphetamine therapy in the treatment of hyperkinetic children. *Pediatrics*, 1967, *40*, 96–98.

Copeland, A. P. The relevance of subject variables in cognitive self-instructional programs for impulsive children. *Behavior Therapy*, 1981, *12*, 520–529.

Copeland, A. P. Individual differences factors in children's self-management: Toward individualized treatments. In P. Karoly & F. H. Kanfer (Eds.), *Self-management and behavior change: From theory to practice*. New York: Pergamon, 1982.

Copeland, A. P. Children's talking to themselves: Its developmental significance, function, and therapeutic promise. In P. C. Kendall (Ed.), *Advances in cognitive–behavioral research and therapy* (Vol. 2). New York: Academic Press, 1983.

Copeland, A. P., & Hammel, R. Subject variables in cognitive self-instructional training. *Cognitive Therapy and Research*, 1981, *5*, 405–420.

Cowen, E. L., Pederson, A., Babigian, H., Izzo, L., & Trost, M. A. Long-term follow-up of early detected vulnerable children. *Journal of Consulting and Clinical Psychology*, 1973, *41*, 438–446.

Craighead, W. E. A brief clinical history of cognitive–behavioral therapy with children. *School Psychology Review*, 1982, *11*, 5–13.

Craighead, W. E., Craighead, L., & Meyers, A. New directions in behavior modification with children. In M. Hersen, R. Eisler, & P. Miller (Eds.), *Progress in behavior modification* (Vol. 6). New York: Academic Press, 1978.

Crandall, U. C., Katkovsky, W., & Crandall, V. G. Children's beliefs in their own control of reinforcement in intellectual–academic achievement situations. *Child Development*, 1965, *36*, 91–109.

Cruikshank, W. M. *The brain-injured child in home, school, and community*. Syracuse: Syracuse University Press, 1966. (Revised in 1977 as *Learning disabilities in home, school, and community*.)

Cullinan, D., Epstein, M. H., & Silver, L. Modification of impulsive tempo in learning disabled pupils. *Journal of Abnormal Child Psychology*, 1977, *5*, 437–444.

Cunningham, C. E., & Barkley, R. A. The effects of Ritalin on the mother–child interactions of hyperkinetic twin boys. *Developmental Medicine and Child Neurology*, 1978, *20*, 634–642.

Delfini, L. F., Bernal, M. E., & Rosen, P. M. Comparison of deviant and normal boys in home settings. In E. J. Mash, L. A. Hamerlynck, & L. C. Handy (Eds.), *Behavior modification and families*. New York: Brunner/Mazel, 1976.

Denhoff, E. The natural life history of children with minimal brain dysfunction. *Annals of the New York Academy of Science*, 1973, *205*, 188–205.

Dodge, K. A., & Frame, C. L. Social cognitive biases and and deficits in aggressive boys. *Child Development*, 1982, *53*, 620–635.

Dodge, K. A., Murphy, R. R., & Buchsbaum, K. The assessment of intention-cue detection skills in children: Implication for developmental psychopathology. *Child Development*, 1984, *55*, 163–173.

Douglas, V. I. Stop, look and listen: The problem of sustained attention and impulse control in hyperactive and normal children. *Canadian Journal of Behavioral Science*, 1972, *4*, 259–281.

Douglas, V. I. Sustained attention and impulse control: Implication for the handicapped child. In J. A. Swets & L. L. Elliott (Eds.), *Psychology and the handicapped child*. Washington, D.C.: U.S. Office of Education, 1974.

Douglas, V. I. Perceptual and cognitive factors as determinants of learning disabilities: A review chapter with special emphasis on attentional factors. In R. M. Knights & D. J. Bakker (Eds.), *The psychology of learning disorders: Theoretical approaches*. Baltimore: University Park, 1976.

Douglas, V. I. Higher mental processes in hyperactive children: Implications for training. In R. M. Knights & D. J. Bakker (Eds.), *Rehabilitation, treatment, and management of learning disorders*. Baltimore: University Park, 1980.

Douglas, V. I., Parry, P., Marton, P., & Garson, C. Assessment of a cognitive training program for hyperactive children. *Journal of Abnormal Child Psychology*, 1976, *4*, 389–410.

Douglas, V. I., & Peters, K. G. Toward a clearer definition of the attentional deficit of hyperactive children. In G. A. Hale & M. Lewis (Eds.), *Attention and the development of cognitive skills*. New York: Plenum, 1979.

Drabman, R. S., Spitalnik, R., & O'Leary, K. D. Teaching self-control to disruptive children. *Journal of Abnormal Psychology*, 1973, *82*, 10–16.

Drummond, D. Self-instruction training: An approach to disruptive classroom behavior (Doctoral dissertation, University of Oregon, 1974). *Dissertation Abstracts International*, 1975, *35*, 4167B–4168B. (University Microfilms No. 75-3, 869)

Dunn, L. M. *Expanded manual for the Peabody Picture Vocabulary Test*. Minneapolis: American Guidance Services, 1965.

Durrell, D. D. *Durrell Analysis of Reading Difficulty*. New York: Harcourt, Brace and World, 1955.

D'Zurilla, T. J., & Goldfried, M. R. Problem solving and behavior modification. *Journal of Abnormal Psychology*, 1971, 107–126.

D'Zurilla, T. J., & Nezu, A. Social problem solving in adults. In P. C. Kendall (Ed.), *Advances in cognitive–behavioral research and therapy* (Vol. 1). New York: Academic Press, 1982.

Egeland, B., Bielke, P., Kendall, P. C. Achievement and adjustment correlates of the Matching Familiar Figures test. *Journal of School Psychology*, 1980, *18*, 361–372.

Egeland, B., & Weinberg, R. A. The Matching Familiar Figures test: A look at its psychometric credibility. *Child Development*, 1976, *47*, 483–491.

Elkin, A. Group work with children and youth. In A. Ellis & M. E. Bernard (Eds.), *Rational emotive approaches to the problems of childhood*. New York: Plenum, 1983.

Ellis, A. *Reason and emotion in psychotherapy*. New York: Stuart, 1962.

Enright, R. D. *Social cognitive development: A training model for intermediate school-age children*. St. Paul, Minn.: Pupil Personnel Division, Minnesota State Department of Education, 1977.

Eyberg, S. M., & Johnson, S. M. Multiple assessment of behavior modification with families: Effects of contingency contracting and order of treated problems. *Journal of Consulting and Clinical Psychology*, 1974, *42*, 594–606.

Feldhusen, J., & Houtz, J. Problem-solving and the concrete–abstract dimension. *Gifted Child Quarterly*, 1975, *19*, 122–129.

Feldhusen, J., Houtz, J., & Ringenbach, S. The Purdue Elementary Problem-Solving Inventory. *Psychological Reports*, 1972, *31*, 891–901.

Ferster, C. B., Nurnberger, J. I., & Levitt, E. B. The control of eating. *Journal of Mathetics*, 1962, *1*, 87–109.

Finch, A. J. Jr., Kendall, P. C., Deardorff, P. A., Anderson, J., & Sitarz, A. M. Reflection–impulsivity, persistence behavior, and locus of control in emotionally disturbed children. *Journal of Consulting and Clinical Psychology*, 1975, *43*, 748. (a)

Finch, A. J. Jr., Wilkinson, M. D., Nelson, W. M. III, & Montgomery, L. E. Modification of impulsive cognitive tempo in emotionally disturbed boys. *Journal of Abnormal Child Psychology*, 1975, 3, 49–52. (b)

Fischler, G. L. *Qualitative and process measures of social–cognitive problem-solving skills in elementary school children: Relationships with social and emotional adjustment*. Doctoral dissertation, University of Minnesota, 1984.

Fischler, G. L., & Kendall, P. C. *Social cognitive problem-solving and childhood adjustment: Qualitative and topological analyses*. Manuscript submitted for publication, University of Minnesota, 1984.

Fish, B. The "one child, one drug" myth of stimulants in hyperkinesis. *Archives of General Psychiatry*, 1971, *25*, 193–203.

Flavell, J. H. Metacognitive aspects of problem-solving. In L. B. Resnick (Ed.), *The nature of intelligence*. Hillsdale, N.J.: Erlbaum, 1976.

Flavell, J. H. *Cognitive development*. Englewood Cliffs, N.J.: Prentice-Hall, 1977.

Ford, M. E. The construct validity of egocentrism. *Psychological Bulletin*, 1979, *86*, 1169–1188.

Forehand, R., King, H. E., Peed, S., & Yoder, P. Mother–child interactions: Comparison of a noncompliant clinic group and a nonclinic group. *Behaviour Research and Therapy*, 1975, *13*, 79–84.

Forehand, R., & Peed, S. Training parents to modify noncompliant behavior of their children. In A. J. Finch & P. C. Kendall (Eds.), *Treatment and research in child psychopathology*. New York: Spectrum, 1979.

Foster, S. L. Family conflict management: Skill training and generalization procedures (Doctoral dissertation, State University of New York at Stony Brook, 1978). *Dissertation Abstracts International*, 1979, *39*, 5063B–5064B. (University Microfilms No. 79-08, 689)

Friedling, C., & O'Leary, S. G. Effects of self-instructional training on second- and third-grade hyperactive children: A failure to replicate. *Journal of Applied Behavior Analysis*, 1979, *12*, 211–219.

Gal'perin, P. Y. Stages in the development of mental acts. In M. Cole & I. Maltzman (Eds.), *A handbook of contemporary Soviet psychology*. New York: Basic Books, 1969.

Genshaft, J. L., & Hirt, M. Race effects in modifying cognitive impulsivity through self-instruction and modeling. *Journal of Experimental Child Psychology*, 1979, *27*, 185–194.

Giebink, J. W., Stover, D., & Fahl, M. Teaching adaptive responses to frustration to emotionally disturbed boys. *Journal of Consulting and Clinical Psychology*, 1968, *32*, 366–368.

Glogower, F., & Sloop, E. W. Two strategies of group training parents as effective behavior modifiers. *Behavior Therapy*, 1976, *7*, 177–184.

Glueck, S., & Glueck, E. T. *Unraveling juvenile delinquency*. New York: Commonwealth Fund, 1950.

Golden, M., Montane, A., & Bridger, W. Verbal control of delay behavior in two-year-old boys as a function of social class. *Child Development*, 1977, *48*, 1107–1111.

Goldfried, M. J. Anxiety reduction through cognitive–behavioral intervention. In P. C. Kendall & S. D. Hollon (Eds.), *Cognitive–behavioral interventions: Theory, research, and procedures*. New York: Academic Press, 1979.

Goldiamond, I. Self-control procedures in personal behavior problems. *Psychological Reports*, 1965, *17*, 851–868.

Goldstein, K., & Sheerer, M. Abstract and concrete behavior: An experimental study with special tests. *Psychological Monographs*, 1941, *53*, 1–151.

Goodwin, S., & Mahoney, M. J. Modification of aggression through modeling: An experimental probe. *Journal of Behavior Therapy and Experimental Psychiatry*, 1975, *6*, 200–202.

Gordon, T. *Parent effectiveness training*. New York: Wyden, 1970.

Goyette, C. H., Conners, C. K., & Ulrich, R. F. Normative data on revised Conners Parent and Teacher Rating Scales. *Journal of Abnormal Child Psychology*, 1978, *6*, 221–236.

Graziano, A. M., & Mooney, K. C. Family self-control instruction for children's nighttime fear reduction. *Journal of Consulting and Clinical Psychology*, 1980, *48*, 206–213.

Graziano, A. M., Mooney, K. C., Huber, C., & Ignasiak, D. Self-control instruction for children's fear-reduction. *Journal of Behavior Therapy and Experimental Psychiatry*, 1979, *10*, 221–227.

Guralnick, M. J. Solving complex perceptual discrimination problems: Techniques for the development of problem-solving strategies. *American Journal of Mental Deficiency*, 1976, *81*, 18–25.

Harlow, H. F., & Mears, C. *The human model: Primate perspectives.* New York: Wiley, 1979.

Harter, S. *A model of intrinsic motivation in children: Individual differences and developmental change.* Invited address presented at the Minnesota Symposium on Child Psychology, Minneapolis, October 1979.

Harter, S. The Perceived Competence Scale for Children. *Child Development*, 1982, *53*, 87–97.

Hartup, W. W. Peer relations. In P. Mussen (Ed.), *Handbook of child psychology* (Vol. 4) (4th ed.). New York: Wiley, 1983.

Haynes, S. N. *Principles of behavioral assessment.* New York: Gardner, 1978.

Hechtman, L., Weiss, G., Finkelstein, J., Wener, A., & Benn, R. Hyperactives as young adults. Preliminary report. *Canadian Medical Association Journal*, 1976, *115*, 625–630.

Hetherington, E. M., Cox, M., & Cox, R. *The development of children in mother-headed families.* Paper presented at the Conference on Families in Contemporary America, Washington, D.C., 1977.

Hobbs, S. A., Moguin, L. E., Tyroler, M., & Lahey, B. B. Cognitive behavior therapy with children: Has clinical utility been demonstrated? *Psychological Bulletin*, 1980, *87*, 147–165.

Homatidis, S., & Konstantareas, M. M. Assessment of hyperactivity: Isolating measures of high discriminant validity. *Journal of Consulting and Clinical Psychology*, 1981, *49*, 533–541.

Homme, L. E. Perspectives in psychology: XXIV. Control of coverants, the operants of the mind. *Psychological Record*, 1965, *15*, 501–511.

Hopkins, J., Perlman, T., Hechtman, L., & Weiss, G. Cognitive style in adults originally diagnosed as hyperactives. *Journal of Child Psychology and Psychiatry*, 1979, *20*, 209–216.

Hoy, E., Weiss, G., Minde, K., & Cohen, N. The hyperactive child at adolescence: Cognitive, emotional, and social functioning. *Journal of Abnormal Child Psychology*, 1978, *67*, 311–324.

Hudson, L. M. On the coherence of role-taking abilities: An alternative to correlational analysis. *Child Development*, 1978, *49*, 223–227.

Huessy, H. R. Study of the prevalence and therapy of the choreatiform syndrome or hyperkinesis in rural Vermont. *Acta Paedopsychiatrica*, 1967, *34*, 130–135.

Huessy, H. R. Hyperkinetic problems continue to teens. *Clinical Psychiatry News*, 1974, *2*, 5.

Huessy, H., Metoyer, M., & Townsend, M. 8–10 year follow-up of 84 children treated for behavioral disorder in rural Vermont. *Acta Paedopsychiatrica*, 1974, *10*, 230–235.

Hughes, H. M., & Haynes, S. N. Structured laboratory observation in the behavioral assessment of parent–child interactions: A methodological critique. *Behavior Therapy*, 1978, *9*, 428–447.

Irwin, F. W. *Intentional behavior and motivation: A cognitive view.* Philadelphia: Lippincott, 1971.

Jacob, R. G., O'Leary, K. D., & Rosenblad, C. Formal and informal classroom settings: Effects on hyperactivity. *Journal of Abnormal Child Psychology*, 1978, *6*, 47–60.

Jahoda, M. The meaning of psychological health. *Social Casework*, 1953, *34*, 349–354.

Jahoda, M. *Current concepts of positive mental health.* New York: Basic Books, 1958.

Jastak, J. F., Bijou, S. W., & Jastak, S. R. *Wide Range Achievement Test.* Wilmington, Del.: Guidance Associates, 1965.

Johnson, S. M., Bolstad, O. D., & Lobitz, G. K. Generalization and contrast phenomena in behavior modification with children. In E. J. Mash, L. A. Hamerlynck, & L. C. Handy (Eds.), *Behavior modification and families.* New York: Brunner/Mazel, 1976.

Johnson, S. M., & Lobitz, G. K. The personal and marital status of parents as related to observed child deviance and parenting behaviors. *Journal of Abnormal Child Psychology,* 1974, *3,* 193–208.

Kagan, J. Reflection–impulsivity: The generality and dynamics of conceptual tempo. *Journal of Abnormal Psychology,* 1966, *71,* 17–24.

Kagan, J., & Messer, S. B. A reply to "Some misgivings about the Matching Familiar Figures test as a measure of impulsivity." *Developmental Psychology,* 1975, *11,* 244–248.

Kagan, J., Rosman, B. L., Day, D., Albert, J., & Phillips, W. Information processing in the child: Significance of analytic and reflective attitudes. *Psychological Monographs,* 1964, *78* (1, Whole No. 578).

Kane, J. S., & Lawler, E. E. Methods of peer assessment. *Psychological Bulletin,* 1978, *85,* 555–586.

Kane, J. S., & Lawler, E. E. In defense of peer assessment: A rebuttal to Brief's critique. *Psychological Bulletin,* 1980, *88,* 80–81.

Kanfer, F. H. Self-regulation: Research issues and speculations. In C. Nuringer & J. L. Michael (Eds.), *Behavior modification in clinical psychology.* New York: Appleton-Century-Crofts, 1970.

Kanfer, F. H. The many faces of self-control, or behavior modification changes its focus. In R. B. Stuart (Ed.), *Behavioral self-management: Strategies, techniques, and outcome.* New York: Brunner/Mazel, 1977.

Kanfer, F. H., Karoly, P., & Newman, A. Reduction of children's fear of the dark by competence-related and situational threat-related verbal cues. *Journal of Consulting and Clinical Psychology,* 1975, *43,* 251–258.

Karoly, P. Behavioral self-management in children: Concepts, methods, issues, and directions. In M. Hersen, R. Eisler, & P. Miller (Eds.), *Progress in behavior modification* (Vol. 5). New York: Academic Press, 1977.

Karoly, P. Self-management problems in children. In E. J. Mash & L. G. Terdal (Eds.), *Behavioral assessment of childhood disorders.* New York: Guilford, 1981.

Kazdin, A. E. Covert modeling, model similarity, and reduction of avoidance behavior. *Behavior Therapy,* 1974, *5,* 325–340.

Kazdin, A. E. Imagery elaboration and self-efficacy in the correct modeling treatment of unassertive behavior. *Journal of Consulting and Clinical Psychology,* 1979, *47,* 725–733. (a)

Kazdin, A. E. Nonspecific treatment factors in psychotherapy outcome research. *Journal of Consulting and Clinical Psychology,* 1979, *47,* 846–851. (b)

Kendall, P. C. On the efficacious use of verbal self-instructional procedures with children. *Cognitive Therapy and Research,* 1977, *1,* 331–341.

Kendall, P. C. Cognitive–behavioral interventions with children. In B. B. Lahey & A. E. Kazdin (Eds.), *Advances in clinical child psychology* (Vol. 4). New York: Plenum, 1981. (a)

Kendall, P. C. One-year follow-up of concrete versus conceptual cognitive–behavioral self-control training. *Journal of Consulting and Clinical Psychology,* 1981, *49,* 748–749. (b)

Kendall, P. C. Assessment and cognitive–behavioral interventions: Purposes, proposals, and problems. In P. C. Kendall & S. D. Hollon (Eds.), *Assessment strategies for cognitive–behavioral interventions.* New York: Academic Press, 1981. (c)

Kendall, P. C. Cognitive processes and procedures in behavior therapy. In C. M. Franks,

G. T. Wilson, P. C. Kendall, & K. D. Brownell, *Annual review of behavior therapy* (Vol. 8). New York: Guilford, 1982. (a)

Kendall, P. C. Individual versus group cognitive–behavioral self-control training: One-year follow-up. *Behavior Therapy*, 1982, *13*, 241–247. (b)

Kendall, P. C. Integration: Behavior therapy and other schools of thought. *Behavior Therapy*, 1982, *13*, 559–571. (c)

Kendall, P. C. Social cognition and problem solving: A developmental and child-clinical interface. In B. Gholson & T. Rosenthal (Eds.), *Applications of cognitive-developmental theory*. New York: Academic Press, 1984.

Kendall, P. C., & Bemis, K. M. Thought and action in psychotherapy: The cognitive-behavioral approaches In M. Hersen, A. E. Kazdin, & A. S. Bellack (Eds.), *The clinical psychology handbook*. New York: Pergamon, 1983.

Kendall, P. C., & Braswell, L. Cognitive–behavioral assessment: Model, measures, and madness. In J. N. Butcher & C. D. Spielberger (Eds.), *Advances in personality assessment* (Vol. 1). Hillsdale, N.J.: Erlbaum, 1982. (a)

Kendall, P. C., & Braswell, L. Cognitive–behavioral self-control therapy for children: A components analysis. *Journal of Consulting and Clinical Psychology*, 1982, *50*, 672–689. (b)

Kendall, P. C., & Braswell, L. (Producers). *Cognitive behavioral self-control therapy for children* (45-minute videocassette). Minneapolis: University of Minnesota, 1982. (c) (Available from the first author, Department of Psychology, Weiss Hall, Temple University, Philadelphia, Pa. 1922.)

Kendall, P. C., & Brophy, C. Activity and attentional correlates of teacher ratings of hyperactivity. *Journal of Pediatric Psychology*, 1981, *6*, 451–458.

Kendall, P. C., & Finch, A. J. Jr. A cognitive–behavioral treatment for impulsivity: A case study. *Journal of Consulting and Clinical Psychology*, 1976, *44*, 852–857.

Kendall, P. C., & Finch, A. J. Jr. A cognitive–behavioral treatment for impulsivity: A group comparison study. *Journal of Consulting and Clinical Psychology*, 1978, *46*, 110–118.

Kendall, P. C., & Finch, A. J. Changes in verbal behavior following a cognitive-behavioral treatment for impulsivity. *Journal of Abnormal Child Psychology*, 1979, 7, 455–463. (a)

Kendall, P. C., & Finch, A. J. Developing nonimpulsive behavior in children: Cognitive-behavioral strategies for self-control: In P. C. Kendall & S. D. Hollon (Eds.), *Cognitive–behavioral interventions: Theory, research, and procedures*. New York: Academic Press, 1979. (b)

Kendall, P. C., & Finch, A. J. Jr. Reanalysis: A reply. *Journal of Consulting and Clinical Psychology*, 1979, *47*, 1107–1108. (c)

Kendall, P. C., Finch, A. J., Little, V. L., Chirico, B. M., & Ollendick, T. H. Variations in a construct: Quantitative and qualitative differences in children's locus of control. *Journal of Consulting and Clinical Psychology*, 1978, *46*, 590–592.

Kendall, P. C., & Fischler, G. L. Behavioral and adjustment correlates of problem-solving: Validational analyses of interpersonal cognitive problem-solving measures. *Child Development*, 1984, *55*, 879–892.

Kendall, P. C., & Hollon, S. D. (Eds.). *Cognitive–behavioral interventions: Theory, research, and procedures*. New York: Academic Press, 1979.

Kendall, P. C., & Korgeski, G. P. Assessment and cognitive–behavioral interventions. *Cognitive Therapy and Research*, 1979, *3*, 1–21.

Kendall, P. C., & Norton-Ford, J. D. *Clinical psychology: Scientific and professional dimensions*. New York: Wiley, 1982. (a)

Kendall, P. C., & Norton-Ford, J. D. Therapy outcome research methods. In P. C. Kendall & J. N. Butcher (Eds.), *Handbook of research methods in clinical psychology*. New York: Wiley, 1982. (b)

Kendall, P. C., Pellegrini, D., & Urbain, E. S. Approaches to assessment for cognitive–behavioral interventions with children. In P. C. Kendall & S. D. Hollon (Eds.), *Assessment strategies for cognitive–behavioral interventions.* New York: Academic Press, 1981. (a)

Kendall, P. C., & Urbain, E. S. Cognitive–behavioral intervention with a hyperactive girl: Evaluation via behavioral observations and cognitive performance. *Behavioral Assessment,* 1981, *3,* 345–357.

Kendall, P. C., & Wilcox, L. E. Self-control in children: Development of a rating scale. *Journal of Consulting and Clinical Psychology,* 1979, *47,* 1020–1029.

Kendall, P. C., & Wilcox, L. E. A cognitive–behavioral treatment for impulsivity: Concrete versus conceptual training in non-self-controlled problem children. *Journal of Consulting and Clinical Psychology,* 1980, *48,* 80–91.

Kendall, P. C., & Zupan, B. A. Individual versus group application of cognitive–behavioral strategies for developing self-control in children. *Behavior Therapy,* 1981, *12,* 344–359.

Kendall, P. C., Zupan, B. A., & Braswell, L. Self-control in children: Further analyses of the Self-Control Rating Scale. *Behavior Therapy,* 1981, *12,* 667–681. (b)

Kifer, R. E., Lewis, M. A., Green, D. R., & Phillips, E. L. Training pre-delinquent youths and their parents to negotiate conflict situations. *Journal of Applied Behavior Analysis,* 1974, *7,* 357–364.

Kirmil-Gray, K., Duckham-Shoor, L., & Thoresen, C. E. *The effects of self-control instruction and behavior management training on the academic and social behavior of hyperactive children.* Paper presented at the meeting of the Association for Advancement of Behavior Therapy, New York, November 1980.

Klahr, D., & Robinson, M. Formal assessment of problem-solving and planning processes in preschool children. *Cognitive Psychology,* 1981, *13,* 113–148.

Klein, N. C., Alexander, J. F., & Parsons, B. V. Impact of family systems intervention on recidivism and sibling delinquency: A model of primary prevention and program evaluation. *Journal of Consulting and Clinical Psychology,* 1977, *45,* 469–474.

Kohlberg, L., Yaeger, J., & Hjentholm, E. Private speech: Four studies and a review of theories. *Child Development,* 1968, *39,* 671–690.

Kopel, S., & Arkowitz, H. The role of attribution and self-perception in behavior change: Implications for behavior therapy. *Genetic Psychology Monographs,* 1975, *92,* 175–212.

Kopp, C. B. Antecedents of self-regulation: A developmental perspective. *Developmental Psychology,* 1982, *18,* 199–214.

Kurdek, L. A. Structural components and intellectual correlates of cognitive perspective taking in first through fourth grade children. *Child Development,* 1977, *48,* 1503–1511.

Lahey, B. B., Green, K. D., & Forehand, R. On the independence of ratings of hyper-activity, conduct problems, and attentional deficit in children: A multiple regression analysis. *Journal of Consulting and Clinical Psychology,* 1980, *48,* 566–574.

Lambert, H. M., Sandoval, J., & Sassone, D. *Multiple prevalence estimates of hyper-activity in school children.* Paper presented at the meeting of the American Psychological Association, San Francisco, August 1977.

Larcen, S., Spivack, G., & Shure, M. B. *Problem-solving thinking and adjustment among dependent–neglected pre-adolescents.* Paper presented at the meeting of the Eastern Psychological Association, Boston, April 1972.

Laufer, M. W., & Denhoff, C. Hyperkinetic behavior syndrome in children. *Journal of Pediatrics,* 1957, *50,* 463–474.

Ledwidge, B. Cognitive behavior modification: A step in the wrong direction? *Psychological Bulletin,* 1978, *85,* 353–375.

Lick, J., & Bootzin, R. Expectancy factors in the treatment of fear: Methodological and theoretical issues. *Psychological Bulletin*, 1975, *82*, 917–931.

Little, V. L. The relationship of role-taking ability to self-control in institutionalized juvenile offenders (Doctoral dissertation, Virginia Commonwealth University, 1978). *Dissertation Abstracts International*, 1979, *39*, 2992B. (University Microfilms No. 78-22, 701)

Lobitz, G. K., & Johnson, S. M. Normal versus deviant children: A multimethod comparison. *Journal of Abnormal Child Psychology*, 1975, *3*, 353–374.

Locke, E. A. Behavior modification is not cognitive—and other myths: A reply to Ledwidge. *Cognitive Therapy and Research*, 1979, *3*, 119–126.

Loney, J. The intellectual functioning of hyperactive elementary school boys: A cross-sectional investigation. *American Journal of Orthopsychiatry*, 1974, *44*, 754–762.

Loney, J., Comly, H. H., & Simon, B. Parental management, self-concept, and drug response in minimal brain dysfunction. *Journal of Learning Disabilities*, 1975, *8*, 187–190.

Loney, J., Langhorne, J., & Paternite, C. An empirical basis for subgrouping the hyperkinetic/minimal brain dysfunction syndrome. *Journal of Abnormal Psychology*, 1978, *87*, 431–441.

Loper, A. B. Metacognitive development: Implications for cognitive training. *Exceptional Education Quarterly*, 1980, *1*, 1–8.

Lorber, N. M. The Ohio Social Acceptance Scale. *Educational Research*, 1970, *12*, 240–243.

Lovaas, O. I. Cue properties of words: The control of operant responding by rate and content of verbal operants. *Child Development*, 1964, *35*, 245–256.

Luria, A. R. The directive function of speech in development and dissolution. *Word*, 1959, *15*, 341–352.

Luria, A. *The role of speech in the regulation of normal and abnormal behaviors.* New York: Liveright, 1961.

Lytton, H. The socialization of two-year-old boys: Ecological findings. *Journal of Child Psychology and Psychiatry*, 1976, *17*, 287–304.

Mahoney, M. J. Personal science: A cognitive learning therapy. In A. Ellis & R. Grieger (Eds.), *Handbook of rational psychotherapy*. New York: Springer, 1977. (a)

Mahoney, M. J. Reflections on the cognitive-learning trend in psychotherapy. *American Psychologist*, 1977, *32*, 5–13. (b)

Mahoney, M. J., & Arnkoff, D. B. Cognitive and self-control therapies. In S. L. Garfield & A. E. Bergin (Eds.), *Handbook of psychotherapy and behavior change* (2nd ed.). New York: Wiley, 1978.

Marlatt, G. A. Aclohol use and problem drinking: A cognitive–behavioral analysis. In P. C. Kendall & S. D. Hollon (Eds.), *Cognitive–behavioral interventions: Theory, research, and procedures*. New York: Academic Press, 1979.

Mash, E. J., & Terdal, L. G. Behavioral assessment of childhood disturbance. In E. J. Mash & L. G. Terdal (Eds.), *Behavioral assessment of childhood disorders*. New York: Guilford, 1981.

Mash, E. J., Terdal, L., & Anderson, K. The response-class matrix: A procedure for recording parent–child interactions. *Journal of Consulting and Clinical Psychology*, 1973, *40*, 163–164.

McClure, L. F., Chinsky, J. M., & Larcen, S. W. Enhancing social problem-solving performance in an elementary school setting. *Journal of Educational Psychology*, 1978, *70*, 504–513.

McCord, W., McCord, J., & Gudeman, J. *Origins of alcoholism*. Palo Alto, Calif.: Stanford University Press, 1960.

Meacham, J. A. Verbal guidance through remembering the goals of action. *Child Development*, 1978, *49*, 188–193.

Meichenbaum, D. Examination of model characteristics in reducing avoidance behavior. *Journal of Personality and Social Psychology*, 1971, *17*, 298–307.

Meichenbaum, D. Self-instructional methods. In F. Kanfer & A. Goldstein (Eds.), *Helping people change.* New York: Pergamon, 1975.

Meichenbaum, D. *Cognitive-Behavior Modification Newsletter,* No. 2, April 1976. (a)

Meichenbaum, D. Toward a cognitive theory of self-control. In G. Schwartz & D. Shapiro (Eds.), *Consciousness and self-regulation* (Vol. 1). New York: Plenum, 1976. (b)

Meichenbaum, D. *Cognitive-behavior modification: An integrative approach.* New York: Plenum, 1977.

Meichenbaum, D. Cognitive behavior modification: The need for a fairer assessment. *Cognitive Therapy and Research,* 1979, *3,* 127–132. (a)

Meichenbaum, D. Teaching children self-control. In B. B. Lahey & A. E. Kazdin (Eds.), *Advances in clinical child psychology* (Vol. 2). New York: Plenum, 1979. (b)

Meichenbaum, D., & Asarnow, J. Cognitive–behavioral modification and metacognitive development: Implications for the classroom. In P. C. Kendall & S. D. Hollon (Eds.), *Cognitive–behavioral interventions: Theory, research, and procedures.* New York: Academic Press, 1979.

Meichenbaum, D., & Goodman, J. Training impulsive children to talk to themselves: A means of developing self-control. *Journal of Abnormal Psychology,* 1971, *77,* 115–126.

Mendelson, N., Johnson, N., & Stewart, M. Hyperactive children as teenagers: A follow-up study. *Journal of Nervous and Mental Diseases,* 1971, *153,* 272–279.

Messer, S. B. Reflection–impulsivity: A review. *Psychological Bulletin,* 1976, *83,* 1026–1052.

Milich, R. S., Loney, J., & Landau, S. Independent dimensions of hyperactivity and aggression: A validation with playroom observation data. *Journal of Abnormal Psychology,* 1982, *91,* 183–198.

Minde, K., Lewin, D., Weiss, G., Lavigueur, H., Douglas, V. I., & Sykes, E. The hyperactive child in elementary school: A five-year controlled follow-up. *Exceptional Children,* 1971, *38,* 215–227.

Minde, K., Weiss, G., & Mendelson, N. A five year follow-up study of 91 hyperactive school children. *Journal of American Academy of Child Psychiatry,* 1972, *11,* 595–610.

Mischel, W. Processes in delay of gratification. In L. Berkowitz (Ed.), *Advances in experimental social psychology* (Vol. 7). New York: Academic Press, 1974.

Mischel, W., & Patterson, C. J. Substantive and structural elements of effective plans for self-control. *Journal of Personality and Social Psychology,* 1976, *34,* 942–950.

Monohan, J., & O'Leary, K. D. Effects of self-instruction on rule-breaking behavior. *Psychological Reports,* 1971, *29,* 1051–1066.

Moore, S. F., & Cole, S. O. Cognitive self-mediation training with hyperkinetic children. *Bulletin of the Psychonomic Society,* 1978, *12,* 18–20.

Morrison, J. R., & Stewart, M. A. A family study of the hyperactive child syndrome. *Biological Psychiatry,* 1971, *3,* 189–195.

Mussen, P. H. *The psychological development of the child.* Englewood Cliffs, N.J.: Prentice-Hall, 1963.

Nay, W. R. Analogue measures. In A. R. Ciminero, K. S. Calhoun, & H. E. Adams (Eds.), *Handbook of behavioral assessment.* New York: Wiley, 1977.

Neilans, T. H., & Israel, A. C. Towards maintenance and generalization of behavior change: Teaching children self-regulation and self-instructional skills. *Cognitive Therapy and Research,* 1981, *5,* 189–196.

Nelson, W., & Birkimer, J. C. Role of self-instruction and self-reinforcement in the modification of impulsivity. *Journal of Consulting and Clinical Psychology,* 1978, *46,* 183.

Nowicki, S. Jr., & Strickland, B. R. A locus of control scale for children. *Journal of Consulting and Clinical Psychology,* 1973, *40,* 148–154.

Nye, F. I. *Family relationships and delinquent behavior.* New York: Wiley, 1958.

O'Leary, K. D. The effects of self-instruction on immoral behavior. *Journal of Experimental Child Psychology*, 1968, *6*, 297–301.

O'Leary, S. G., & Steen, P. L. Subcategorizing hyperactivity: The Stony Brook Scale. *Journal of Consulting and Clinical Psychology*, 1982, *50*, 426–432.

Palkes, H., Stewart, M., & Freedman, J. Improvement in maze performance of hyperactive boys as a function of verbal-training procedures. *Journal of Special Education*, 1972, *5*, 337–342.

Palkes, H., Stewart, M., & Kahana, B. Porteus maze performance of hyperactive boys after training in self-directed verbal commands. *Child Development*, 1968, *39*, 817–826.

Parry, P. *The effect of reward on the performance of hyperactive children.* Unpublished doctoral dissertation, McGill University, 1973.

Parsons, B. V., & Alexander, J. F. Short-term family intervention: A therapy outcome study. *Journal of Consulting and Clinical Psychology*, 1973, *41*, 195–201.

Parsons, J. A. The reciprocal modification of authentic behavior and program development. In G. Semb (Ed.), *Behavior analysis and education: 1972.* Lawrence: University of Kansas Support and Development Center for Follow Through, 1972.

Paternite, C. E., Loney, J., & Langhorne, J. E., Jr. Relationships between symptomatology and SES-related factors in hyperkinetic/MBD boys. *American Journal of Orthopsychiatry*, 1976, *46*, 291–301.

Patterson, C., & Mischel, W. Effects of temptation-inhibiting and task-facilitating plans on self-control. *Journal of Personality and Social Psychology*, 1976, *33*, 207–217.

Patterson, G. R. The aggressive child: Victim and architect of a coercive system. In E. Mash, L. Hamerlynck, & L. Handy (Eds.), *Behavior modification and families: I. Theory and research.* New York: Brunner/Mazel, 1976.

Patterson, G. R., Ray, R. S., Shaw, D. A., & Cobb, J. A. *Manual for coding of interactions.* (1969 rev.). New York: Microfiche, 1969.

Patterson, G. R., Reid, J. B., Jones, R. R., & Conger, R. E. *A social learning approach to family intervention: Families with aggressive children* (Vol. 1). Eugene, Ore.: Castalia, 1975.

Paulauskas, S. L., & Campbell, S. B. G. Social perspective-taking and teacher ratings of peer interaction in hyperactive boys. *Journal of Abnormal Child Psychology*, 1979, 7, 483–494.

Pellegrini, D. S. *The social–cognitive qualities of stress-resistant children.* Unpublished doctoral dissertation, University of Minnesota, 1980.

Piaget, J. *The language and thought of the child.* New York: Harcourt-Brace, 1926.

Piaget, G. W. Training parents to communicate. In A. A. Lazarus (Ed.), *Clinical behavior therapy.* New York: Brunner/Mazel, 1972.

Piers, E. V., & Harris, D. B. *The Piers–Harris Children's Self-Concept Scale.* Nashville: Counselor Recordings and Tests, 1969.

Pitkanen, L. The effect of similation exercises on the control of aggressive behavior in children. *Scandinavian Journal of Psychology*, 1974, *15*, 169–177.

Platt, J. J., & Spivack, G. Problem-solving thinking of psychiatric patients. *Journal of Consulting and Clinical Psychology*, 1972, *39*, 148–151. (a)

Platt, J. J., & Spivack, G. Social competence and effective problem-solving thinking in psychiatric patients. *Journal of Clinical Psychology*, 1972, *28*, 3–5. (b)

Platt, J. J., & Spivack, G. Studies in problem-solving thinking of psychiatric patients: Patient–control differences and factorial structure of problem-solving thinking. *Proceedings, 81st Annual Convention of the American Psychological Association*, 1973, *8*, 461–462.

Platt, J. J., Spivack, G., Altman, N., Altman, D., & Peizer, S. B. Adolescent problem-solving thinking. *Journal of Consulting and Clinical Psychology*, 1974, *42*, 787–793.

Porteus, S. D. *The maze test and mental differences.* Vineland, N.J.: Smith, 1933.

Porteus, S. D. *The maze test: Recent advances*. Palo Alto, Calif.: Pacific Books, 1955.

Pressley, M. Increasing children's self-control through cognitive interventions. *Review of Educational Research*, 1979, *49*, 319–370.

Pressley, M., Reynolds, W. M., Stark, K. D., & Gettinger, M. Cognitive strategy training and children's self-control. In M. Pressley & J. R. Levin (Eds.), *Cognitive strategy research: Psychological foundations*. New York: Springer, 1983.

Prinz, R., Connor, P., & Wilson, C. Hyperactive and aggressive behaviors in childhood: Intertwined dimensions. *Journal of Abnormal Child Psychology*, 1981, *9*, 191–202.

Prinz, R., & Loney, J. Teacher-rated hyperactive elementary school girls: An exploratory developmental study. *Child Psychiatry and Human Development*, 1974, *4*, 246–257.

Rapoport, J. L., Quinn, P. O., Burg, C., & Bartley, L. Can hyperactivities be identified in infancy? In R. L. Trites (Ed.), *Hyperactivity in children: Etiology, measurement, and treatment implications*. Baltimore: University Park, 1979.

Reynolds, W. M., & Stark, K. D. Cognitive behavior modification: The clinical application of cognitive strategies. In M. Pressley & J. R. Levin (Eds.), *Cognitive strategy research: Psychological foundations*. New York: Springer, 1983.

Riddle, M., & Roberts, A. H. *The Porteus Mazes: A critical evaluation*. Report No. PR-74-3, Department of Psychiatry, University of Minnesota, 1974.

Riddle, M., & Roberts, A. H. Delinquency, delay of gratification, recidivism, and the Porteus Maze tests. *Psychological Bulletin*, 1977, *84*, 417–425.

Roberts, M. A., Milich, R., Loney, J., & Caputo, J. A multitrait–multimethod analysis of variance of teachers' ratings of aggression, hyperactivity, and inattention. *Journal of Abnormal Child Psychology*, 1981, *9*, 371–380.

Robin, A. L., Fischel, J. E., & Brown, K. E. The measurement of self-control in children: Validation of the Self-Control Rating Scale. *Journal of Pediatric Psychology*, 1984, *9*, 165–175.

Robin, A. L., Kent, R., O'Leary, K. D., Foster, S., & Prinz, R. An approach to teaching parents and adolescents problem-solving communication skills: A preliminary report. *Behavior Therapy*, 1977, *8*, 639–643.

Robin, A. L., & Schneider, M. *The turtle-technique: An approach to self-control in the classroom*. Unpublished manuscript, State University of New York at Stony Brook, 1974.

Robin, A. L., Schneider, M., & Dolnick, M. The turtle technique: An extended case study of self-control in the classroom. *Psychology in the Schools*, 1976, *13*, 449–453.

Robins, L. *Deviant children grow up*. Baltimore: Williams & Wilkins, 1966.

Rochester Social Problem-Solving Group. *Social problem solving (SPS): Open middle test scoring and reliability report*, 1978–1979. (Available from the Center for Community Study, 575 Mt. Hope Avenue, Rochester, N.Y. 14620.)

Roff, M. Childhood social interactions and young adult bad conduct. *Journal of Abnormal and Social Psychology*, 1961, *63*, 333–337.

Roff, M., Sells, S. S., & Golden, M. M. *Social adjustment and personality development in children*. Minneapolis: University of Minnesota Press, 1972.

Rondal, J. Investigation of the regulatory power of impulsive and meaningful aspects of speech. *Genetic Psychology Monographs*, 1976, *94*, 3–33.

Rosenthal, T., & Bandura, A. Psychological modeling: Theory and practice. In S. L. Garfield & A. E. Bergin (Eds.), *Handbook of psychotherapy and behavior change* (2nd ed.). New York: Wiley, 1978.

Ross, A. O. *Psychological disorders of children: A behavioral approach to theory, research, and therapy*. New York: McGraw-Hill, 1980.

Ross, D. M., & Ross, S. A. *Hyperactivity: Research, theory, and action*. New York: Wiley, 1976.

Rotter, J. B. Generalized expectancies for internal versus external control of reinforcement. *Psychological Monographs*, 1966, *30* (Whole No. 1).

Rotter, J. B., & Hochreich, D. J. *Personality.* Glenview, Ill.: Scott, Foresman, 1975.

Routh, D. K. Developmental aspects of hyperactivity. In C. K. Whalen & B. Henker (Eds.), *Hyperactive children: The social ecology of identification and treatment.* New York: Academic Press, 1980.

Rubin, K., & Krasnor, L. Social cognitive and social behavioral perspectives on problem solving. In M. Perlmutter (Ed.), *Social cognition: Minnesota Symposium on Child Psychology* (Vol. 18). Hillsdale, N.J.: Erlbaum, 1984.

Russell, M. L., & Thoresen, C. E. Teaching decision-making skills to children. In J. D. Krumboltz & C. E. Thoresen (Eds.), *Counseling methods.* New York: Holt, Rinehart & Winston, 1976.

Rutter, M. Epidemiological and conceptual considerations in risk research. In E. J. Anthony & C. Koupernik (Eds.), *The child in his family: Children at psychiatric risk.* New York: Wiley, 1974.

Rutter, M., Cox, A., Tupling, C., Berger, M., & Yule, W. Attainment and adjustment in two geographical areas: I. Prevalence of psychiatric disorders. *British Journal of Psychiatry,* 1975, *126,* 493–509.

Salkind, N. J. *The development of norms for the Matching Familiar Figures test.* Manuscript available from the author, University of Kansas, 1979.

Sanders, L. W. Issues in early mother–child interaction. *Journal of the American Academy of Child Psychiatry,* 1962, *1,* 141–166.

Sarason, I. G. Verbal learning, modeling and juvenile delinquency. *American Psychologist,* 1968, *23,* 254–266.

Sarason, I. G. Test anxiety and the self-disclosing model. *Journal of Consulting and Clinical Psychology,* 1975, *43,* 148–153.

Sarason, I. G., & Ganzer, V. J. Modeling and group discussion in the rehabilitation of juvenile delinquents. *Journal of Counseling Psychology,* 1973, *20,* 442–449.

Sarason, I. G., & Sarason, B. R. Teaching cognitive and social skills to high school students. *Journal of Consulting and Clinical Psychology,* 1981, *49,* 908–918.

Schallow, J. R. Locus of control and success at self-modification. *Behavior Therapy,* 1975, *6,* 667–671.

Scherer, M., & Nakamura, C. Y. Children's fear survey. *Behaviour Research and Therapy,* 1968, *6,* 178–182.

Schleifer, M., Weiss, G., Cohen, N., Elman, M., Cvejic, H., & Kruger, E. Hyperactivity in preschoolers and the effect of methylphenidate. *American Journal of Orthopsychiatry,* 1975, *45,* 38–50.

Schlesser, R., Meyers, A., & Cohen, R. Generalization of self-instructions: Effects of general versus specific content, active rehearsal, and cognitive level. *Child Development,* 1981, *52,* 335–340.

Schneider, M. Turtle technique in the classroom. *Teaching Exceptional Children,* 1974, *8,* 22–24.

Schneider, M., & Robin, A. L. The turtle technique: A method for the self-control of impulsive behavior. In J. D. Krumboltz & C. E. Thoresen (Eds.), *Counseling methods.* New York: Holt, Rinehart & Winston, 1976.

Schrag, P., & Divoky, D. *The myth of the hyperactive child.* New York: Pantheon, 1975.

Schunk, D. H. Effects of effort attributional feedback on children's perceived self-efficacy and achievement. *Journal of Educational Psychology,* 1982, *74,* 548–556.

Selman, R. L. *The growth of interpersonal understanding: Developmental and clinical analyses.* New York: Academic Press, 1980.

Selman, R. L., & Byrne, D. A structural–developmental analysis of levels of role-taking in middle childhood. *Child Development,* 1974, *45,* 803–806.

Selman, R. L., & Jaquette, D. Stability and oscillation in interpersonal awareness: A clinical–developmental analysis. In C. B. Keasey (Ed.), *The XXVth Nebraska Symposium on Motivation.* Lincoln: University of Nebraska Press, 1978.

Selman, R. L., Jaquette, D., & Lavin, R. Interpersonal awareness in children: Toward an integration of developmental and clinical child psychology. *American Journal of Orthopsychiatry*, 1977, *47*, 264–274.

Shantz, C. U. The development of social cognition. In E. M. Hetherington (Ed.), *Review of child development research* (Vol. 5). Chicago: University of Chicago Press, 1975.

Shure, M. B., & Spivack, G. *Problem-solving capacity, social class and adjustment among nursery school children.* Paper presented at the meeting of the Eastern Psychological Association, Atlantic City, N.J., 1970.

Shure, M. B., & Spivack, G. Means–end thinking, adjustment and social class among elementary school-aged children. *Journal of Consulting and Clinical Psychology*, 1972, *38*, 348–353.

Shure, M. B., & Spivack, G. *Problem-solving techniques in childrearing.* San Francisco: Jossey-Bass, 1978.

Shure, M. B., Spivack, G., & Jaeger, M. Problem-solving thinking and adjustment among disadvantaged preschool children. *Child Development*, 1971, *42*, 1791–1803.

Speedie, S. M., Houtz, J., Ringenbach, S., & Feldhusen, J. Abilities measured by the Purdue Elementary Problem-Solving Inventory. *Psychological Reports*, 1973, *33*, 959–963.

Spivack, G., Haimes, P. E., & Spotts, J. *Devereux Adolescent Behavior Rating Scale.* Devon, Pa.: Devereux Foundation, 1967.

Spivack, G., & Levine, M. *Self-regulation in acting-out and normal adolescents* (Report No. M-4531). Washington, D.C.: National Institute of Mental Health, 1963.

Spivack, G., Platt, J. J., & Shure, M. B. *The problem-solving approach to adjustment.* San Francisco: Jossey-Bass, 1976.

Spivack, G., & Shure, M. B. *Social adjustment of young children: A cognitive approach to solving real-life problems.* San Francisco: Jossey-Bass, 1974.

Spivack, G., & Swift, M. The classroom beahvior of children: A critical review of teacher-administered rating scales. *Journal of Special Education*, 1973, *7*, 55–89.

Stewart, M. A., Pitts, F. N., Craig, A. B., & Dieruf, W. The hyperactive child syndrome. *American Journal of Orthopsychiatry*, 1966, *36*, 861–867.

Stone, G., Hinds, W., & Schmidt, G. Teaching mental health behaviors to elementary school children. *Professional Psychology*, 1975, *6*, 34–40.

Stuart, R. B. Behavioral control of overeating. *Behaviour Research and Therapy*, 1967, *5*, 357–365.

Tant, J. L. *Problem-solving in hyperactive and reading disabled boys.* Unpublished doctoral dissertation, McGill University, 1978.

Taplin, P. S., & Reid, J. B. Changes in parent consequation as a function of family intervention. *Journal of Consulting and Clinical Psychology*, 1977, *45*, 973–981.

Tavormina, J. B. Relative effectiveness of behavioral and reflective group counseling with parents of mentally retarded children. *Journal of Consulting and Clinical Psychology*, 1975, *43*, 22–31.

Thackwray, D., Meyers, A., Schlesser, R., & Cohen, R. Achieving generalization with general versus specific self-instructions: Effects on academically deficient children. *Cognitive Therapy and Research*, in press.

Thomas, A., Chess, S., & Birch, H. G. *Temperament and behavior disorders in children.* New York: New York University Press, 1968.

Tolman, E. C. *Purposive behavior in animals and men.* New York: Century, 1932.

Tolman, E. C. *Collected papers in psychology.* Reprinted as *Behavior and psychological man.* Berkeley: University of California Press, 1951.

Torgesen, J. K. The role of nonspecific factors in the task performance of learning disabled children: A theoretical assessment. *Journal of Learning Disabilities*, 1977, *10*, 27–34.

Trites, R. L. Prevalence of hyperactivity in Ottawa, Canada. In R. L. Trites (Ed.), *Hyperactivity in children: Etiology, measurement, and treatment implications.* Baltimore: University Park, 1979.

Turkewitz, H., O'Leary, K. D., & Ironsmith, M. Generalization and maintenance of appropriate behavior through self-control. *Journal of Consulting and Clinical Psychology*, 1975, *43*, 577–583.

Urbain, E. S. *Interpersonal problem-solving training and social perspective-taking training with impulsive children via modeling role-play and self-instruction.* Unpublished doctoral dissertation, University of Minnesota, 1979.

Urbain, E. S. *Social skills training workshop and friendship group manual.* St. Paul, Minn.: Wilder Child Guidance Clinic, 1982.

Urbain, E. S., & Kendall, P. C. Review of social–cognitive problem-solving interventions with children. *Psychological Bulletin*, 1980, *88*, 109–143.

Urbain, E. S., & Kendall, P. C. *Interpersonal problem-solving, social perspective-taking, and behavioral contingencies: A comparison of group approaches with impulsive–aggressive children.* Unpublished manuscript, University of Minnesota, 1981.

Varni, J. W., & Henker, B. A self-regulation approach to the treatment of three hyperactive boys. *Child Behavior Therapy*, 1979, *1*, 171–191.

Vygotsky, L. *Thought and language.* New York: Wiley, 1962.

Wagner, I. *Reflection–impulsivity re-examined: Analysis and modification of cognitive strategies.* Paper presented at the Biennial Meeting of the Society for Research in Child Development, Denver, April 1975.

Wahler, R. G., House, A. E., & Stambaugh, E. E. *Ecological assessment of child problem behavior.* New York: Pergamon, 1976.

Walker, H. M. *The Walker Problem Behavior Identification Checklist.* Los Angeles: Psychological Services, 1970.

Wechsler, D. *Weshsler Intelligence Scale for Children.* New York: Psychological Corp., 1949.

Weiner, B., Frieze, I., Kukla, A., Reed, L., Rest, S., & Rosenbaum, R. M. *Perceiving the causes of success and failure.* Morristown, N.J.: General Learning Press, 1971.

Weinreich, R. J. *Inducing reflective thinking in impulsive, emotionally disturbed children.* Unpublished thesis, Virginia Commonwealth University, 1975.

Weiss, G. A natural history of hyperactivity in childhood and treatment with stimulant medication at different ages: A summary of research findings. *International Journal of Mental Health*, 1975, *4*, 213–226.

Weiss, G., Minde, K., Werry, J. S., Douglas, V. I., & Nemeth, E. Studies on the hyperactive child. VIII: Five year follow-up. *Archives of General Psychiatry*, 1971, *24*, 409–414.

Weissberg, R. P., Gesten, E. L., Rapkin, B. D., Cowen, E. L., Davidson, E., de Apodaca, R. F., & McKim, B. J. Evaluation of a social-problem-solving training program for suburban and inner-city third-grade children. *Journal of Consulting and Clinical Psychology*, 1981, *49*, 251–261.

Wender, P. H. *Minimal brain dysfunction in children.* New York: Wiley, 1971.

Werry, J. S. Developmental hyperactivity. *Pediatric Clinics of North America*, 1968, *19*, 9–16.

Werry, J. S., & Quay, H. C. The prevalence of behavior symptoms in younger elementary school children. *American Journal of Orthopsychiatry*, 1971, *41*, 136–143.

Wikler, A., Dixon, J., & Parker, J. Brain function in problem children and controls: Psychometric, neurological and electroencephalographic comparisons. *American Journal of Psychiatry*, 1970, *127*, 634–655.

Wilkins, W. Expectancy of therapeutic gain: An empirical and conceptual critique. *Journal of Consulting and Clinical Psychology*, 1973, *40*, 69–77.

Wilkins, W. Expectancies in therapy research: Discriminating among heterogeneous nonspecifics. *Journal of Consulting and Clinical Psychology*, 1979, *47*, 837–845.

Williams, D. Y., & Akamatsu, T. J. Cognitive self-guidance training with juvenile delinquents. *Cognitive Therapy and Research*, 1978, *2*, 285–288.

Witkin, H. A., Oltman, P. K., Raskin, E., & Karp, S. *A manual for the Embedded Figures Test*. Palo Alto, Calif.: Consulting Psychologists Press, 1971.

Wilson, G. T. Cognitive behavior therapy: Paradigm shift or passing phase? In J. P. Foreyt & D. P. Rathjen (Eds.), *Cognitive behavior therapy: Research and applications*. New York: Plenum, 1978.

Wright, J. C. *The KRISP: A technical report*. Unpublished manuscript, 1973.

Zivin, G. (Ed.). *The development of self-regulation through private speech*. New York: Wiley, 1979.

Author Index

O

P

Q

R

Subject Index